Marching Students

Marching Students

Chicana and Chicano Activism in Education, 1968 to the Present

EDITED BY

MARGARITA BERTA-ÁVILA

ANITA TIJERINA REVILLA

JULIE LÓPEZ FIGUEROA

UNIVERSITY OF NEVADA PRESS

RENO & LAS VEGAS

University of Nevada Press, Reno, Nevada, 89557 USA
Copyright © 2011 by University of Nevada Press
All rights reserved
Manufactured in the United States of America

Library of Congress Cataloging-in-Publication Data
Marching students: Chicana and Chicano activism in education, 1968 to
the present / edited by Margarita Berta-Ávila, Anita Tijerina Revilla, and
Julie López Figueroa.

p.   cm.

Includes bibliographical references and index.

ISBN 978-0-87417-841-8 (pbk. : alk. paper)

1. Hispanic American students—Social conditions. 2. Educational
equalization—United States. 3. Student movements—United States—
History—20th century. 4. United States—Ethnic relations. I. Berta-Ávila,
Margarita, 1972–   II. Tijerina Revilla, Anita, 1973–
III. López Figueroa, Julie, 1969–
LC2670.M36 2011
373.18'108968'72073–dc22
2010035066

The paper used in this book is a recycled stock made from
30 percent post-consumer waste materials, certified by FSC,
and meets the requirements of American National Standard
for Information Sciences—Permanence of Paper
for Printed Library Materials, ANSI/NISO Z39.48-1992 (R2002).
Binding materials were selected for strength and durability.

21   20   19   18   17   16   15   14   13   12   11
5   4   3   2

To César, Liliana, Santiago, Delia, Dee Dee,

Brenda, Destiny, Rae Ana, Michael, Anthony, Chito,

Macedonio, Maria, Marina, Raul, and Alfredo

CONTENTS

Conclusion: Learning from the Chicana/o Blowouts 188

MARGARITA BERTA-ÁVILA AND JULIE LÓPEZ FIGUEROA

ILLUSTRATIONS

Forty years ago, during the month of March 1968, Mexican American high school students shocked the city of Los Angeles and the nation when thousands of them walked out of the segregated public schools located in the eastside barrios of the city. I was one of the college student activists who marched with them through the streets of East Los Angeles to peacefully protest the racism and educational inequality we faced in the schools.

The walkouts lasted for a week and a half and disrupted the nation's largest public-school system and captured front-page headlines and national attention. More than ten thousand students participated, including students from the predominantly African American Thomas Jefferson High School in South Central Los Angeles who walked out in solidarity with us.

Three months after the walkouts, I was one of thirteen walkout organizers who were indicted for conspiracy to disrupt the Los Angeles city school system, the largest in the nation. At the time, I was a first-year graduate student and the president of my campus chapter of the United Mexican American Students. I was arrested in the early-morning hours while hard at work on a term paper due for one of my graduate seminars. The trauma my family and I were forced to endure during my arrest and subsequent imprisonment was a life-changing experience for me.

The thirteen of us who were indicted faced sixty-six years in prison if convicted of the conspiracy charges. It took two years for our case to be decided by the California State Appellate Court. The court finally ruled that we were innocent of the conspiracy charges by virtue of the First Amendment to the U.S. Constitution granting freedom of speech.

The walkouts were the first major mass dramatic protest against racism and educational inequality ever staged by Mexican Americans in the history of the United States. It was carried out in the nonviolent protest tradition of the Civil Rights movement. Its historical significance was similar to the 1960 black student sit-ins in Greensboro, North Carolina. As the Greensboro student protest fueled the flames of the civil rights struggle in the South, the East Los Angeles walkouts ignited the emergence of the Mexican

American civil rights movement—which came to be known as the Chicano movement—throughout the southwestern United States.

The Chicana/o movement opened doors for equal opportunity in higher education to young people who had been systematically excluded and led to the creation of Chicana/o studies departments and programs throughout the nation. It also contributed to equal opportunity in employment for Mexican Americans and other Latinas/os. It produced thousands of professionals that included writers, poets, artists, filmmakers, lawyers, teachers, medical doctors, health workers, and social workers as well as hundreds of community and labor organizers and political leaders at the local, state, and national levels of government.

The movement also resulted in a generation of scholar activists deeply committed to playing a role in the struggle for civil and human rights and social justice in our society. The scholars and activists represented in this volume are outstanding examples of those who continue to follow the path charted by the 1960s generation. The work they have produced for this volume places the 1968 walkouts and the Chicana/o civil rights movement in historical context. Their exemplary work provides a critical understanding of, and insight into, the continuing struggle being waged by Latina/os for educational equality in the United States.

I am pleased the editors of this volume decided to commemorate those historic walkouts with this outstanding collection of essays.

Carlos Muñoz Jr.
Professor Emeritus, University of California, Berkeley

PREFACE

This book seeks to commemorate the 1968 Chicana/o student walkouts, or blowouts, that occurred throughout the Southwest. Birthed from the Chicana/o *movimientos,* the student blowouts in East Los Angeles were a visible social critique of the ways traditional education underserved and marginalized Chicana/os. With careful planning led by students, approximately ten thousand Chicana/o students walked out of classes on March 1, 1968, to protest educational inequity. Within the process of protest for a more inclusive pedagogy, the student blowouts served as a reminder that identity politics continue to mediate the quality of education students receive.

This is a timely book that not only presents an analysis of the walkouts of 1968 but also traces a development in various sectors of education to the present. This edited volume highlights and draws parallels between the students who marched in 1968, 2006, and the present. Most importantly, the essays explore what these kinds of student movements indicate about the state of our society. As a result, the contributors in this volume ground their scholarship in critical resistance, queer, critical race, and Chicana feminist theories to frame and to ask new and provocative questions on Chicana/o identity and activism as they relate to education and the student protests of today. We explore Chicana/o identity and activism through student and community marches, flag waving, and chanting that have been stereotyped as radical instead of progressive. Oftentimes, this portrayal has impeded dialogue and the exchange of potentially beneficial ideas. In terms of theories and pedagogies in education, highlighting the transformative contributions those with a Chicana/o consciousness have made, and continue to make, is long overdue. As the fortieth anniversary for the "East L.A. Blowouts" approached, we thought it timely and necessary to collect the stories and work of our colleagues to show that the struggle for better education for Chicanas/os and Latinas/os is constant and fierce.

Lastly, we would like to acknowledge how the idea for this book developed. We presented our work with colleague Luis Urrieta at a panel at the American Educational Research Association conference titled "Chicana/o

Activism and Education: Theories and Pedagogies of Trans/formation." The panel was part of the Critical Educators for Social Justice Symposium, and it was chaired by Dr. Antonia Darder, a scholar who has led the way and mentored many of us on this path toward creating social change with education. After the presentation, it was solidified. Even though we come from many walks of life with similarities and differences across gender, sexuality, race/ethnicity, age, and citizenship/immigration, it became critical that as educators we unite with the same intent—to use education as a tool for transformation. Thus we were inspired to share our stories and research collectively and publish this work.

We would also like to acknowledge Urrieta's early contributions to the project. He brought about a conceptual framework that guided this work. Our belief in this project compelled us as volume editors to bring it to fruition upon his departure.

Marching Students

Introduction

ANITA TIJERINA REVILLA

In the 1960s and 1970s, students from predominately Chicana/o schools organized massive protests to demand a host of educational reforms that included improved schooling conditions, better preparation for higher education, the implementation of bilingual instruction, and much more. Overall, they demanded an educational system that would treat them with greater dignity and respect. Decades before that, with the Lemon Grove incident (1931) and the *Mendez v. Westminster School District* (1947) case, Mexican and Chicana/o parents were among the first to file lawsuits denouncing the practice of school segregation for Mexican-origin children (Alvarez 1986; Bermudez forthcoming). There have been numerous instances of the continued unrest and dissatisfaction with the education of Chicanas and Chicanos in the United States. For example, in 1968, thousands of East Los Angeles students walked out of school, denouncing the poor educational practices within the Los Angeles Unified School District. They were building on the legacy of protests of Mexican-origin activists from the 1930s to 1950s, the broader Chicana/o and civil rights movements, and the anti–Vietnam War protests of the time. The 1968 East L.A. Walkouts or Blowouts became a model of student resistance and youth empowerment wherein students used direct action to demand social justice. It is no mistake that in 2006 and still today, students have staged walkouts demanding justice for their communities. Similar walkouts and acts of resistance by students have been seen in opposition to unfair legislation such as California Propositions 187 (anti-immigrant), 227 (antibilingual education), and 21 (youth criminalization), as well as many more that go unreported by the national media.

As a result of social movements in education, there have been several developments, including desegregation, bilingual education, affirmative action, multicultural education, Chicana/o studies, better school financing, migrant education, and much more. Still, students and their families continue to feel underserved and dismissed by institutions of education. According to the Chicana/o educational pipeline based on U.S. Census data, fewer than 10 percent of Chicanas/os who start elementary school in the United States pursue and complete a bachelor's degree. An overwhelming 56 percent of Chicana/o students drop out or are "pushed out" of school—a statistic that has remained the same or worsened since the 1970s (Yosso 2006, 3). As critical educators, we use the phrase "push out" instead of "drop out" to recognize the role of institutions in the increasing number of students who leave school early, recognizing that students' decisions to pursue high school diplomas and higher education are impacted by outside forces as well, including teachers, counselors, administrators, and legislators.

In 2006 we witnessed a nationwide Chicana/o and Latina/o community protest against the unfair treatment of immigrants in the United States. With the passing of HR 4437 in the House of Representatives in December 2005, students once again took to the streets to make it known that they would not stand for the continued and exacerbated criminalization of undocumented immigrants. HR 4437 (the Border Protection, Antiterrorism, and Illegal Immigration Control Act of 2005) called for a seven hundred–mile fence along the U.S.-Mexico border, local legal authorities to aid in deportation procedures, an increase in fines and criminal charges for undocumented people and their employers, and a host of other demands. It further declared undocumented people and anyone who "aids or assists" them felons. There was a national outcry against the inhumanity and criminalization that the bill suggested for immigrants. Currently, we are dealing with the positive and negative aftermath of HR 4437. The bill was not passed in the Senate, but several items within the bill were reintroduced and passed into law at a later time. Deportations and increased anti-immigrant sentiment and legislation are soaring. However, the large-scale resistance to social injustice that was catalyzed in 2006 has left us with a legacy that continues through activism, organizing, voting, civic engagement, and consciousness raising. The numbers of youth engaged in this movement are extremely significant. Throughout the nation, Latina/o students and their parents were at the forefront of organizing efforts, including student walkouts. Their efforts of resistance went beyond the immigration debate as they denounced racism, classism, sexism, and homophobia. Student contingencies at immigrant rights marches held posters that read: "Brown Is Beautiful!" "Chican@ Consciousness for All," "What Happened to No Child Left Behind?" and "Queers Are Immigrants Too!" This book speaks to many of the concerns of these students and their educators; it provides a space wherein their voices are represented.

THEORETICAL OVERVIEW

This book is a collaborative effort by Chicana/o scholars in the fields of Chicana/o studies, ethnic studies, women's studies, and education to collect the research and experiences of people who have worked historically and are working presently on a vision of social justice for Chicana and Chicano youth and communities. Most often, we envision our path to social justice through education. Thus, we closely study the work and struggles of Chicana/o scholars, parents, teachers, students, and community members to learn from their practices, their acts of resistance against subordination, and their transformative movements toward social justice.

At the forefront of critical education research are theories that contest schooling practices that maintain the subordination of "oppressed" people, including but not limited to poor, working-class, female, ethnic/linguistic minority, undocumented, disabled, and queer students, as well as many other marginalized and discriminated populations.[1] Paulo Freire's work is the foundation for many of our efforts in this area, as he outlined a theoretical model for working with oppressed students many years ago. He primarily focused on people oppressed by their condition as exploited workers, but his theories have been expanded to include many more discriminated groups. Freire argued that dehumanization is the "result of an unjust order that engenders violence in the oppressors, which in turn dehumanizes the oppressed." He also asserted that "sooner or later being less human leads the oppressed to struggle against those who made them so" (1994, 26). Hence, the oppressed will not be able to tolerate their continued oppression and dehumanization and will eventually have no other recourse but to resist and seek out their own liberation. According to Freire, the oppressed can and should be transformers of their world, and they can do this through a liberatory praxis, which includes critical consciousness/education, or *conscientización,* and action.

Henry Giroux (1983) wrote that a radical pedagogy will be achieved only when we better understand the relationships among power, resistance, and human agency. That is, there are power dynamics at play within schools that are systematically disenfranchising particular students based on certain aspects of their identities and background. However, there are also many ways that these students and their educators are strategically resisting oppression and "push-out" factors. Marginalized students and their allies have human agency, and they are surviving and thriving using their education and critical consciousness to navigate an unjust system. The majoritarian perspective that posits that all students have an equal opportunity and access to education is heavily contested by the work of critical scholars. We recognize the injustices, but also realize there are ways to change the expected outcomes.

Chicana and Chicano critical race education scholars Daniel Solórzano and Dolores Delgado Bernal expand on Giroux's discussion of resistance as they examine the oppositional behavior of students from a critical race perspective. They analyze the experiences of the students involved in the 1968 East Los Angeles school walkouts and the 1993 UCLA Chicana and Chicano studies protests to explore a kind of student behavior called "transformational resistance." Solórzano and Delgado Bernal wrote, "*Transformational resistance* . . . refers to student behavior that illustrates both a critique of oppression and a desire for social justice. With a deeper level of understanding and a social justice orientation, transformational resistance offers the greatest possibility for social change" (2001, 319).

Whereas some people believe that oppositional behavior and resistance are static, we recognize that there is much fluidity within them. For instance, an individual can exhibit behavior that can be both conformist and transformative in that we sometimes choose to work within institutions that are extremely conformist and reduce our visions of social change based on our limitations within those institutions. However, even when we participate in institutions that maintain racist, classist, sexist, homophobic and heterosexist, and citizenist perspectives and hierarchies, we may be working toward transformative social change by challenging these structures from within them as well as outside of them.[2] We believe this to be dramatically evident in the work of educators and students participating in institutions of education. As critical race theorists in education indicate, education has the power to both oppress and liberate (Solórzano and Delgado Bernal 2001). Furthermore, Alejandro Covarrubias and Anita Tijerina Revilla extended Solórzano and Delgado Bernal's resistance paradigm to shift from a "critique of social oppression" to a "multidimensional consciousness of social oppression" to extrapolate on the idea that a critical consciousness, or *conscientización,* is complicated by examining the intersectionality of race, class, gender, sexuality, citizenship, and many other socially constructed categories that reinforce power dynamics in our society. They wrote, "*Multidimensional consciousness* consists of a sophisticated critique of how multiple, intersecting structures of domination (e.g., racism, capitalism, sexism, heteronormativity, etc.) interact with each other and impact one's social and political situation as part of an historical condition" (2003, 466). Hence, a critical multidimensional consciousness is not simply being race conscious or gender conscious but rather a commitment to developing a *conscientización* about *all* forms of injustice. In addition, there is a shift in the resistance diagram from "motivated for social justice" to commitment to social justice. "Commitment to social justice in this context is understood as the commitment to engage in a process of transforming all relations of inequality, whether they are individual or systemic, both understood as political" (ibid., 467).

It is the concept of transformational resistance that this book focuses on as we examine the role of activism in the educational past and present of Chicanas and Chicanos. Hence, this book and the contributors of this book actively seek to document and problematize the experiences of people who are working to build individual and collective multidimensional consciousness while also committing to social justice movements. We view the positive changes for Chicanas and Chicanas in education as a result of activism that can be seen as transformational resistance.

In chapter 1, Carlos Tejeda writes from the perspective of a decolonizing pedagogue, challenging the educational system's desire to create "schooling for subservience." He points to the 1968 East Los Angeles Walkouts or Blowouts as an important event in history in which a shift took place for those being educated for the purpose of creating a subordinated workforce. Beginning in this chapter and filtered throughout the book, we commemorate the walkouts for the significant impact they make on the legacy of Chicana/o student and community activism in the area of education.

Adriana Katzew and Lilia R. De Katzew focus on the production of art and media by Chicana/o youth as a form of protest. They point to art as one of the core elements of the Chicana/o movement that served as a consciousness-building tool and nurtured a sense of pride for the community historically. They further argue that art and visual culture continue to play a central role in Chicana/o social movements today.

Alejandro Covarrubias builds on his earlier work on "Agencies of Transformational Resistance" to offer a more descriptive analysis of the function and potential of such organizations. ATRs are organizations or collectives that work to create community, offer resources and skills, promote multidimensional consciousness, and provide hope for members of the collectives that social change is possible. Covarrubias shares an example of an ATR by describing the success of one Los Angeles community-based organization.

Edward M. Olivos and Carmen E. Quintana discuss the importance of the role of parents in the commitment to social justice. They examine the history of the walkouts and compare the experiences of bilingual and bicultural students and parents from the 1960s to the present. Despite all the work that was done, the problems of the past have persisted. Olivos and Quintana advocate for the need to politicize parental involvement and call on parents to look at the role they played in the 1968 walkouts as a model for ways to deal with the discrimination that Chicana/o students are facing in schools today.

Rita Kohli and Daniel G. Solórzano follow up by discussing racial discrimination between People of Color and within groups of color. They draw connections among racism, white supremacy, and racial hierarchies to illustrate how these phenomena transfer into internalized problems of People of Color. They call upon People of Color to critically assess the impact of such discrimination and to work toward coalitions as they document the experiences of high school students in Los Angeles who are taking the initiative to build cross-race coalitions.

Xico González, Eracleo Guevara, Alejo Padilla, and Marianna Rivera describe concretely a school called La Academia del Barrio Telpochcalli, which was created as a direct result of Chicana/o activism in education. This school is an example of praxis—theory and action that connect a multi-dimensional consciousness with a commitment to social justice. Both educators and students push forward a vision based on transformational resistance. In this chapter, the authors give an overview of the creation of the school, a historical context and its connection to critical pedagogy, and the lessons learned from the perspective of the educators.

In chapter 7, the authors discuss the current status of Chicana/o education and the outcome that we witnessed nationally in 2006. Evelyn M. Rangel-Medina and Anita Tijerina Revilla document the experiences of the Las Vegas Activist Crew who were responsible for the grassroots movement that shut down the Las Vegas Strip—the epicenter of commerce in town—on May 6, 2006. Again, they draw parallels to the 1968 Blowouts, but they further document the status of schools and the backlash on immigrant people from the perspective of the student activists organizing the movement locally. In their chapter, they illustrate the incredible work of student activists who essentially were the driving force of the immigrant rights movement in Las Vegas, Nevada.

Finally, Margarita Berta-Ávila and Julie López Figueroa conclude this book by illustrating the role of identity and activism in the schooling experiences of Mexican-origin students. They argue that based on the lessons learned from the legacy of Chicana/o activism in education, we are poised at an important place where we can draw on these experiences to create and implement a Chicana/o pedagogical framework that does not ignore the history of Chicana/o discrimination and actively rejects student subordination.

NOTES

1. The use of the word "queer" is related to the community-activist practice of using the term "queer" as a reclaimed and redefined label that acts as an umbrella for many nonheteronormative identifications including lesbian, gay, bisexual, transgender, intersexed, questioning, allies, and fluid. It is a term that holds political significance and is heavily associated with the gay and queer rights movement.

2. "Citizenism" is anti-immigrant behavior or ideologies that result in the belief of the superiority of people who are classified by the state as citizens of a nation. This

state- and federally sanctioned classification results in a system of unearned advantages for citizens and unwarranted discrimination of noncitizens, such as denial of basic human rights and dignity.

REFERENCES

Alvarez, R. 1986. "The Lemon Grove Incident: The Nation's First Successful Desegregation Court Case." *Journal of San Diego History* 32, no. 2. http://www.sandiego history.org/journal/86spring/lemongrove.htm.

Bermudez, N. Forthcoming. "*Mendez v. Westminster:* The Story of a Mexican American Community's Struggle to End Race Discrimination in Their Neighborhood Schools." Ph.D. diss., University of California at Los Angeles.

Covarrubias, A., and A. Tijerina Revilla. 2003. "Agencies of Transformational Resistance." *Florida Law Review* 55, no. 1: 459–77.

Freire, P. 1994. *Pedagogy of the Oppressed.* New York: Continuum Press.

Giroux, H. 1983. *Theory and Resistance in Education: A Pedagogy of the Opposition.* South Hadley, Mass.: Bergin and Garvey Press.

Solórzano, D. G., and D. Delgado Bernal. 2001. "Examining Transformational Resistance Through a Critical Race and LatCrit Theory Framework: Chicana and Chicano Students in an Urban Context." *Urban Education* 36, no. 3: 308–42.

Yosso, T. 2006. *Critical Race Counterstories Along the Chicana/o Educational Pipeline.* New York: Routledge Press.

CHAPTER 1

Genealogies of the Student "Blowouts" of 1968

CARLOS TEJEDA

I wrote the following passage in a doctoral dissertation that focused on the production and workings of *social space* in an elementary classroom:

> I read the passage and I could see myself sitting in the classroom as a child. It was me who didn't care if they thought I was a Carlos or a Juan, as long as I could avoid being singled out. It was I who had been afraid to occupy the very space of my existence in the classrooms of my childhood. For years, school was the place where I sat in fear that I'd be called on to read aloud or give an answer. It was I who wanted to be a nobody because a nobody could avoid being singled out, exposed as an unintelligent boy who couldn't read and didn't speak correctly. I was the Mexican reduced to the occupation of an inexistence: the loudness of my accent, Indian features, and dark skin compelled me to inhabit the silence of the classroom. (Tejeda 2000, 13–14).

This passage was written because I found it impossible to explain my interest in social space—that space that is a product of social practice and socially constructed meaning, which people act upon as it simultaneously acts on them—without referencing my past. It is part of a chapter where I narrate memories and feelings that were conjured while reading a text when I was a freshman in college. That text, written by Mexican author Elena Poniatowska, chronicled the lives of the poor who migrated from Mexico's

9

countryside to Mexico City—people Poniatowska described as "voiceless nobodies" who avoided giving their names because they feared "to be a bother, to occupy a space and time that didn't belong to them." It described people who when interviewed and asked to give their names would respond that she could "just put Juan," or "whatever name she wished," that they could "answer to any name she wanted," because "any name would be okay" (1995, 11). The text was a mirror in which, as a young man lost in college, I began to find myself within a reflection of thoughts and feelings that had marked my life—a life, I was learning, that indexed an experience shared by countless others.

To begin to understand my life and what it indexes, it is necessary to focus on the larger *historical contexts* and *social spaces* of my being-in-the-world, on the *time-spaces* of my lived experience. The concept of a *time-space* is informed by the work of Lefebvre (1991) and Bakhtin (1981). Lefebvre argues that our *being in the world* is simultaneously social, historical, and spatial, and that these dimensions of our existence can neither exist nor be understood independently of one another. Bakhtin argues that there is an intrinsic connectedness of temporal and spatial relationships, and he uses the term "chronotope" to refer to what he sees as the inseparability of time and space. Hence, when I use the term "time-space," I am referring to a being-in-the-world in which the social, historical, and spatial are ontologically equivalent and in which time and space are inseparable and thoroughly interrelated. From this concept of a *time-space,* to contextualize a person's life, one must look not only at social indicators (such as gender, race, and class) and historical periods (for example, colonial times, the era of de jure segregation, the 1960s) but also at geographical locations (a slave state, the Southwest, East Los Angeles).

It is impossible, then, to begin to account for how phenotype and language could have had so much to do with what I thought and felt as a boy in school without accounting for the *racialization* of social relations and the forms of *deculturalization* that characterized the southwestern United States of the early 1970s, without accounting for the inferiorization and subordination that characterized the positionality of Spanish-speaking Mexicans in states like California and cities like Los Angeles. What's more, it is not possible to explain the types of racialization and forms of cultural domination that were commonplace in the time-space of the southwest-

ern United States of the early 1970s without an understanding of their origins and development throughout the larger time-spaces of what today is
known as the United States. What I experienced in 1971 as a dark-skinned,
Spanish-speaking boy in an Anglo-American school in East Los Angeles had
a lot to do with ideologies, social practices, and institutional arrangements
whose origins can be traced to the enslavement of Africans, the genocide
and forced removal of indigenous people, and the imperialist expansion of
the United States into what was then the northern half of the nation-state
of Mexico. Similarly, to begin to understand how a boy who was afraid to
inhabit his existence in a classroom could grow to occupy the academic
spaces that afforded him the opportunity to theorize that space, it is necessary to consider the larger social and historical context—the time-space—in
which occupying those academic spaces was made possible. It is impossible
to begin to account for my access to the social spaces of an undergraduate
and graduate education without locating that access in the larger time-space
born of the struggle for civil rights and educational equality in American
society. The opportunities I enjoyed as a young adult were made possible
by a long-fought struggle that forced rearrangements in "American" society
that included the restructuring of educational opportunity. In other words,
what we commonly refer to as the *present* is unintelligible, a reality that can
be neither decoded nor discursively constructed without a reading of what
we commonly refer to as the *past*.

It is not possible to begin to understand the recent past or immediate present of specific lives and the larger time-space in which those lives
transpire without being firmly grounded in a critical understanding of
the present that interpretively gazes toward the past—which must also be
understood as social, historical, and spatial. To understand the present, it
is necessary to map the paths of ideologies and practices through which the
past extends into the present. What's more, I contend that without a critical
understanding of the present terrain and an interpretive mapping of what
we commonly refer to as the past, we are ontologically lost, readily constructed as this or that, and easily positioned in this or that social location:
we can be their "Mexicans," "Hispanics," "Latinos," "beaners," "illegals," or
the "nobodies" that will answer to any name they give us because any that
they choose for us will be okay. The lack of a critical understanding of our
present and an interpretive mapping of our past reduces us to ontological

orphans who are unfamiliar with and disconnected from the genealogy of our *being* in the social world, to people who may be afraid to occupy the very space of our existence because, not knowing who we are or where we come from, we can easily be told what does and does not belong to us, where we are from, and where we do not belong.

Gazing down the paths of conquest, colonization, and capitalist expansion to map the ideologies and practices through which the past has trekked into the present, we can locate strands of ideological and material practices that weigh us down with what has been while compelling us to move from that which is. We can see that ideological and material practices from the past simultaneously *enable* and *constrain* us, and that they do so in a manner that calls for us to both commemorate and condemn the past. Those ideological and material practices can be mapped from moments and locations in time and space when and where the actions of social subjects disrupt the larger time-space of their occurrence. The 1968 East Los Angeles High School Walkouts (commonly referred to as the "Blowouts") constitute one of those moments and locations in time and space that allow for a mapping of the strands of ideologies and practices through which the past extends into the present.

In this chapter, I contend that the "Blowouts" must be commemorated for vividly exposing and valiantly opposing the condemnable ideologies and practices of a *schooling for subservience* and educational exclusion that constrained Chicanas/os in American society. I use the term "schooling for subservience" to refer to schooling whose curricular contents (both hidden and overt) and pedagogical practices aim to socialize groups of students *to* and *through* norms, values, and worldviews that facilitate their social and cultural domination. It refers to forms of schooling that operate to construct in students identities and subjectivities that compel them to participate in, acquiesce to, or ignore their social and cultural subordination by dominant groups. As a decolonizing pedagogue (see Tejeda, Espinoza, and Gutierrez 2003), I work from the following premises: that forms of schooling from our colonial and capitalist anterior, which find both direct and mutated manifestations in the present, are inextricably tied to the workings of contemporary forms of domination and exploitation in American society; that the forms of schooling for subservience practiced and perfected throughout the history of racial domination and capitalist exploitation in Anglo-American society function at the service of today's social and cultural domination; and that without the effective workings of a schooling for subservience, the type of social, political, cultural, and economic hegemony enjoyed by the dominant classes in American society would not be possible. In what follows, I use the work of various scholars to trace a genealogy of the ideological and material practices that produced the educational experience Chicana/o students protested by walking out of their high schools in 1968. I then use the work of scholars to highlight that the Blowouts were made possible by a set of ideological and material practices with a genealogy of their own.

THE EAST LOS ANGELES HIGH SCHOOL BLOWOUTS OF 1968

I am the boy who was afraid to occupy the space of my existence in the classrooms of my childhood and the young man in college who was haunted by the memories of that boy. But I am also a professor in the field of education with a doctorate degree from one of the leading graduate schools of education in the United States. In either case, and they are both my case, I find it impossible to begin to explain who I am or what I have lived, to narrate the identity I want to assume, or to define the educational politics I want to practice without looking back into what is commonly referred to as the past to interpret what is understood to be the present. But in looking at the past, I see neither landscapes of absolute certitude about that which has "passed" nor transcendental "truths" to make sense of the present. The past is not a set of fixed phenomena with inherent meanings that is out there waiting to be seen, nor are there global positioning devices to be had when attempting to map the past's paths into the present. I understand that while mapping the past it is important to survey the terrain with both conceptual caution and epistemological humility. It is one thing to know that there is a past to which we are directly connected, but it is quite another to believe that we can know that past with absolute certainty. Scholars like Trouillot insistently remind us that there is a real difference "between *what happened* and *that which is said to have happened*" (1995, 3; emphasis added). Others like White (1999) argue that historical discourse is incapable of producing "truths" about the past—that it yields only interpretations. The work of these scholars warns that attempts to construct understandings of the past will have to unfold without access to a "god's-eye view" or a transcendental vantage from whence to gaze at *what happened*. I understand that in using the historical narratives of the various scholars cited below I am building on *interpretations of what happened,* and not *what actually happened.* Despite these understandings, I do not believe that the past is entirely unknowable, or that we are completely lost in the present. Although I agree that there is neither an epistemologically pristine position from which to view the past nor a correct historical interpretation to be had, I also agree with Somekawa and Smith (1988) that rather than looking for or believing in the absolute truth or complete objectivity of the historical narratives we construct, we should believe in the moral or political positions we are taking with our narratives. Hence, this chapter's mapping of the past into the present, while striving toward the ideal of objectivity and attempting to be as approximate as possible to *what happened,* is more concerned with the moral and political value of constructing a counternarrative that contextualizes and highlights the importance of commemorating and condemning that which constituted the 1968 Blowouts—a counternarrative from whence we can move from what has been to what should be. With this in mind, and the understanding that my vision can be neither perfectly focused nor impartial, I briefly map genealogical strands of ideologies and practices that marked the time-space of the 1968 Blowouts.

When I gaze into past, into the immediate time-space of my life and the larger time-space I have shared with others, I see strands of ideologies and practices that ought to be condemned aloud. But I see also, with no less clarity, ideologies and practices that ought to be commemorated with conviction. I see the sacrifice my parents practiced to ensure their children survived as exiles from equality in a society that openly ostracized the "other." I see ideologies and practices that led to the 1968 Blowouts, when thousands of high school students in East Los Angeles and surrounding areas walked out of schools protesting against their education. Those actions and events should be commemorated because they constitute an integral part of a struggle that opened doors for people to enter spaces that had been systematically denied to them and because they serve as a clear example of the past's constraining and enabling force upon the present. They are a vivid example of the need to both commemorate and condemn an inheritance of ideologies and practices that have shaped who and where we are and can serve as a road map for where we need to move and who we want to be.

According to various scholars, the East Los Angeles Student Walkouts

(Blowouts) of 1968 began during the first week of March and continued for more than a week and a half (Bernal 1998; Inda 1990; Muñoz 1989; Rosales 1997). At least two scholars pinpoint the first walkout to the Friday morning of March 1, when a few hundred students walked out of Wilson High School in protest against their principal's decision to cancel a school play (Inda 1990; Rosales 1997). But these same scholars emphasize that the cancellation of the play was not the real cause behind the walkout; they attribute it to people's feelings regarding fundamental issues, and they point out that students "would not return to classes unless they got smaller class sizes, more emphasis on Chicana/o history and culture, and expanded student rights" (Inda 1990, 14). The walkout at Wilson High School, like the walkouts that followed, was essentially a protest against an inferior education. The students at Wilson were followed by more than a thousand students at Lincoln High School who walked out on the morning of March 4. On Tuesday, March 5, more than two thousand students walked out of Garfield High School. Students at Roosevelt High School walked out on Wednesday, and by Friday March 8 the walkouts had extended beyond the east side and were occurring throughout Los Angeles, including Belmont, Jefferson, and Venice high schools. They continued for more than a week and a half, with as many as ten to fifteen thousand students walking out in protest (see Acuña 1981; Bernal 1998; Inda 1990; Muñoz 1989; and Rosales 1997).

As mentioned above, the Blowouts were a protest against profound issues affecting large sectors of the Mexican American population, the most significant and concrete of these being an inferior education. Rosales explains that the call for educational reform was a major element of the 1960s Chicana/o movement and that Chicana/o students used the walkouts "to dramatize what they considered the abysmally poor educational conditions affecting their schools" (1997, 185). Scholars who have examined the Blowouts highlight the following about the educational practices and circumstances faced by Chicana/o students: high school dropout or push-out rates of more than 50 percent, which could be contrasted to dropout rates of 3.1 percent and 2.6 percent for Palisades and Monroe high schools in West Los Angeles (Acuña 1981; Bernal 1998; Inda 1990); an average of only 7.1 years of schooling, which could be contrasted with 9 years of schooling for African Americans and 12 years of schooling for Anglos (Inda 1990); the lowest reading scores in the Los Angeles school district; a highly disproportionate placement of students in special education classes and classes for the mentally retarded and the emotionally disturbed; schools that were overcrowded and undermaintained in comparison to schools that served Anglos and African Americans; curricular contents and practices that ignored Chicana/o culture and functioned to prepare students for low-skilled jobs; and teachers and administrators who lacked an understanding of working-class communities or were openly racist against Chicana/o students or both (Acuña 1981; Bernal 1998). Inda summarizes the practices and circumstances students protested against in the following terms:

> From the moment Chicano children entered school, they were made to feel ashamed of their culture. Five out of ten barrio schools did not allow students to speak Spanish. Not only was their language demeaned, but also their style of dress. They were often told, "stop looking like pachucos," and forbidden to wear certain clothes, which were a source of pride for students. Thomas Carter in *Mexican Americans in Schools: A History of Neglect,* documented racist teacher attitudes that contributed to the negative self-image of Chicanos. Most teachers believed that Mexican culture produced a lack of motivation in students. They were pessimistic about the Mexican's ability to learn. Teachers saw the Chicano child as inferior to the white child, an inferiority which the overt racists attributed to innate stupidity and which more "open-minded" racists attributed to laziness or apathy in the culture. (1990, 2–3)

CONDEMNING GENEALOGIES OF SCHOOLING FOR SUBSERVIENCE AND EDUCATIONAL EXCLUSION

The practices and circumstances students protested in 1968 were far from a temporary aberration in an otherwise egalitarian society with equality of social and educational opportunity. Inda (1990) argues that it was years of unsuccessful attempts by Chicanas/os to improve the schooling they received that led to the walkouts. Bernal reminds us that the struggle for a quality education predated the walkouts by a number of decades and that many of the issues and concerns of participants and supporters "were very similar to those voiced in Mexican communities in the United States since before the turn of the century" (1998, 117). Referring to schooling conditions and outcomes for Chicana/o students decades after the Blowouts, in the 1990s, Valencia writes: "School failure among Chicanos is not a new situation. On the contrary, it is an old and stubborn condition. It refuses to relent. It continues even in the face of opposition. Imagine having a toothache that never goes away and you can have a sense of the persistent nature of the poor academic performance of a substantial portion of the Chicano school population. In short, Chicano school failure is deeply rooted in history" (1991, as cited in Valencia 2002, 3).

What students were protesting against during the Blowouts was far from new, but tracing the walkouts' "deeply rooted" origins requires examining more than a number of decades or even the most recent centennial. Referring to the schooling of indigenous populations, Grande writes that "the miseducation of American Indians precedes the 'birth' of this nation," and that schooling was "a well-established weapon in the arsenal of American Imperialism long before the first shots of the revolutionary war were ever fired" (2004, 11). In an introductory passage to his history of the education and *deculturalization* of dominated cultures in American society, Spring argues, "Violence and racism are a basic part of American history and the history of the schools." He continues:

> *Cultural genocide*—the attempt to destroy other cultures—is an important part of the history of violence in the U.S. Often, U.S. educational policies have involved cultural genocide. "Deculturalization" is the term I use for the process of cultural genocide. . . .
>
> *Deculturalization is the educational process of destroying a people's culture and replacing it with a new culture.* Language is an important part of culture. In the case of the United States, schools have used varying forms of this method in attempts to eradicate the cultures of Native Americans; African Americans; Mexican Americans; Puerto Ricans; and immigrants from Ireland, Southern and Eastern Europe, and Asia. Believing that Anglo-American culture was the superior culture and the only culture that would support republican and democratic institutions, educators forbade the speaking of no-English languages, particularly Spanish and Native American tongues, and forced student to learn Anglo-American centered curriculum. . . .
>
> European invaders and early U.S. government leaders were able

to rationalize their conquest and expropriation of Native American lands by thinking of Indians as culturally and racially inferior. These attitudes were woven into educational plans to deculturalize Native Americans so that they would willingly sell their lands to Anglo-American settlers. This pattern of linguistic and cultural genocide continued into the twentieth century. (2004, 3, 15)

What students were walking out against in 1968 were the concrete manifestations of ideological and material practices whose genealogies can be mapped throughout a temporal extension of centuries and across a spatial expanse of continents. Gazing down historical paths of state-sponsored schooling in the United States, we see that those ideological and material practices worked to impose *schooling for subservience* and establish educational exclusion.

Focusing specifically on the school failure of impoverished racial and ethnic minority students in the United States, Valencia and other scholars offer a particular interpretation and mapping of those genealogies. Valencia contends that of the different explanations for the school failure of minority students, "deficit thinking theory has held the longest currency among scholars, educators and policymakers." He defines "deficit thinking" as a model with several explanatory variants, which generally "posit that students who fail do so because of alleged internal deficiencies (such as cognitive and/or motivational limitations) or shortcomings socially linked to the youngster—such as familial deficits and dysfunctions." It is described as an explanatory model that "overwhelmingly locates school failure and its causes in students and their families," while ignoring important structural factors such as school segregation, differences in school funding, curriculum differentiation, or a combination thereof (1997b, xi). Valencia (1997a) explains deficit thinking in terms of the following major characteristics: it blames the victim, it is oppressive, it is pseudoscientific, it is a dynamic model that changes according to the exigencies of the times, it is a model of educability that calls for specific educational policy and practice, and it is a model whose controversial nature produces contesting perspectives and countering discourses.

Menchaca traces the roots of deficit thinking to the time-space of the early 1600s. She argues that between 1620 and 1870 non-Europeans were enslaved or reduced to servitude because it economically benefited whites, which rationalized their economic interests through racial ideologies that claimed nonwhites were inferior. Among the various inferiorizing notions articulated during that period were the following: that as "god's chosen people" Anglo-Saxons were destined to populate, own, and govern the lands of the "new world" in order to "salvage" them from the paganism of "savage" and "barbarian" peoples who were "descendants of the devil"; that "Africans were not human beings," and their enslavement was in accordance with the will of God (1997, 15); that all humans were children of God, but nonwhite peoples were inferior due to racial differences that resulted from their migrations and acclimations to particular environmental niches and climates; that the different races were different species and only Caucasians were human beings; that Native Americans "were only three-fifths of a person"; that Africans "were a race of degenerate people who were dull and inclined to laziness" (21); that the physical differences and intellectual inferiority of dark-skinned people were "a result of the cultural degeneration they experienced proceeding their exodus from the Garden of Eden" (23); that "non-whites spoke primitive languages reflecting a simplistic mentality"; that "blacks had evolved from gorillas and Indians from monkeys," with whom "they shared similar behavior characteristics" (27); that all races were Homo sapiens, but "Caucasians had larger brain cases" and "were cognitively superior to nonwhites," whom they were entitled to govern (31); that Anglo-Saxons were superior in intellect to all other races—including other whites (34); and that intelligence and all other social characteristics were genetically inherited, resulting in a social order that was "an outcome of intellectual differences between inferior and superior peoples" (34–35). Menchaca argues that by the late 1800s these types of views had amalgamated into a commonsense racial ideology composed of a set of values, images, and constructs used by whites to interpret their world and make sense of the nonwhite peoples in the world.

Despite the heinous nature of those racial ideologies, their depravity was easily surpassed by the material practices they served to rationalize and from which they became inseparable. The enslavement of millions of Africans and the genocide and dislocation of millions of indigenous people are two of the most telling manifestations of the synergistic effect of the wide array of ideological and material practices that would impact virtually every dimension of nonwhite people's lives.

In the 1600s both British missionaries and the Quakers established schools to "educate" Africans and indigenous peoples. Although missionaries argued that Africans and Indians were human and could be religiously converted, they maintained the idea that they were savages whose cultures had not allowed them to reach the cognitive level of Caucasians. The purpose of their schooling was to teach Christianity in order to save souls (Menchaca 1997). Referring specifically to the education of Native peoples, Axtell writes that the goal of English missionaries was to convert them "to a totally new way of life and thought" (1985, 179). During the Revolutionary period, abolitionists in the North began educating freed slaves, but the education offered to former slaves (which consisted primarily of reading and writing in English, had a strong religious orientation, and served to replace African cultures with Anglo culture) was not intended to create an opportunity for social equality with whites. Africans found freedom from slavery in the North, but with it came an intense discrimination. That discrimination included segregated schooling, which was firmly established by the end of the eighteenth century and became a centerpiece of educational exclusion and inequity until the middle of twentieth century when the Supreme Court ruled against it. In the South, literacy for Africans was outlawed; states established compulsory ignorance laws that prohibited educating slaves and maintained these laws until 1868 (Franklin and Moss 1988; Spring 2004).

Despite the fact that formal public education in the United States was offered by states as early as 1825, there is no evidence indicating that racial minorities participated in the public education system during the nineteenth century. After 1868 state governments afforded local school boards decision-making power over the schooling of racial minorities, but the states simultaneously prevented school boards from exercising that power by passing funding laws to ensure that blacks and other racial groups would not be schooled despite the intentions of local school boards (Menchaca 1997).

In the case of indigenous people, formal public education was denied, but Anglos were far from uninterested in "schooling" Indians, and the salvation of souls was far from the only motive behind their interest in educating Indians. In addition to the initial attempts to "civilize" and "save" the "savage" Indian, after the Revolutionary period the U.S. government attempted to use schooling and *deculturalization* policies to appropriate lands without incurring the costs of waging war. Adhering to a strategy developed by George Washington, Thomas Jefferson attempted to use trading houses to "civilize" Native peoples who occupied lands wanted by the government. He believed that a cultural transformation "was key to acquiring native lands," and the cultural transformation he proposed included *teaching* a desire for the accumulation of property, extinguishing the practice of sharing, having Natives form nuclear families, and transforming Indians into yeoman farmers living on farms (Spring 2004, 13).

Thomas McKenney, the first head of the Office of Indian Affairs, also believed that education was fundamental to social control and societal improvement; he argued that a school system controlled by missionary teachers could transform Native Americans in a single generation (Spring 2004). McKenney's beliefs about the transforming capacity of schooling were put into practice with the Civilization Act of 1819. The work of schooling Indians on the lands neighboring the "frontier" settlements of the United States and the lands to which indigenous groups were being relocated was then undertaken primarily by Protestant missionary educators, who believed that learning English was essential for the intended cultural transformation. At the end of the 1820s, however, President Jackson had concluded that Washington's and Jefferson's civilization policies and the Civilization Act of 1819 "had failed to educate the southern tribes to the point where they would want to sell their lands," and he was concerned that "education was actually resulting in Indians gaining the tools to resist the policies of the U.S. government." This led to the Indian Removal Act of 1830, which gave the president the power to set aside lands located west of the Mississippi to be exchanged for Indian lands located east of the Mississippi, as well as the authority "to provide assistance to the tribes for their removal and resettlement on new lands" (ibid., 23).

By the second half of the late 1850s, however, government leaders were coming to the realization that white settlement would require more land and that dealing with indigenous groups who refused to acquiesce to the government was again a major concern. According to Spring (2004), the U.S. government considered a combination of allotment programs (which distributed commonly held tribal land to individual "Indians"), the reservation system, and educational policies as the best method of dealing with the groups who refused to give up their lands. He explains that during the last part of the nineteenth century, educational policies included eliminating indigenous cultural practices, replacing indigenous languages with English, and creating allegiance to the U.S. government and that boarding schools played a fundamental role in the implementation of those educational policies. Indigenous children sent to boarding schools were taken from their families by force in order to separate them from their language and cultural practices. The following were among the primary goals of the boarding schools: teaching English, offering vocational training for jobs, instilling the work ethic and capitalist values, the inculcation of patriotism, and the teaching of allegiance to the U.S. government. Between 1879 and 1905, twenty-five nonreservation boarding schools were opened throughout the United States. Spring writes that the boarding schools used paramilitary forms of organization and financed themselves with the labor of students who were forced to work raising crops and tending animals. Children were awakened at five in the morning, marched from place to place, constantly drilled, given little time for recreation, and punished with floggings. He adds that during the 1920s, investigators were horrified by the conditions they encountered, and he quotes an anthropologist who referred to the boarding schools as "penal institutions—where little children were sentenced to hard labor for a term of years to expiate the crime of being born of their mothers" (ibid., 31). Spring summarizes the experience of indigenous people with Anglo-American schooling as follows:

> During periods of conquest, education provided Europeans with a means to cultural and linguistic genocide of Native Americans. By defining Native Americans as the culturally and inferior other, Europeans could justify the Indian wars and the resulting expropriation of lands. The defeat of Native Americans opened vast territories for European Americans' exploitation.
>
> The problem for the U.S. government was ensuring that Native American armies would never again challenge the incursion of white settlers. To avoid any future challenges from the vanquished, the U.S. government instituted educational policies of deculturalization. To a certain extent these educational policies were effective. However, con-

tinued resistance by Native Americans eventually led to demands on the U.S. government in the latter part of the twentieth century for restoration of tribal cultures and languages. The federal government only responded positively to these demands when it appeared that Native Americans were no longer a military threat. (ibid., 32)

Unfortunately, neither schooling for subservience nor the denial of access to the literacies necessary for an equitable participation in Anglo-American society ended with the effective subjugation of Africans and Native peoples.

Valencia's discussion of what he refers to as the *genetic pathology model* allows us to continue tracing the genealogy of ideological and material practices that resulted in the educational practices and circumstances Chicana/o students protested against in 1968. According to Valencia, the genetic pathology model essentially argued that intelligence and inferiority were genetic. He explains that it was founded in social Darwinism, Galtonian eugenics, Mendelian genetics, and the anthropometric assessment and classification of intelligence. It held currency between the 1890s and 1930s, and it was well established by the 1920s. Citing Cravens, Valencia explains that individuals who held hereditarian perspectives included scholars, researchers, professors, designers of widely used standardized tests, officers of scholarly organizations, and government consultants who were frequently in positions of stature and authority and that their ideas "were seized upon by men in public life who possessed a direct stake in their application to American society" (Cravens 1997, 45, cited in Valencia 1997c, 41). He further explains that "hereditarian ideas became a rational for white racial superiority" (43), and he adds that the deficit thinking of hereditarians directly affected the policy and practice of schooling in American society. Two sets of practices that emerged from hereditarian ideas were those directly related to eugenics and intelligence testing.

Eugenics and the Innate Superiority of Whites

Citing Chorover, Valencia explains that it was the United States and not Nazi Germany that first established laws providing for eugenic sterilization aimed at racial purification (Chorover 1979, 43, cited in Valencia 1997c, 47). Valencia explains that Galtonian eugenics gave "impetus to the forced sterilization practices vis-à-vis the 'mentally defective' and other undesirables"

(45). Between 1907 and 1931, thirty-one states established sterilization laws, and it is believed that during that period 12,145 forced sterilizations were performed—7,548 of them in California. By 1958, 60,926 sterilizations sanctioned by state laws had been performed.

Mendelian genetics were misused to argue that miscegenation between "intellectually superior whites" and "intellectually inferior Blacks, Mexican Americans, and American Indians" would produce "disharmonious, baleful unions." Valencia points out that despite the fact that the alleged consequences of racial mixing were found to be fallacious, "Mendelian genetics held currency as a prominent ideological foundation for deficit thinking during the era of the genetic pathology model" (52).

Intelligence Testing and the Intellectual Superiority of Whites

Between 1908 and 1911, H. H. Goddard, a student of Galtonian hereditarianist Stanley Hall, translated Binet and Simon's French intelligence test and argued that it could be used to measure innate intelligence. Then, between 1911 and 1915, Lewis Terman (who was also a student of Stanley Hall) substantially revised the Binet scale into what came to be known as the Stanford-Binet Intelligence Test. The test, which claimed the capacity to measure a person's intelligence quotient (IQ), utilized a scale that was standardized on a group that was white and middle class. By 1918, a test development team (which included Goddard and Terman) headed by Robert Yerkes, a Harvard professor and the president of the American Psychological Association, had designed two group-administered intelligence tests for the U.S. Army. Yerkes argued that mental testing of recruits would provide valuable information for their proper placement in the army. During 1918 and 1919, the army undertook the universal testing of recruits, assessing the mental ability of 1,726,966 enlisted men (Valencia 1997c). Citing the work of Gould (1981), Valencia highlights three conclusions drawn from the test results that would influence social policy long after the test scores had been forgotten: that the measured average mental age of white American adults was 13.08 years, that men from southern and eastern Europe were less intelligent than those from Nordic ancestry, and that the average mental age of "negro" recruits was 10.41 years. Valencia writes: "Given the strength of the circular nature of this argument, the massive data base, and the prominent reputations of the Army test developers, the value of deficit thinking on the American stock market of social thought would rise dramatically. Already on the increase, the eugenics, anti-miscegenation, and restrictionist immigration movements looked to the Army data to bolster their political agendas" (1997c, 55). But racial purists and nativists were not the only ones who used the results of intelligence tests to translate their agendas into social policy. Educators and educational policy makers also misused intelligence testing, and they did so while enunciating its emerging racial ideologies and institutionalizing the type of social stratification those tests "scientifically" legitimized.

By 1920, several intelligence tests had been developed and were ready for use by public school systems. Concerned with promoting efficiency, schools were highly receptive to those tests: "By the mid 1920s group-administered intelligence tests were used with great frequency in our public schools, and bureaucracies arose to handle the mass testing and use of test results" (ibid., 57). Valencia points out that the proliferation of group-administered intelligence tests allowed scholarly research on racial differences in mental ability to become firmly established. He writes the following about that research:

> To be sure, 1920s race psychology research of racial/ethnic differences in intelligence was a prominent activity. As we have seen, the conclusions drawn about intellectual differences between whites and some children of color (i.e., African American; Mexican American) were, in frequency, predominantly hereditarian based. Children of color, it was alleged, performed lower than their white peers largely because of inferiority in native intelligence. This research claim, in and of itself, is indeed a significant social statement of the nature of race relations during the height of the genetic pathology era. The allegation of the intellectual inferiority of these racial/ethnic minority groups speaks to the descriptive and explanatory aspects of deficit thinking during this period. The question remains, however, about the prescriptive role of intelligence testing research and the use of tests in shaping school curriculum. (ibid., 71)

This question can be addressed through Gonzalez's research on Mexican American students in Los Angeles's public schools during that period. Gonzalez (1974a, 1974b) finds that in the 1920s, practices such as intelligence testing, homogenous groupings, curriculum differentiation, and counseling programs served to stratify students according to race or ethnicity and socio-economic status. IQ test results, for example, were used to place students at elementary schools in one of four different types of classes: *normal* classes, *opportunity* rooms, *adjustment* rooms, or *development* centers. Opportunity rooms were further divided into Opportunity A rooms and Opportunity B rooms; the former were designed for "mentally superior" students, while the latter were for "slow learners" whose IQ scores were higher than 70 but below the "normal" range. Adjustment rooms were designed for "normal" students with an average-range IQ who had specific skill problems, were "educationally maladjusted," or were in need of remediation in reading or English. Development centers were for students—typically referred to as "mentally retarded" or "mentally deficient"—whose IQ scores were below 70. Based on the median IQ score (91.2) of Mexican children, Gonzalez (1974b) suggests that it was highly probable that nearly one-half of Mexican students would have been placed in "slow learner" and "development" centers—that is, 50 percent of Mexican students were placed in classes for the mentally retarded or the mentally subaverage. According to Gonzalez (1974a), in 1929 there were eleven development centers in Los Angeles, with a total enrollment of twenty-five hundred students. Ten of the eleven centers were located in working-class communities, and Mexican children were highly overrepresented in five of those centers. Mexican American students constituted the entire enrollment in one center, a third of the enrollment in two centers, and a fourth of the enrollment in the other two centers. Gonzalez explains that some development centers served as producers of cheap labor, training students for unskilled and semiskilled occupations in restaurants, laundries, and agriculture.

Gonzalez's research also focused on intelligence testing and curriculum differentiation in Los Angeles's secondary schools. He found that by the middle of the 1920s, there had been established a four-tiered tracking system, with each track having specific teaching methods, curricula, educational objectives, and consequences. The following were the four curricular tracks: very superior, normal, dull normal, and mentally retarded. The tracks were designed by using IQ testing to identify the type of course work that was compatible with students' mental capacity. Citing Gonzalez (1990), Valencia writes: "Given the widespread belief that Mexican American children were not cut out for 'book study' and thus should be trained for hand

work, it is not at all surprising that Los Angeles schools undertook a systematic curricula plan of 'training for occupational efficiency for Mexican Americans'" (1997c, 78). According to Gonzalez (1974b), by 1929 there were seventy regular vocational education courses in approximately one-half of the
school district's high schools, but an overwhelming number of these courses
were located in poor, working-class, and non-Anglo neighborhoods. Given
the genealogy of practices and circumstances I am trying to trace to illustrate
the significance of the Blowouts, what Gonzalez finds with regards to vocational courses and specific high schools in Los Angeles is highly telling: a
total of forty-five of the aforementioned seventy vocational courses were
offered in three of the city's east-side high schools—Lincoln, Roosevelt, and
Jefferson—and a total of thirty-five of those courses were offered in Lincoln
and Roosevelt alone. He also finds that in 1932 the school district was offering a total of thirty-one "class A vocational courses" to male students in its
high schools. "Class A vocational courses" offered students about five hours
of trade instruction and one and a half hours of academic instruction. Lincoln, Roosevelt, and Fremont high schools, located in working-class neighborhoods, accounted for as many as twenty-six of the thirty-one courses,
while not a single "class A vocational course" was offered in high schools on
the west side—an area that was predominantly white and of a higher socioeconomic status (as cited in Valencia 1997c).

Valencia cites Gonzalez's research to point out that the situation was
probably worst for Mexican American females, whose vocational training
was often limited to preparing them for menial jobs as domestic servants,
laundry workers, and seamstresses. He also highlights the fact that the geo-
graphic distribution of vocational education for females in the school district was very similar to that found for males in that the vocational courses
were disproportionately offered in schools with working-class and minority
students. He cites Gonzalez as follows:

> For instance, homemaking was offered at only four schools: Lafay-
> ette Junior High School (with an enrollment of 36 per cent Black,
> 14 per cent Mexican, and 30 per cent Jewish), Belvedere Junior High
> (51 per cent Mexican) Hollenbeck (Mexican and Jewish) and Jefferson
> (mixed working class). Lincoln offered dressmaking, millinery and
> power-sewing. Roosevelt offered dressmaking, sewing, power-sewing,

and personal hygiene. Fremont offered dressmaking and personal hygiene. What this in fact meant, was that of six vocational subjects for females Lincoln offered three, Roosevelt four, Fremont two. Only seven schools taught vocational courses for women. All of them were located in working class neighborhoods. (Gonzalez 1974b, 180, cited in Valencia 1997c, 80)

Although it is clear that intelligence testing and curriculum differentiation served as "oppressive sorting tools" leading to inferior schooling for racial minorities and the poor, Valencia contends that it would be "inaccurate" to see intelligence testing and its related practices as solely responsible for the educational inequity of the 1920s and 1930s. He insists that we not forget "extrascientific" factors such as the already entrenched perspective that perceived the educability of racial minorities and the poor as very limited, or the racial segregation whose ideological foundations could be traced to the nineteenth-century belief that whites should avoid social interaction with racial groups that were biologically inferior (1997c, 81). In California, those ideological foundations were so strong and the racial segregation so intense that 85 percent of the schools surveyed by the state in 1930–31 indicated that they were segregating Mexican Americans through the use of either separate schools or separate classrooms within their schools (Valencia 1997c).

Unfortunately, neither intelligence testing nor the racial ideology that predated and accompanied that testing was the last "oppressive sorting tool" wielded against racial minorities and directly related to the practices and circumstances Chicana/o students protested in 1968. Maintaining a focus on the lineage of deficit thinking and concomitant practices traced by Menchaca and Valencia, Foley (1997) explains that around 1930 deficit thinking based on genetics began a rapid decline in acceptance and began to be replaced by a deficit thinking based on cultural traits and behaviors.

According to Foley, Oscar Lewis's culture of poverty theory was fundamental to the type of explanations for school failure that would replace explanations based on genetic inferiority. Lewis's work argued that people living in poverty created a unique and self-sustaining way of life defined by a set of negative values, norms, and social practices that were allegedly passed on to successive generations. Foley explains that public policy makers seeking to blame the poor combined the culture of poverty theory with theories of cultural deficit to articulate an interdisciplinary discourse on poverty and the poor. Citing Michael Katz (1989), Foley points out that several generations of policy makers wielded a "poverty discourse" that extended from the "War on Poverty" liberals of the 1960s to Reagan conservatives in the 1980s—the latter utilizing the poverty discourse to articulate an effective rhetoric against big government and the welfare state.

Pearl continues tracing deficit thinking from the *culture of poverty model* to the *cultural depravation model* that dominated deficit thinking when Chicana/o students walked out against their schooling in the late 1960s. He explains that once genetic interpretations of racial differences began losing favor in the 1950s, differences in school achievement had to be explained as resulting from something other than genetic differences. Those differences could have been explained as the product of persistent unequal treatment in society, or they could have been explained as resulting from a deficit other than innate intelligence. To the misfortune of racial minorities and the poor, the greater part of social policy and social science thinking adopted the latter explanation, clearing the way for the rise to prominence of the *cultural deprivation model and its cultural deficit thesis.* Pearl writes, "The *cultural deprivation model,* also know as the *cultural disadvantagement* or *social pathology model,* singled out the family unit (rather than genes) as the transmitter of deficiencies. Although culture (or the alleged lack of it) was central to the cultural deprivation model, the family was the key. The family unit—mother, father, home environment—was pegged as the carrier of pathology" (1997, 133). Pearl explains that the child of this model's hypothesized family was characterized in the following ways: as intellectually and linguistically impaired, having pathogenic personality characteristics, fatalistic and mistrustful, lacking self-esteem, lacking impulse control, unable to distinguish right from wrong, and anti-intellectual. He further explains that three different cultural theses were employed to explain differences in school achievement and that those theses "had a powerful influence on public opinion and social policy":

> *Cultural deprivation* (which became, inaccurately, a rubric for the cultural thesis) is drawn from sociology and anthropology and postulates the existence of alienated cultures that are too antagonistic to schooling to effectively prevent members from succeeding in school. A sec-

ond cultural thesis, *inadequate socialization,* derives from psychoanalysis and postulates a chaotic home situation resulting in the character disorder of arrested development, for example, an inability to delay gratification, thus negatively affecting school performance. A third thesis, *accumulated environmental deficits,* based on cognitive development theory, contends that accumulated environmental deficits in the critical early years lead to irreversible cognitive deficits. All three meet our criteria of deficit thinking because they are used to explain behaviors and attitudes that are inimical with school success. (ibid., 134)

Of the three theses, the last two appear to have been the most significant throughout the 1960s. Whereas "inadequate socialization" became the primary explanation for the deficits ascribed to racial minorities, it was the ideas of the "accumulated environmental deficits" thesis that had the greatest impact on policy and practice. The latter is said to have been at the heart of the Great Society programs and the attempts at compensatory education—including programs like Head Start and Follow Through. Pearl emphasizes that these deficit theses allowed scholars and policy makers to ignore "the complex makeup of macrolevel and microlevel mechanisms that helped structure schools as inequitable and exclusionary institutions" (151).

Given what Pearl explains, it is clear that said theses functioned to refine and expand the arsenal of ideological practices wielded against dominated groups by offering what I would refer to as a *discourse of denial and deceit.* Said discourse, disguised in the semantics of social science and leveraging its legitimacy, made it possible for many to "understand" and explain away the disproportionate underachievement of racial minority students while ignoring the centuries of schooling for subservience and educational exclusion that had been part and parcel of the plethora of social practices and policies employed to ensure the ideological inferiorization and social subordination of racial groups in American society.

COMMEMORATING THE CONTRIBUTIONS OF THE BLOWOUTS

Informed by the scholars cited above, one can argue that the inferiorization and educational practices Chicana/o students protested against in 1968 descended from a schooling for subservience and educational exclusion whose ancestry had established roots in Anglo-American society since the 1600s. The prohibition against speaking Spanish in the schools, the highly disproportionate placement in special education classes for the mentally retarded and emotionally disturbed, the alarming push-out and dropout rates, the curricular contents that lacked relevancy for Chicana/o students, the courses designed to condition students for low-skilled jobs, the over-crowded classrooms and dilapidated facilities, the openly racist teachers and administrators (who saw in the Chicana/o child an inferiority resulting from innate or cultural stupidity, laziness, and apathy), and the overall context that made Chicana/o students feel ashamed can be understood as the instantiation of ideologies and practices from time-spaces that unfolded as far back as the 1600s and stretched into the time-space of 1968. The aforementioned were the more contemporary forms of a schooling for subservience and educational exclusion that was indicted by the Blowouts and condemned by the demands of marching students whose testimonies identified these forms as conduits of crimes against social and educational equality. But as mentioned above, the Blowouts also highlight ideologies and practices that ought to be commemorated.

What happened in March 1968 was more than a mass of students walking out of school; people from dominated groups, historically excluded from the type of literacies tied to social mobility and success, had been "walking out" on *schooling for subservience* since its inception in Anglo-American society. The events of 1968 were different because the corporeal-contextual syntax of the bodies that walked out of Lincoln, Roosevelt, Garfield, Wilson, Belmont, and Jefferson high schools explicitly articulated that it was schooling as a social institution that was failing and that students intended to make their schools places where the rhetoric of educational equality was realized. The walkouts of 1968 were fundamentally important because, far from simply turning away from schooling, Chicana/o students intended to take back their schooling.

Leading up to the Blowouts and then communicated in an official list presented to the school board a few weeks after, students voiced the following demands: a curriculum that focused on the contributions of Mexican Americans and made students aware of the injustices suffered by Chicanas/os in American society; bilingual education; the hiring of more

Mexican American teachers and administrators; training for teachers, administrators, and staff that reflected local conditions; greater community input and control of schools; smaller class sizes; and a more liberal approach to the rights of students. As a powerful indictment and compelling testimony against ideas and practices that inferiorized Chicanas/os, the narrative articulated by those marching students needs to be commemorated in the same manner as Rosa Parks's refusal against racial segregation or Cesar Chavez's challenge to the conscience of consumers.

As a set of actions and events, the walkouts should be commemorated because they formed an integral part of a larger time-space in which the collective actions of individuals marked a qualitative change in the larger social and historical context of when and where our lives transpire. They must be understood, in Inda's words, as "a key event in contemporary Chicano history" (1990, 23). Muñoz explains that the Blowouts were "the first major mass protest explicitly against racism undertaken by Mexican Americans in the history of the United States." He states that the student strike "had a profound impact on the Mexican American Community in Los Angeles and other parts of the country" and that it generated both "an increased political awareness" and "efforts to mobilize the community," resulting in the "revitalization of existing community political organizations and the emergence of new ones" (1989, 64–65). Acuña (1981) points out that the Blowouts highlighted the educational plight of Chicanas/os and encouraged other walkouts throughout the country. Among the walkouts in other cities and states, he mentions those in Denver, San Antonio, Phoenix, Santa Clara, Elsa, and Abilene. According to Muñoz, the student walkouts in Denver contributed to the further development of the Crusade for Justice and made Corky Gonzales a national leader of the emerging Chicana/o movement. Muñoz credits the walkouts in Crystal City, Texas, with contributing directly to the founding of La Raza Unida Party, to an electoral revolt that led to the party's takeover of that city's government and school system, and to making José Angel Gutiérrez into a national leader of the movement. He further credits the concerns and momentum built up among Mexican American students who participated in the Blowouts (as well as those within the ranks of student organizations on college campuses) with breaking "the ideological bonds that characteristically keep student organizations, and students in general, from questioning authority and the status quo" (1989, 65). Muñoz writes:

The strike of 1968 went beyond the objectives of [Sal] Castro and others concerned only with improving education. It was the first loud cry for Chicano Power and self-determination, serving as the catalyst for the Chicano student movement as well as the larger Chicano Power Movement of which it became the most important sector. . . .

The student strikes in the community and on the college campus, in conjunction with the political upheavals of the late sixties, thus generated the framework for the eventual transformation of student activist organizations into a full-blown student movement with clear social and political goals and an ethnic nationalist ideology that came to be known as cultural nationalism. (ibid., 66, 72)

According to Acuña (1981), in California the number of Mexican American studies programs had increased to approximately fifty by the fall of 1969. As a set of actions and ideals that profoundly impacted the Mexican American community and served as a catalyst for both the Chicana/o student movement and the larger Chicana/o power movement, it is appropriate to frame the importance of the Blowouts in the terms Rosales uses to describe the importance of the overall Chicana/o movement they helped to set in motion:

No Mexican American can escape its inheritance: not the individuals who hated the movimiento, nor those who became too sophisticated for it, nor the ones who were indifferent to it. The movimiento's legacy, in fact, affects a greater portion of the present-day U.S.-Mexican population than when it was at its apogee. Most present-day Chicano civil rights leaders and politicians no longer insist on the Plan Espiritual de Aztlán as a guide to action, nor do they look to "Corky" Gonzales and José Angel Gutierrez for leadership. But consciously or unconsciously, everyone follows more than one precept established during the movement. (1997, 250)

As a tenured professor who was once afraid to occupy the very space of his existence in a classroom, I am a living expression of the debt of gratitude that is owed to the students of 1968, of the need to commemorate the fragile lineage of educational opportunity they helped engender with the conception and labor of their struggle. I was born only three years before the Blowouts began, and I walked into public schooling in East Los Angeles only two years after Chicana/o students had walked out. My arrival at the University of California at Santa Cruz in 1983 was enabled by their departure from the high schools in 1968.

COMMEMORATING THE GENEALOGY OF IDEALS AND PRACTICES BEHIND THE BLOWOUTS

The Blowouts were a response to socially *constraining* ideologies and practices whose genealogies stretch across the time-space of several centuries and continents, but they were also the product of *enabling* ideologies and practices with a lineage of their own. Just as Chicana/o students did not simply get up and walk out because their schools had suddenly begun to fail them, they did not stand up and walk out in the demand-driven and highly organized manner that they did without a set of enabling ideas and practices whose origins predate the actual actions and events that took place during that explosive week and a half in 1968.

In terms of anticolonial resistance and social struggle by dominated peoples, the Blowouts can be seen as a branch on a family tree whose roots extend as deep as the colonial domination and social subjugation that have characterized Anglo-American society since its inception in the 1600s. The scholars whose work spotlights the schooling for subservience and educational exclusion that have been integral components of that colonial domination and social subjugation also make it possible to trace an accompanying genealogy of struggle and resistance against that schooling for subservience and educational exclusion. Although the limitations of this chapter do not allow for a detailed discussion of that extensive genealogy, it is possible to highlight the more immediate lineage of practices and circumstances that directly predated and enabled the Blowouts by reviewing the work of scholars who have specifically examined them.

Bernal's work on the Blowouts (1998) is an ideal place to begin this brief illustration. Pointing out that women's roles and voices have been omitted from accounts of the Blowouts, Bernal builds on data from the oral histories of eight women (who directly participated in the Blowouts) to argue for a reconceptualization of grassroots leadership that acknowledges Chicanas as important leaders in said movements. Originating from a women's studies tradition, the reconceptualized notion of leadership she articulates is characterized by the following: it locates women at the center of its analysis, it rejects paradigms that define leaders as individuals who occupy visible or high positions in an organization, it avoids divorcing the tasks of organizing from the tasks of leading, and it understands leadership as a collective process in which the dynamic roles of men and women who engage toward a common goal or vision are mutually important and reinforcing. This reconceptualization of leadership, explains Bernal, allows for the inclusion of women's voices, a capturing of the manner in which women emerge as leaders, and an alternative understanding of the differing *dimensions of grassroots leadership.* This alternative understanding of the different dimensions of grassroots leadership is fundamental to the reconceptualization of leadership Bernal puts forth, and given that she identifies and examines five different types of activities that could be considered dimensions of grassroots leadership in the Blowouts, her work spotlights some of the immediate ideas and practices that predated and enabled the Blowouts—that is, the ideas and practices that paved the paths through which a past of struggle and resistance trekked into the present.

Bernal identifies *organizing, developing consciousness, networking, holding office,* and *acting as a spokesperson* as dimensions of grassroots leadership in the Blowouts, and she asserts that the women she interviewed participated in these different dimensions in distinct ways and to varying degrees. Although all five of these were fundamentally important to the unfolding of the Blowouts, Bernal's discussion of *organizing* and *developing consciousness* helps substantiate my argument that the Blowouts were both a response to *constraining* ideologies and practices whose genealogies stretch across a vast and protracted time-space and a product of *enabling* ideologies and practices with an immediate lineage that formed part of a larger genealogy of struggle and resistance against schooling for subservience and educational exclusion.

Organizing for the Blowouts. Working from a definition of organizing that includes attending meetings and planning or implementing events and activities related to what resulted as the Blowouts, Bernal writes that all eight of the women she interviewed participated in community, PTA, school board, and Blowout committee meetings. Active participation in meetings that "helped to develop or support the demonstrations" is said to have been "an important component of organizing the Blowouts" (1998, 126). As a concrete example of this type of leadership, Bernal narrates that prior to and during the Blowouts Mita Cuaron (one of her interviewees) participated in meetings where community members generated lists of issues and demands that were later brought before the school board. Several of the participants interviewed by Bernal attempted to address and remedy educational inequities by implementing various strategies before resorting to the walkouts. As members of the Young Citizens for Community Action (YCCA), for example, they regularly held meetings to discuss educational issues, and at one point conducted a needs-assessment survey to gather information on the situation in the schools. Bernal documents what one of her interviewees, Vickie Castro, explains about those surveys: "We wanted to compile complaints and I guess we were trying to develop, even in our simple perspective, something like a needs assessment. We would talk to kids, What do you think about your school? Do they help you? Do they push you out? Are you going to college? . . . I know we compiled quite a bit of complaints and that's where during the walkouts when you hear about the demands, a lot of that was based on these complaints. So we had a process in mind" (ibid., 126).

After those surveys were completed, several members of the YCCA (including three of Bernal's interviewees) actively worked in support of Julian Nava's campaign for election to the school board. Another interviewee speaks of organizing efforts related to the antiwar movement and the issue of police brutality in the community. Bernal writes that "without the organizing efforts and persistence of these and other young Chicanas the Blowouts may not have taken place and the attention needed to expose poor educational conditions may not have been garnered" (ibid., 127).

Developing the consciousness that sparked and fueled the Blowouts. Bernal identifies helping others to gain consciousness of social and educational inequities through discussions or the use of print media as another dimension of leadership leading up to the Blowouts. All of the participants Bernal interviews engaged in raising consciousness by engaging in informal dialogues with family members, peers, and community members. To illustrate the importance placed on raising consciousness and the role Chicanas played, Bernal quotes Rachael Ochoa Cervera: "You raised consciousness in any way that you could do it, subtly or outright" (ibid.). She writes that two of her other interviewees, Tanya Luna and Mita Cuaron, used mimeograph machines to make copies of leaflets and flyers that were distributed in the schools and surrounding communities. She also points out that her interviewees were involved with the two community activist newspapers—*Inside*

Eastside and *La Raza*—directly connected to the Blowouts. She confirms that all the women she interviewed read these newspapers and encouraged others to do so, while Tanya Luna and Paula Crisostomo actually wrote for and distributed the newspapers.

Although not as significant in terms of highlighting ideologies and practices that predated the Blowouts, the role of Chicanas in the other three dimensions of grassroots leadership was no less significant in terms of the unfolding and relative success of the Blowouts. Hence, that role in those dimensions merits mention here.

Networking. Referring to networking as activities that link diverse groups to build a base of support, Bernal explains that during the Blowouts it was necessary to count on support from both the community members and people outside the community who could lend legitimacy to the efforts undertaken by the students (ibid., 130).

Holding office. Four of Bernal's interviewees held an elected or appointed office that was directly or indirectly related to the walkouts. Vickie Castro served as the first president of the YCCA, which played a significant role in the organization of the Blowouts, and both Mita Cuaron and Cassandra Zacarías were elected as student body officers shortly after the Blowouts. Rosalinda Méndez González was appointed to the Mexican American Education Commission—originally an advisory board to the school board—months after the Blowouts, acting as spokesperson.

Acting as a spokesperson. Although during the Blowouts it was most often males who assumed the role of official or unofficial spokespersons for the cameras and newspapers, there were occasions in which females served as spokespersons. Rosalinda Méndez González and Paula Crisostomo served as official spokespersons when they testified before the U.S. Commission on Civil Rights hearing in Los Angeles. González, Vickie Castro, and other Chicanas also testified before the Los Angeles School Board in the effort to reinstate Sal Castro as a teacher.

Bernal's focus on what people actually did to organize and sustain the walkouts serves as a window to the ideologies and practices that enabled the walkouts to materialize into the historically significant event we are called on to commemorate forty years after it took place. What's more, her work allows us to begin to trace the immediate lineage of those ideologies and practices.

Bernal states that four of the women she interviewed for her study had participated in the Mexican American Youth Leadership Conferences for high school students held at Camp Hess Kramer in Malibu, California. The annual conferences, which began in 1963, "were important to the development of the 1968 Blowouts because a number of students who participated in the conferences later became organizers in the Blowouts" (ibid., 118). Referring to the same conferences, Rosales writes: "While it is difficult to trace the idea of the Blowouts to any one group or individual, it is certain that Camp Hess Kramer veterans, some who became Brown Berets, were core planners" (1997, 189). The conferences, sponsored by the Los Angeles County Commission on Human Relations and led by Mexican American veterans of war who became teachers and social workers, were designed to promote good citizenship, but they were also forums for discussing problems in the communities and schools of the participants (Muñoz 1989). According to the women Bernal interviewed, the conferences at the camp provided a framework to conceptualize inequities and helped develop in them a sense of community and familial responsibility. One of the interviewees stated, "These conferences were the first time we began to develop a consciousness." Bernal explains that in addition to encouraging civic responsibility and good citizenship, the conferences also led students to focus on more radical and progressive issues. Rosalinda Méndez González is quoted as follows with regard to the impact of the conferences: "Well, when we started going to these youth conferences, there were older Mexican Americans. Now we were high school kids, so older was probably twenties and early thirties. They would talk to us, and explain a lot of things about what was happening, and I remember they were opening up our eyes. After those youth conferences, then we went back and started organizing to raise support for the farmworkers and things like that" (1998, 118).

From Rosales's discussion of the Blowouts (1997), we know that two of those "things" were the establishment of the Piranya Coffee House and the forming of the YCCA. In 1967, David Sanchez, who attended Camp Hess Kramer in 1966 and 1967, was funded by the California Council of Churches to start the Piranya as a place to keep teenagers out of trouble after school. That same year, Sanchez brought together a group of fellow Camp Hess Kramer participants, including Vickie Castro, and they formed the YCCA. The Piranya is said to have served as a headquarters for the YCCA (Rosales

1997), which initially worked within the system surveying high school students, meeting with educational officials to discuss problems, and endorsing candidates for the school board (Bernal 1998), but it was increasingly radicalized and evolved into the Brown Berets. Inda (1990) writes that the YCCA used Piranya to organize classes on history and culture, and Rosales (1997) explains that young patrons at la Piranya were "excited" by articles in *La Raza* that exposed police brutality and articulated "blistering" attacks against the educational system. Inda credits *La Raza* and *Inside Eastside* with being highly influential in the development of the Blowouts. In an issue published in December 1967, *La Raza* included an article that outlined statistics of the educational inequity suffered by Chicanas/os, and it ran another article that stated: "The goal for 1968 is to change our educational system; change is not only desirable but it is ESSENTIAL." Before the walkouts, Inda states, the newspaper ran ads asking people to "Turn On, Join In, Walkout" (1990, 11). Referring to the Camp Hess Kramer veterans who were core planners and the many other activists, groups, and organizations that were crucial in the organizing, Rosales writes:

> They devoted numerous hours to discussing educational inadequacies and how they could be changed. Perhaps influenced by the Black cultural movement, they all agreed that education of Mexican Americans lacked cultural relevancy.
>
> Soon planners favored the idea of a walkout as a means of dramatizing their issues. They then printed propaganda broadsides designed to persuade students to abandon their classes. Their activities became so overt that weeks before the strike, students, teachers, and administrators knew about the impending walkout. In fact, one month before the incident, teachers openly debated the issue and started taking sides. Meanwhile Chicano newspapers *La Raza, Inside Eastside,* and *The Chicano Student* helped fuel the passions of students and boycott supporters by spreading an "awareness" among students and non-students alike. (1997, 189)

Although the discussion above merely skims the surface of the ideological and material practices that led up to and enabled the Blowouts, it should highlight that these events were far from being the products of spontaneous ideas and actions. There was a genealogy to the practices that enabled and constituted the week and a half of protests in March 1968 as surely as there was a genealogy of the practices that were protested against. The former should be commemorated as surely as the latter should be condemned.

CONCLUSION

The Chicanas/os who walked out of their schools in March 1968 marked that time-space of American society with a corporeal-contextual syntax that could not be ignored. Their bodies wrote a counternarrative to a national history that had consistently ignored or erased their existence and its inconsistency with the ideals of social equality and opportunity. The explosion of thousands of bodies that marched out of schools protesting against the social and educational inequity suffered by Chicanas/os spotlighted genealogies of both social domination and social struggle against domination, instantiating much that is to be commemorated and much that is to be condemned forty years after the actions and events. It is not possible to comprehend the beauty of the actions and ideals we are called on to commemorate without an understanding of the horror of the ideologies and practices they courageously condemned. To that generation of marching students is owed a debt that can never be repaid. It is only right that we ensure it is forever acknowledged—and honored in our ideals and practices.

REFERENCES

Acuña, R. 1981. *Occupied America: A History of Chicanos.* 2nd ed. New York: Harper and Row.

Axtell, J. 1985. *The Invasion Within: The Conquest of Cultures in Colonial North America.* New York: Oxford University Press.

Bakhtin, M. M. 1981. *The Dialogic Imagination: Four Essays.* Austin: University of Texas Press.

Bernal, D. D. 1998. "Grassroots Leadership Reconceptualized: Chicana Oral Histories and the 1968 East Los Angeles High School Blowouts." *Frontiers: A Journal of Women Studies* 19, no. 2: 113–42.

Chorover, S. L. 1979. *From Genius to Genocide: The Meaning of Human Nature and the Power of Behavior Control.* Cambridge: MIT Press.

Cravens, H. 1998. *The Triumph of Evolution: American Scientists and the Heredity-Environment Controversy, 1900–1941.* Philadelphia: University of Pennsylvania Press.

Foley, E. F. 1997. "Deficit Thinking Models Based on Culture: The Anthropological

Protest." In *The Evolution of Deficit Thinking: Educational Thought and Practice,* edited by Richard R. Valencia, 113–31. Washington, D.C.: Falmer Press.

Franklin, J. H., and A. A. Moss Jr. 1988. *From Slavery to Freedom: A History of Negro Americans.* 6th ed. New York: Alfred A. Knopf.

Gonzalez, G. G. 1974a. "Racism, Education, and the Mexican Community in Los Angeles, 1920–1930." *Societas* 4: 287–301.

———. 1974b. "The System of Public Education and Its Function Within the Chicano Communities, 1919–1930." Ph.D. diss., University of California at Los Angeles.

———. 1990. *Chicano Education in the Era of Segregation.* Philadelphia: Balch Institute Press.

Gould, S. J. 1981. *The Mismeasure of Man.* New York: W. W. Norton.

Grande, S. 2004. *Red Pedagogy: Native American Social and Political Thought.* Lanham, Md.: Rowman and Littlefield.

Inda, J. J. 1990. *La comunidad en lucha: The Development of the East Los Angeles High School Blowouts.* Working Papers Series, no. 29. Stanford: Stanford Center for Chicano Research.

Katz, M. B. 1989. *The Undeserving Poor: From the War on Poverty to the War on Welfare.* New York: Pantheon.

Lefebvre, H. 1991. *The Production of Space.* Translated by D. Nicholson-Smith. 1974. Reprint, Cambridge: Blackwell.

Menchaca, M. 1997. "Early Racist Discourses: The Roots of Deficit Thinking." In *The Evolution of Deficit Thinking: Educational Thought and Practice,* edited by Richard R. Valencia, 13–40. Washington, D.C.: Falmer Press.

Muñoz, C. 1989. *Youth, Identity, Power: The Chicano Movement.* New York: Verso.

Pearl, A. 1997. "Cultural and Accumulated Environmental Deficit Models." In *The Evolution of Deficit Thinking: Educational Thought and Practice,* edited by Richard R. Valencia, 132–59. Washington, D.C.: Falmer Press.

Poniatowska, E. 1985. *Fuerte es el silencio.* Mexico City: Ediciones ERA.

Rosales, F. A. 1997. *Chicano: The History of the Mexican American Civil Rights Movement.* Houston: Arte Público Press of the University of Houston.

Somekawa, E., and E. A. Smith. 1988. "Theorizing the Writing of History; or, 'I Can't Think Why It Should Be So Dull, for a Great Deal of It Must Be Invention.'" *Journal of Social Theory* 22, no. 1: 149–61.

Spring, J. 1992. *Images of American Life: A History of Ideological Management in Schools, Movies, Radio, and Television.* New York: State University of New York Press.

———. 2004. *Deculturalization and the Struggle for Equality: A Brief History of the Education of Dominated Cultures in the United States.* 4th ed. Boston: McGraw-Hill.

Tejeda, C. 2000. "Mapping Social Space: A Study of Spatial Production in an Elementary Classroom." Ph.D. diss., University of California at Los Angeles.

Tejeda, C., M. Espinoza, and K. Gutierrez. 2003. "Toward a Decolonizing Pedagogy: Social Justice Reconsidered." In *Pedagogy of Difference,* edited by P. Trifonas. New York: Routledge.

Trouillot, M.-R. 1995. *Silencing the Past: Power and the Production of History.* Boston: Beacon Press.

Valencia, R. R., ed. 1997a. "Conceptualizing the Notion of Deficit Thinking." In *The Evolution of Deficit Thinking: Educational Thought and Practice,* edited by Richard R. Valencia, 1–12. Washington, D.C.: Falmer Press.

———, ed. 1997b. *The Evolution of Deficit Thinking: Educational Thought and Practice.* Washington, D.C.: Falmer Press.

———. 1997c. "The Genetic Pathology Model of Deficit Thinking." In *The Evolution of Deficit Thinking: Educational Thought and Practice,* edited by Richard R. Valencia, 41–112. Washington, D.C.: Falmer Press.

———, ed. 2002. *Chicano School Failure and Success: Past, Present, and Future.* 2nd ed. New York: Routledge Falmer.

White, H. 1999. *Figural Realism: Studies in the Mimesis Effect.* Baltimore: John Hopkins University Press.

CHAPTER 2

Visual Culture and Art in Activism

ADRIANA KATZEW

LILIA R. DE KATZEW

Art for art's sake had no place in the Chicana/o movement of the 1960s and 1970s. At a time when Mexican Americans protested against societal injustices and demanded changes, art did not have the luxury to remain an activity for private consumption. Art became instrumental; it was created to have a social and political impact in the struggle of Chicanas/os to redefine their identity in the United States, in their struggle for fair labor and pay for the farmworkers, in their struggle for better education for students, and in the struggle to end racism and police brutality, which affected a large proportion of Mexican Americans in the United States.[1]

This chapter examines the educative role of visual culture and visual arts during the Chicana/o *movimiento* of the 1960s and 1970s. To do so, we first provide a historical context of that time period, with a focus on a central event that catapulted the Chicana/o movement—the East Los Angeles High School Blowouts, or walkouts. The essay then considers the role of Chicana/o leaders in bringing visual iconography, visual culture, and visual arts to the forefront of the *movimiento*. We then address the educative role of visual artists in the *movimiento*, especially through posters, murals, and films. We conclude with an analysis of the use of visual culture and arts in recent marches to protect immigrant rights. In our conclusion we pose questions as to the role of the artist as a cultural worker and producer of visual education.

At the heart of this chapter is the concept that art was not an auxiliary but at the very core of the Chicana/o movement. It played an essential role in providing a sense of pride in Chicanas'/os' pre-Columbian past, in educating the community about Mexican and Chicana/o history, and in bringing people together in the struggle for civil rights. The vital role that visual culture played during the *movimiento* has endured, evident in the visual iconography deployed in the most recent marches for immigrants' rights and in the continuing work of Chicana and Chicano artists to create art that may have an impact in today's social, cultural, and political arenas.

THE CHICANA/O MOVEMENT: A HISTORICAL CONTEXT

The key element that energized and propelled the Chicana/o movement toward national recognition was the East Los Angeles high school walkouts in March 1968, otherwise known as the "Blowouts." In one week, more than fifteen thousand Chicana/o high school students left their classes throughout the Los Angeles area to protest the poor educational conditions that endemically afflicted their schools and to demand educational reforms. At that time, 60 percent of Mexican American students dropped out of high school before graduating from the twelfth grade (Rosales 1996). Mexican American students were, as a matter of internal school policy, tracked to vocational areas and not encouraged to pursue a college education. Most of them had an eighth grade reading level when and if they graduated from high school (Galán 1996b).

When Chicana/o students formed picket lines carrying placards that read "Chicano Power," "Viva La Raza," and "Viva La Revolución," a new image of themselves began to form, similar to that created by Cesar Chavez when he marched with farmworker strikers to Sacramento carrying placards that read "Justicia para los Campesinos y Viva la Virgen de Guadalupe" (Justice for the farmworkers and long live the Virgin of Guadalupe) in 1966. These Chicana/o high school students called for reform of poor school conditions, demanded the firing of prejudiced teachers and administrators, and insisted that school curricula recognize the existence and contributions of Chicanas/os to the U.S. sociohistorical fabric. They also demanded bilingual education and the hiring of qualified Mexican American teachers, as well as the end of corporal punishment. Essentially, these Chicana/o students agreed that Chicanas'/os' educational journey in the public system lacked any cultural relevancy or significance. They were determined to overcome the invisible status as second-class U.S. citizens imposed on them by the mainstream U.S. society.

Ironically, the high school walkouts were organized at a time when the number of Mexican Americans enrolling in institutions of higher education was growing and when many U.S. colleges and universities were radicalizing, thus allowing the creation of many student organizations. By the end of 1967, more than thirty-five Chicana/o organizations had been formed in Southern California, and numerous publications such as *El Grito, La Raza, El Pocho Ché, Regeneración,* and many others flourished in California. By that time, and specifically with the walkouts, California Chicana/o youth, especially students, had taken the leadership role in the Chicana/o movement and incorporated visual iconography in their protests to speak to the community at large. Their efforts were supported by other integral members of the Chicana/o movement—the Brown Berets, "the largest nonstudent radical youth organization in the Mexican American community" (Muñoz 1989, 84), whose leadership and rank-and-file membership were composed predominantly from street youth (Muñoz 1989).

Thus, the impact of the East Los Angeles High School Blowouts on Chicano communities in the U.S. Southwest was enormous. It inspired other Chicana/o high school students to stage walkouts in California, Texas, Colorado, New Mexico, and other areas, and it finally brought national attention to their cause. One factor that allowed Chicanas/os throughout the Southwest to more easily organize walkouts was that nearly 80 percent lived in urban areas where they had numerous sources of information and communication (Meier and Ribera 2001). However, the East Los Angeles Walkouts were soon followed by increased police harassment that targeted not only Chicana/o students but also the Mexican American community at large, and many Chicana/o students were jailed, fined, or put on probation.

As a consequence of the East Los Angeles Walkouts, the Chicana/o civil rights movement blueprint started to take shape. The 1968 walkouts or strikes were "the first loud cry for Chicano Power and self-determination, serving as the catalyst for the formation of the Chicano student movement as well as the larger Chicano Power Movement of which it became the most important sector" (Muñoz 1989, 66). Soon after the walkouts, a national Chicana/o youth meeting attended by more than two thousand young

Chicanas/os from all over the country materialized in Denver in 1969. This meeting, called "The First National Chicano Youth Group Liberation Conference," was sponsored and organized by Rodolfo "Corky" Gonzales, who was the founder of the Crusade for Justice organization. Gonzales had issued "El Plan del Barrio," a socioeconomic and political blueprint for separate public housing for Chicanas/os, bilingual education, barrio self-sufficient economic growth, and internal development—inspired by the Chicago Black Muslim group—and the restitution of land taken from Hispanos in Colorado and New Mexico. During this conference, the young *movimiento* leaders explored ideology and identity questions, and they came up with the most significant outcome from the conference: *El Plan Espiritual de Aztlán,* which advocated separatism, a position they justified because of the "brutal Gringo invasion of our territories" (*El Plan de Aztlán* n.d., 1) and the alienation that ensued for Chicanas/os in the United States. *El Plan Espiritual de Aztlán* recognized Chicanas/os as the original inhabitants of the northern land of Aztlán—the land of their forebears, and the cultural and spiritual homeland of Chicanas/os in the U.S. Southwest. Chicanas/os were not to be perceived any longer as foreigners in their own land, and the legend of Aztlán became the rallying cry in search for the roots that predated Chicano links with Mexico. The use of the term "Aztlán" by these young Chicanas/os was an affirmation of their pre-Columbian ancestry that was rooted geographically in the U.S. Southwest and had a unique history, tradition, and language distinct from the Anglo dominant culture. *El Plan* addressed the importance of cultural production in spreading this ideology and in educating Chicanas/os about their culture, as discussed later in this chapter.

El Plan Espiritual de Aztlán brought forth a cathartic experience for these young Chicana/o activists in terms of identity. They recognized that they had been living under the shadow of denial displayed by their parents who had fought to gain access to the U.S. mainstream through an ideology of assimilation that advocated working within the system to solve problems facing Mexican Americans in the United States. The Chicana/o movement generation recognized that their parents' efforts of working within the system had not succeeded and that they were still not sharing in the benefits of the American dream (Rosales 1996). The walkouts brought an awareness in young Chicanas/os that they were discriminated against and that their aspirations for a better education, economic opportunities, social equality, and political representation were denied to them by the Anglo-American system. They saw that one-third of Mexican Americans lived in poverty with an unemployment rate double the national average, and that only four Mexican Americans served in Congress—an underrepresentation of a population of seven million Mexican Americans, with four million concentrated in the U.S. Southwest (Acuña 2000; Galán 1996a). They also saw that most Chicana/o communities were segregated from the Anglo mainstream.

By formulating the *Plan de Aztlán,* the Chicana/o movement generation also rejected their parents' ideology of shedding their *mestizaje* as a way to work within the system in order to gain acceptance from Anglo society. The Chicana/o movement youth proudly embraced their *mestizaje* by classifying themselves as brown people. In fact, the poem *I Am Joaquin* written by Corky Gonzales was adopted as the anthem of the *movimiento* since it lauded Chicanas'/os' *mestizaje,* emphasizing their *indigenismo* and proclaiming separatism for Chicanas/os; assimilation was no longer the desired condition for Chicanas/os. The concept of Aztlán presented the *mestizo*-Indian aesthetic with dignity rather than a negative association. Myths and cultural identification reinforced the desire of the members of the *movimiento* to find unifying cultural and ethnic roots for Chicanas/os as *mestizos* proud of their Indian past.

The search for a unifying Chicana/o identity formulated in the *Plan de Aztlán* was initiated in the East Los Angeles Walkouts. By calling themselves Chicanas/os during the walkouts, this generation of youth was committing an act of defiance against the older generation. "Chicano" was a term that many of their parents used pejoratively to identify lower classes of Mexican Americans or new Mexican immigrants who were still the generation of *los de abajo* (the ones down below) because they "did not transcend their working-class Mexicanness that persisted beyond the first generation" (Rosales 1996, 252). The use of the term "Chicana/o" by the youth was also a way for them to shape a new identity with a more positive perception when looking at themselves, a perception that also identified them with the inherent dignity of *los de abajo.*

The walkouts produced the rank and file of a youth-oriented movement, and a revolutionary movement grew, motivated by a new Chicanismo ideology that was also inspired by Latin American and Mexican revolutionaries such as Ernesto "Che" Guevara, an Argentinean who worked with Castro and the Cuban Revolution, and Emiliano Zapata and Pancho Villa, leaders of the Mexican Revolution. The Chicanismo espoused in the walkouts was the foundation of the *movimiento,* that is, the struggle for social justice for Chicanas/os and a cultural consciousness that emphasized language, heritage, ethnic roots, and Chicana/o contributions, as well as the development of political activism and power through grassroots community organizations. Art served as a vehicle to communicate these ideals, as will be discussed later in this chapter.

Historian Arturo Rosales argues that "the ability to bring about change at institutions of higher learning was a crowning achievement of the movement" (1996, 253). Young Chicana/o students designed a plan for higher education called *El Plan de Santa Barbara* that produced a college curriculum that implemented Chicana/o studies programs throughout the University of California system and was later adopted by other universities across the United States. Even though many of the programs did not follow the radical ideological precepts of *El Plan de Santa Barbara,* which spoke of liberation, cultural nationalism, and the creation of grassroots community organizations, Chicana/o students were actively recruited to colleges and universities after *El Plan de Santa Barbara.*

The walkouts' demands for educational reform and social justice were finally addressed. For the first time in U.S. educational history, Chicanas/os were able to find courses and programs that studied, analyzed, and depicted the Chicana/o experience. The *movimiento* brought about a veritable triumph for a group of people. The legacy of the walkouts and of the *movimiento* still permeates all aspects of Chicana/o life and of U.S. culture. Never before had Chicanas/os come together in such force to search, redefine, and reaffirm their identity. Never before had so many Chicanas/os united to demand an active role in their educational, political, economic, cultural, and social destinies. Although previous generations addressed many of the same concerns at different levels and from different perspectives, the *movimiento* brought about the most profound change in the way Chicanas/os perceived themselves. The walkouts and the *movimiento* took at heart the ideals of democracy and freedom that the United States championed. Chicanas/os understood that the system would not change unless they united to take direct action. Scholar Carlos Muñoz points out that the *movimiento* served as the psychological liberating force to decolonize

Chicanas'/os' minds (Galán 1996a). The movement debunked the general perception of Chicanas/os as an invisible minority, and it also destroyed the myth of Chicanas'/os' political apathy by embracing Cesar Chavez and Dolores Huerta's 1965 California-based farmworker struggle, the 1963 Reies "El Tigre" López Tijerina land-grant restoration movement in New Mexico, and the subsequent creation of La Raza Unida Party.

The establishment of Chicana/o studies centers and programs in several universities across the United States came about because of the walkouts and the ensuing *movimiento*. These centers and programs have opened educational opportunities for young Chicanas/os and provided them with access to professions that allow them to exercise a more active role in the sociological, economic, cultural, and political decision-making process in their communities and their country. All of these advances, however, were achieved partly due to the role that the visual arts and culture played in the *movimiento*. The integration of visual iconography and visual arts during the Chicana/o civil rights movement served to educate members in the Mexican American communities, as well as society at large, about issues confronting Chicanas/os.

VISUAL CULTURE IN THE *MOVIMIENTO:*
THE ROLE OF CHICANA/O LEADERS

The incorporation of visual culture and art in the Chicana/o movement was not happenstance. It was clearly and deliberately created and used by Chicana/o leaders, youth, and artists. But why integrate art? What did these folks believe it had to offer in advancing the goals of the *movimiento*? Through visual images political and social messages can be delivered to large numbers of viewers, educating people and bringing them together under a specific cause. The use of visual images as a means to educate the masses was a strategy utilized by Mexican muralists, especially Diego Rivera, José Clemente Orozco, and David Alfaro Siqueiros in a country with a high rate of illiteracy. A number of Chicanas/os knew of these muralists' strategy and adopted it. Not surprisingly, then, visual images during the civil rights period were utilized to educate members of Mexican American communities, bring them together, connect the struggles of the present with the struggles of the past, and advance the ideologies of the Chicana/o civil rights movement.

Chicana/o leaders during the *movimiento* clearly understood the importance of visual culture and arts as vital tools that could allow them to move their ideologies forward. Cesar Chavez, the leader of the United Farm Workers (UFW) movement, understood the power of images and visual symbols to bring Mexican American farmworkers together under one cause. In the early 1960s, he purposefully selected a symbol to represent the UFW—a flag with an Aztec eagle—as a means to attract farmworkers of Mexican descent to join the union whose goal was to improve their working and living conditions (Sorell 1991). Chavez's reasoning was as follows:

> None of the farmworkers had collective bargaining contracts, and I thought it would take ten years before we got that first contract. I wanted desperately to get some color into the movement, to give people something they could identify with, like a flag. I was reading some books about how various leaders discovered what colors contrasted and stood out the best. The Egyptians had found out that a red field with a white circle and a black emblem in the center crashed into your eyes like nothing else.
>
> I wanted to use the Aztec eagle in the center, as on the Mexican flag. So I told my cousin Manuel, "Draw an Aztec eagle." Manuel had a little trouble with it, so we modified the eagle to make it easier for people to draw.
>
> The first big meeting of what we decided to call the National Farm Workers Association was held in September 1962, at Fresno, with 287 people. We had our huge red flag on the wall, with paper tacked over it. When the time came, Manuel pulled a cord ripping the paper off the flag and all of a sudden it hit the people. Some of them wondered if it was a Communist flag, and I said it probably looked more like a neo-Nazi emblem than anything else. They wanted an explanation, so Manuel got up and said, "When that damn eagle flies—that's when the farmworkers [*sic*] problems are going to be solved." (Chavez 1966)

Chicana/o students and other community members, many of whom joined the farmworker cause—*La Causa*—adopted the image of the UFW's Aztec eagle and used it in the student movement's marches and demonstrations. It became a pervasive image throughout the *movimiento* for several reasons. First, Mexican Americans knew what the Mexican flag looked like,

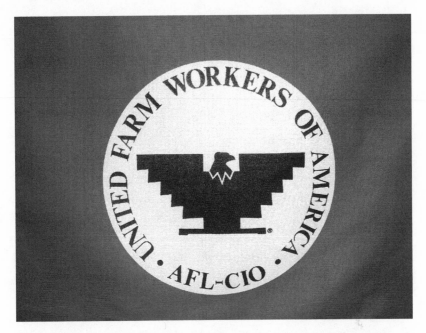

UFW flag used in marches in the 1960s (close-up of logo). Reproduced by permission of Lilia R. De Katzew.

and therefore the UFW's Aztec eagle was an image and symbol that resonated with them. Equally important, the simplified design of the UFW flag—in terms of both shape and colors—allowed for its easy and mass reproduction by artists and nonartists alike.

Chavez also elected to associate *La Causa* with another visual symbol: the *Virgen de Guadalupe*. The *Virgen* served several purposes. As the patron saint of Mexico, the *Virgen* attracted Mexican farmworkers, the majority of whom were Catholic, through the power of religion. Also, at a time when fears of communism were still plaguing U.S. society, and with communism spreading to Cuba and other parts of the world, unions were viewed with suspicion. This union was no exception and was accused of being communist-run. To counter such allegations, UFW leadership underscored the religiosity of its members. According to Chavez, "We wanted them to see that first of all we had the numbers, that we were organized . . . and that we had the virgin with us." The *Virgen* helped the organization project itself as nonradical, further aided by the rally cry of its members: "¡Justicia para los campesinos y viva la Virgen de Guadalupe!" (Rosales 1996, 139). The *Virgen* served, however, as more than a religious symbol for the farmworkers and, later on, for the youth involved in the student movement. She was a cultural icon as well. She represented the mother of Mexico, and therefore symbolized Mexican ancestry and Chicanas'/os' continued connection to Mexico. Furthermore, as a *mestiza,* she was a symbol of pride for Chicanas/os who embraced their *mestizo* and indigenous roots. Finally, she served to create community solidarity among the different constituents in the barrios (Peterson 1992). Not only were flags of the *Virgen de Guadalupe* present in all of the marches and processions led by the UFW, but images of her were also incorporated into later marches and demonstrations led by Chicana/o students and other community members during the *movimiento.*

Another Chicano leader who undoubtedly understood the importance of visual culture in promoting a nationalist Chicana/o ideology was Corky Gonzales, founder of the Chicana/o civil rights organization Crusade for Justice. During the 1969 Chicano Youth Liberation Conference, which he spearheaded, he held a protest march through downtown Denver, and a Mexican flag was carried at the head of the march. The choice to carry the Mexican flag seems coherent in light of the conference, attended mostly by Chicana/o student activists, but also by ex-convicts, nonstudents, and militant youth from street gangs. The purpose of the conference was to set forward a nationalist ideology, whereby all Chicanas/os would be united on the basis of their pride in Mexican ethnicity and culture (Muñoz 1989). The Mexican flag, then, became a symbol of this national ideology. In addition, Gonzales made explicit the role that the arts and artists were to have through a manifesto that emerged during the conference, the *Plan Espiritual de Aztlán* (also referred to as the *Plan*). This document revealed Gonzales's conscious understanding of the role that the arts could play in promoting an ideology, evident in one of the document's organizational goals solely devoted to cultural production: "CULTURAL values of our people strengthen our identity and the moral backbone of the movement. Our culture unites and educates the family of La Raza towards liberation with one heart and one mind. We must insure that our writers, poets, musicians, and artists produce literature and art that is appealing to our people and relates to our revolutionary culture. Our cultural values of life, family, and home will serve as a powerful weapon to defeat the gringo dollar value system and encourage the process of love and brotherhood" (*El Plan de Aztlán* n.d., 6). It is clear from the *Plan* that both art and artists were to be instrumental in educating the community, furthering a "revolutionary culture," and advancing the nationalist ideology that Chicanas/os were developing at that point in time. Corky Gonzales would reiterate this message later on, with even greater force, in a speech he delivered in 1975. In this speech he directly addressed visual artists and writers: "Your paintings, your words, will influence for better or for worse. We urge you to choose for better, speak of growth, of success, tell of tragedy and relate a social message. . . . We urge you to write and paint what we in turn will use as tools to teach our people" (Sorell 1991, 144). In no uncertain terms, the arts were to be created as educational tools and artists were to be what scholar Tomás Ybarra-Frausto later called "producers of visual education" (1993, 56).

Chicano and Chicana youth leaders were also instrumental in integrating art into the student movement. They too understood the importance of visual symbols and employed them during student demonstrations and marches. For instance, during the 1968 high school walkouts, students carried posters that read "Educación" and "Justicia" along with a visual representation of Mexican revolutionary José Miguel Hidalgo y Costilla, chief leader in Mexico's war of independence against Spain in the early nineteenth century. By employing images of Mexican revolutionary leaders, such as Hidalgo, Pancho Villa, and Emiliano Zapata, students demonstrated their interest, knowledge, and connection to Mexican history and culture, which resonated with their demands for an education that included Chicana/o history. Furthermore, they selected Mexican leaders considered revolutionaries because of their fight against those in power who marginalized the less privileged. These visual images went hand in hand with selected slogans that highlighted these young people's pride in their identity. During the Blowouts, for instance, students carried placards that read, "Chicano Power," "Brown Is Beautiful," and "Viva la Raza," as well as posters demanding a better education. Photographs documenting the Blowouts also show students with their hands in the air, sometimes in a clenched fist to symbolize Brown Power (similar to the hand gesture blacks used to symbolize Black Power) and other times making the peace or victory sign, while holding placards that consisted of the UFW eagle and the words "Mexican American Liberation."

Student leaders' repertoire of visual images used during the *movimiento*'s marches and protests grew to include other revolutionary leaders and world events. The image of Che Guevara, the attractive Argentinean revolutionary associated with Fidel Castro and Cuba, became widespread. This was due to the fact that Chicana/o students aligned themselves with other racial minority groups in the United States as well as with colonized people throughout the world (Rosales 1996). This third-world alignment was best exemplified by artists Luis Valdez and Roberto Rubalcava, student activists at San Jose State University in 1964, when they returned from travel to Cuba. Upon their return, they drafted the first radical manifesto written by Chicano student activists, in which they stated, "The Mexican in the United States has been . . . no less a victim of American imperialism than his impoverished brothers in Latin America" (Valdez and Rubalcava 1972, 215). They further added, "As sons of Mexican manual laborers in California, we have traveled to Revolutionary Cuba . . . to emphasize the historical and cultural unanimity of all Latin American peoples, north and south of the border. Having no leaders of our own, we accept Fidel Castro" (ibid., 217). The popularity that the image of Che garnered is evident in photographs taken during the Chicano Moratorium against the Vietnam War in August 1970. The images show the overrepresentation of Chicanos in the armed forces and the high percentage of casualties they constituted. People carried placards of a stylized image of Che's face and the words "Our fight is in the barrio, not Vietnam."

Students also utilized other means of communication as part of the *movimiento,* such as journals and periodicals, to feature pre-Columbian artifacts and introduce works of Mexican and Chicana/o artists. For instance, they featured the works of Mexican muralists Rivera, Orozco, and Siqueiros, whose works were revolutionary and provided social critique. They also included the work of Mexican artist and political and social satirist José Guadalupe Posada, as well as the artwork of Taller de Gráfica Popular, a collective printing studio in Mexico that produced predominantly political work. These periodicals and journals also served as a forum that featured interviews with Chicana/o artists and reproductions of their work. In addition, young Chicana/o artists contributed their artwork to these journals. For instance, artist Harry Gamboa Jr., who had been a high school student leader during the 1968 walkouts, invited other young Chicana/o art-ists, including Patssi Valdez, Gronk, and Willie Herrón, to contribute their artwork to the journal *Regeneración* while he was editor. The inclusion of art in periodicals was deliberate and reflected an understanding by the editors of these venues of visual arts "as essential ingredients in the formation of Chicano pride and identity" (Ybarra-Frausto 1991a, 136).

CHICANA/O ARTISTS AND THE *MOVIMIENTO*: EDUCATING THROUGH POSTERS, MURALS, AND FILMS

Whereas visual artists tend to express their individuality and personal aes-thetic vision through their individual work, this was not the case for a great number of Chicana and Chicano artists during the *movimiento*. Many worked, oftentimes in collectives, creating art that helped further the ide-ology of the Chicana/o movement. Furthermore, their artwork was often intended to promote specific messages and educate the Mexican American community as to particular issues (Maciel 1991). According to scholar Victor Sorell, "At one time or another, virtually all Chicano artists addressed the economic, educational, historical, political, religious, or social chords of the Movement" (1991, 143).

The artistic consciousness of Chicana/o artists was already present; how-ever, before the 1968 Blowouts, artists formed groups and collectives and gathered to discuss the role of art, especially in the *movimiento*. Artist Esteban Villa, member of the Mexican American Liberation Art Front (also known as La Mala Efe or MALAF, later to become the Royal Chicano Air Force), recalls meeting around 1968 with other artists: "We would meet regularly to discuss the role and function of the artist in El Movimiento. . . . Discussions were heated, especially the polemics on the form and content of revolu-tionary art and the relevance of murals and graphic art. Posters and other forms of graphics were especially discussed since many of us were creating *cartelones* [posters] as organizing tools for the various Chicano *mitotes* [spon-taneous happenings] in the Bay Area" (quoted in Ybarra-Frausto 1991a, 130). Other artists addressed the role that the arts and artists should play in more public venues, such as newspaper articles. For example, Manuel J. Marti-nez, a painter and sculptor who served on the board of Corky Gonzales's Crusade for Justice in Denver, exhorted in a 1967 article for the newspaper

El Gallo: La Voz de la Justicia, "I feel that we as Crusaders for Justice should fight to secure and support the arts. Because through art we are enhancing and enriching our movement" (quoted in Sorell 1991, 144).

Posters, murals, and films were three of the most significant and prevalent visual art media that effectively educated members of Mexican American communities as to the messages of the *movimiento.* Posters were utilized as sources of quick visual information. They were relatively easy and inexpensive to reproduce and therefore were appropriate for massive distribution around the barrios and especially during marches and demonstrations. Scholar George Lipsitz argues that "posters functioned as part of the movement, as vital forms that performed important work in the struggle for social change," and they played "crucial roles in constructing organic solidarity and in defining collective ideology" (2001, 73). Initially, Chicana/o artists who created posters were influenced by Mexican artist José Guadalupe Posada and by the Taller de Gráfica Popular because of their strong political voice. Chicana/o artists were also influenced by images of Mexican revolutionaries, such as Villa and Zapata, which they incorporated into their posters. The poster movement, as Shifra Goldman (1984) calls it, was further influenced by the graphics produced during the student movement at the 1968 Olympics in Mexico and the massacre of protesters in Tlatelolco by Mexican troops. An exhibit of Cuban political posters also had a strong impact on Chicana/o artists, especially those in the Bay Area, where the posters were exhibited (Goldman 1984). Ybarra-Frausto argues that Chicana/o posters did not create a new visual vocabulary; instead, they united various stylistic influences and thus reflected a "hybrid expression" (1991a, 138).

The production of posters was not limited to a few Chicana/o artists. This became evident during the Third World Strike at San Francisco State College, which began in November 1968, only a few months after the walkouts. The longest campus strike in the history of the United States, it criticized a poor educational system failing to meet the needs of third-world students, as well as racism and imperialism ("A History of SF State" 2009; Muñoz 1989). During the strike, art students, supported by faculty members, set up a poster-making workshop, which lasted for about a year (Goldman 1984). Artist Rupert García, whose posters from that era have become widely recognized, was one of the students. He explains how the workshop came about:

Well, in the art department we did eventually respond. . . . We had a big meeting of art students and faculty about how to address the campus strike. And one faculty—I guess, a faculty from England, who had just come back from visiting France and Paris—mentioned to us what he saw some students doing there—which was to make posters. And so we—some faculty and students—organized a poster brigade. And we used Dennis Beall's print studios and his instruction on how to do silkscreen and so we learned this technique, like on-the-job training. There was no course, no class. And I was a liaison between the art department and the other members of the Third World Liberation Front organizations. I would go talk to them and come back, and this kind of thing. And so we began to make posters dealing with the issues—issues from racism to better education to police brutality, anti-war, and much more. I mean, all the issues that were being addressed at that time made for a heady experience. Many of those issues were being dealt with in our poster brigade. And the posters were used in the demonstrations on campus, and some were used outside of campus, and some were sold to raise money to get people out on bail, people who had been arrested. And it was going very well. We had really wonderful teamwork. (Smithsonian Institution 1995–96)

In 1968, Rupert García produced a poster of the image of Che Guevara, titled *Right On,* and later produced the poster *Fuera de Indochina* (Out of Indochina) for mass distribution at the Chicano Vietnam Moratorium that took place on August 29, 1970, in Los Angeles (Sorell 1991). Posters created by Chicana/o artists, such as García, therefore reinforced the "organic solidarity" within the Chicana/o movement while also helping "create ideologies that linked *chicanismo* with anticolonial national struggles around the world" (Lipsitz 2001, 78). Artist Malaquías Montoya's 1972 poster *Viet Nam Aztlán* also illustrates this tie between Chicanas/os and other oppressed groups. The poster depicts a Vietnamese man and a Chicano man and includes the phrase "unidos venceran" (together they will overcome).

Not only were the posters educational in their messages, but the actual process of making them entailed a strong educational aspect. Chicana/o artists taught other members of the community how to make posters. García recalls that in 1969, through Artes Seis, a gallery run by Latinos in San Francisco, he taught other members of the gallery how to do silk-screen post-ers (Smithsonian Institution 1995–96). From 1968 to 1975, Chicano artists taught poster making to the public, especially young people at Chicano and Raza centers and galleries, as well as in schools (Goldman 1984). In addition, a number of poster collectives emerged during the Chicana/o movement, including the Royal Chicano Air Force (established in 1970 in Sacramento) and Self-Help Graphics (established in 1972 in East Los Angeles), which did educational outreach in their communities.

Chicana/o artists also produced a large number of murals during this time. Muralism in the barrios was another essential medium that served to edu-cate the community (Cockcroft and Barnet-Sánchez 1993). Ybarra-Frausto has qualified the barrio mural movement as "perhaps the most powerful and enduring contribution of the Chicana/o art movement nationwide" (1991a, 139). He argues that murals, which were based on the Chicana/o struggles of self-determination, "function as a pictorial reflection of the social drama" (1991b, 139). They were also "a cultural medium for disseminating national-ist images" (Maciel 1991, 113). The murals were composed of very specific images: pre-Columbian and indigenous figures; Mexican revolutionaries and leaders; contemporary Chicano leaders such as Cesar Chavez and Reies López Tijerina and, in some cases, leaders from other minority groups, such as Martin Luther King and the Black Panthers (High 1997); everyday life in the barrio; and cultural images such as the *pachucos,* low-riders, and the *Virgen de Guadalupe.* One of the foremost muralists in the *movimiento,* Judith Baca, describes the reclamation of "lost history," a recurring theme of murals of that period (quoted in Sorell 1991, 148). Scholar Freida High (1997) argues that the subjects selected for inclusion in a mural politicized the mural, which in turn politicized the viewers and the community. There-fore, the connection between art in politics and politics in art was clearly established with murals.

Not only were the messages of murals edifying to the viewers, but the process of mural making often had an educational component as well. Murals involved community input and therefore became what Ybarra-Frausto describes as "a large-scale comprehensive public-education system in the barrio" (1991a, 140). Judith Baca's mural projects began in the early 1970s and taught the community about its history through the images painted on the walls. For instance, one of her most renowned murals (and the longest in the world), *The Great Wall of Los Angeles,* which she started in 1974, presents the history of that city from a multicultural perspective. As important, from an educational standpoint, Baca also included hundreds of low-income youth from diverse ethnic backgrounds, many labeled "criminals" and gang youth, in making the murals. In doing so, she provided them with an education that expanded well beyond mural painting and gave them a sense of empowerment (Smithsonian Institution 1986).

The role of murals, however, is incomplete without mention of the art group or collective Asco, whose members were Gronk, Harry Gamboa Jr., Patssi Valdez, and Willie Herrón. As high school students, they had participated in the 1968 walkouts. Later on, they often worked together and stood apart from most other Chicana/o artists in their approach to reaffirm Chicana/o identity. Many other artists utilized traditional Mexican symbols and often painted murals. In contrast, Asco used performance art to convey its political messages, often poking fun at typical Mexican icons and even at the medium of muralism. Such was the case with the group's 1972 performance piece, *The Walking Mural.* In this performance they enacted their own Christmas procession along Los Angeles's Whittier Boulevard. Patssi Valdez was highly made up with white powder on her face, dark lips, and exaggerated red blush on her cheeks, and she was dressed in a black gown, with a black and silver cardboard aura on her head. Asco member Gronk recalls that "Patssi was the Virgin of Guadalupe, but done up in this see-through outfit" (Smithsonian Institution 1997). Gronk, in turn, was dressed up as a Christmas tree. Meanwhile, Herrón was disguised as a "multifaced mural that had become bored with its environment and left," according to Gamboa, who documented the event (1998, 79). Through this performance piece, the group played with the role of murals as the medium of expression for Chicana/o art. As scholar Guisela Latorre puts it, this performance "removed the mural from its site specificity and turned it into yet another icon (or cliché) associated with the Chicana/o culture alongside the Guadalupe and the Christmas tree" (2000, n.p.). Asco's "mural" work was done in this manner because its members were concerned that the traditionalist artists in the community would simply replace old stereotypes of Mexicans and the Mexican community with new ones (Gamboa 1998). It is important to highlight Asco's performance work, which ironically was often mocked, as subversive work not only against the mainstream, dominant society but also against the traditionalist Chicana/o stereotypes. Indeed, the work of Asco highlights the heterogeneity that existed among Chicana/o artists.

Film became another visual means by which Chicanos and Chicanas could educate others and bring about social change in Chicana/o communities. Between 1968 and 1973 a small number of programs were established for minority students, designed to train them for employment in the film industry. The New Communicators program in Los Angeles, funded by the U.S. Office of Economic Opportunity, was created in 1968, though it lasted only eight months. The UCLA Ethno-Communications Program lasted longer, from 1969 to 1973. The University of Southern California also started a special admissions program for minorities during this time, and Stanford University had several Chicana/o students in its film program in the early 1970s. From these programs emerged a cadre of Chicana/o filmmakers (Noriega 2000). Together with other artists in the community, they worked to become "producers of visual education" (Ybarra-Frausto 1993, 56). Documentary filmmaker Sylvia Morales explained the nature of her work and that of fellow students of color in the Ethno-Communications program: "For us there was a sense of urgency, so we set aside our desire to make personal films in order to make ones which reflected our communities" (quoted in Noriega 2000, 101). Their mission was to use their artistic skills to create and produce documentary films and television programs that chronicled the struggles in the Mexican communities around issues that affected them, such as educational inequities, racism, and police brutality. One of their fundamental goals was to educate the Mexican American community about these kinds of issues in order to encourage its members to unite and bring about social and political change (Goldman and Ybarra-Frausto 1991; Lewels 1974; Noriega 2000).

The first documentary film made by a Chicano about Chicanas/os dates back to 1969's *I Am Joaquin* by Luis Valdez, the Chicano playwright, founder of El Teatro Campesino (the Farmworkers Theater) in the mid-1960s, and would-be director of *Zoot Suit* in 1981. *I Am Joaquin* is based on the 1967 poem by Chicano leader Corky Gonzales. Although the technical aspects of the film were very simple—still photography with Valdez's recitation of sections of Gonzales's poem as voice-over—the film powerfully depicted Chicana/o children, families, and farmworkers with dignity. It also featured close-ups of Mexican murals and pre-Columbian objects and places, and

zoomed in on the faces of great Mexican leaders, including Hidalgo y Costilla, Juárez, Villa, and Zapata—to build pride in Mexican roots, as well
as to give examples of revolutionaries who worked to end oppression. The
film ended with contemporary images from the present time, the Chicana/o
movement, as people of Mexican origin marched with posters protesting
the Vietnam War, carrying placards that read "Chicano Power" and "Accept
Me for What I Am: Chicano." Though rudimentary, the film depicted with
clarity the moral conflict of the time, and Chicana/o audiences responded
to it well. According to Ybarra-Frausto, the film was "immediately accepted
as a vibrant and living testimonial of the period" and became a component
of meetings, rallies, and demonstrations of the Chicana/o movement (1991b,
159).

Another important filmmaker from the 1960s was Jesús Salvador Treviño,
a chronicler of that time period. A Chicano film student in the 1960s, he
documented the fight for Chicanas'/os' educational rights. For instance,
he filmed the events that followed the 1968 Blowouts. He also produced
several documentaries for the local Public Broadcasting Station on issues
taking place in the Mexican American community (Treviño 2001). In 1972
Treviño wrote and produced another documentary, *Yo soy Chicano*. It traces
Chicana/o history from its pre-Columbian roots to the civil rights struggles
of Mexican Americans in the early 1970s. In this documentary, he interviewed Chicana/o leaders from the late 1960s and 1970s, including Dolores
Huerta, Reies López Tijerina, José Angel Gutiérrez, and Corky Gonzales,
and he recorded their community activism. This documentary was produced by the local PBS station in Los Angeles (KCET), and aired nationally
in 1972, receiving accolades from, among others, the *Los Angeles Times* and
the *Washington Post* (Noriega 2000; Treviño 2001). He then went on to write
and direct the film *Raices de Sangre* (Roots of blood) (1977), a story about
the struggles of Mexicans and Chicanas/os working in *maquiladoras* (labor-
intensive factories located in Mexico-U.S. border towns) to create a labor
union.

While Valdez's and Treviño's films largely offered a Chicano male perspective, Chicana filmmaker Sylvia Morales provided the other side of the
picture. In 1979 she directed *Chicana*, which is similar in style to Valdez's
film; however, unlike Valdez's *I Am Joaquin* and Treviño's film *Yo soy Chicano*, she provided the history of Mexican and Chicana women. This film

brings to the forefront the vital role women played in the *movimiento*. It also highlights and counters the fact that much of the artistic production during the Chicana/o movement presented men as the protagonists in the *movimiento* and excluded women.

The art collective Asco also created films. Yet it did not follow the documentary-style format. Instead, it created the *No Movie* movies, conceptual pieces through which the group provided an alternative to the portrayals of Mexican Americans supplied by Hollywood—a world that highly influenced them but where they rarely saw Mexican Americans reflected in it. The work of Asco once more stepped outside the boundaries set by the nationalist Chicano ideology and did not resemble the films by Valdez, Treviño, or Morales. However, it is important to note that Asco's films still subverted the dominant image of people of Mexican descent that they witnessed in television and film, and in that sense their work was as revolutionary as any other artist in the community.

In summary, visual production was an integral component of the Chicana/o movement. The *movimiento* was heavily dependent on visual images to transmit its messages to both people within Mexican American communities and outsiders. The link between art and politics, therefore, was inexorable. There was art in politics and politics in art. Furthermore, the inclusion or incorporation of visual culture was an intentional and carefully thought-out action. Whether in placards and posters used in marches and demonstrations, murals painted throughout the barrios, or documentary films, the ultimate purpose of these visual media was to "educate and edify" the community (Ybarra-Frausto 1991a, 128). As Ybarra-Frausto has eloquently stated, "Artists functioned as visual educators, with the important task of refining and transmitting through plastic expression the ideology of a community striving for self-determination" (ibid., 140–41).

CONCLUSION: THE ART SEEDS FROM THE *MOVIMIENTO* TODAY

The power of visual culture and the visual arts to reflect and capture the political narrative of the 1968 Blowouts and the Chicana/o movement of the 1960s and 1970s lives on today. Most recently, in 2006, immigrant rights marches and demonstrations took place nationwide against proposed legislation HR 4437, the Border Protection, Antiterrorism, and Illegal Immigration Control Act of 2005, which would, among other things, criminalize immigrants. The marches took place in the early months of 2006 and built up to a national boycott on May 1, 2006, often dubbed "A Day Without Latinos" or "A Day Without Immigrants." The boycott drew hundreds of thousands of people throughout the United States. Organizers invited students to walk out of schools, businesses to close, people to boycott shopping, and workers to skip work on that day. These marches attracted people of all ages and ethnic groups by the thousands, especially Chicanas/os, other Latinas/os, and immigrant populations from south of the Mexico-U.S. border. Students were often major participants and organizers, with many high school students staging walkouts throughout the country. This is reminiscent of the 1968 student Blowouts and the Chicano Moratorium protests of the 1970s.

What role did visual culture, visual iconography, and the visual arts play in these recent marches, and how does it compare to the integration of art during the *movimiento*? In reviewing photographs and videos of the immigrant rights marches in cities throughout the nation, one of the most important visual icons that stands out is the U.S. flag, which appeared in disproportionately higher numbers than the Mexican flag, in contrast to the Chicana/o movement, where Mexican flags prevailed. The move by organizers and participants toward increasing the number of U.S. flags was intentional and a direct result of criticism and immigrant backlash when more Mexican and Central American flags were present in the earlier marches. This purposeful increase of U.S. flags is reminiscent of Chavez's utilization of the image of the *Virgen de Guadalupe* as a protective shield against outside criticism. The U.S. flag also became a visual icon that served to remind mainstream audiences that Chicanas/os and other Latinas/os are part of the U.S. fabric. It also invited non-Latinas/os to align themselves or come together with Latinas/os under the U.S. flag. In one of the marches, a banner read, "Immigration Is an American Experience," educating and reminding onlookers of the fact that most people in the United States were, at one point or another, immigrants.

Visual images were prevalent throughout the 2006 immigrant rights marches, evidence that the visual legacy of the Chicana/o movement of the 1960s and 1970s lives on. Furthermore, these visual images served to connect the present struggles in the Latina/o community with the struggles that existed during the *movimiento*. For instance, in some of the 2006 marches,

UFW flags with the image of the Aztec eagle created by Cesar Chavez were present. And in one of the marches, an enormous UFW banner included the following phrase, "Labor Rights / Immigrant Rights / The Same Struggle!" Another visual image that was evocative of the *movimiento* was the clenched fist symbolizing Brown Power. One placard from these recent protests had the brown clenched fist with the following words: "Un mundo sin guerra / un mundo sin fronteras" (A world without war / a world without borders). The image of Che also reappeared during the 2006 marches. Interestingly, so did the poster of Chicana artist Yolanda López created in 1978. López's image plays with the image of Uncle Sam pointing his finger at the viewer with the slogan "I want you," used by the U.S. government to recruit people into the armed forces. López's poster features an Aztec man who also points his finger at the viewer, but this time the slogan reads, "Who's the illegal alien, pilgrim?" Lipsitz (2001) argues that the original poster spoke back to power, subverted its authority, and inverted its icons. The resurfacing of López's poster in this new context is as poignant as when it was first created, and once more questions the notion of the Mexican as the "illegal alien" in the United States. López's poster also inspired another one. This new poster uses the same slogan, but instead of an indigenous man pointing at the viewer, his hand is a brown clenched fist, symbolizing Brown Power, with indigenous people in the background. This new version illustrates how ideas are borrowed and re-created.

Visual images and slogans also appeared in a new visual medium: the T-shirt. Some T-shirts only had slogans, such as "Just Cause," "Unidos Estamos" (United We Stand), or "Indigenous Revolution." Other T-shirts combined words with images. One T-shirt, for example, combined the words "Defending Land and Life" with an image of a clenched fist. Another T-shirt had the image of the U.S. flag with the words, "We Come in Peace. We Are Not Criminals." There were also T-shirts with the more typical icons, such as Zapata.

And what role did Chicana and Chicano artists play during these recent marches? Young Chicana/o artists live under a different sociohistorical context than artists did in the 1960s and 1970s during the Chicana/o movement. Yet, as evidenced in the 2006 marches, artists continue to create art that has social meaning. Two young artists who created posters for the recent immigrant rights marches serve as examples. Favianna Rodriguez Giannoni,

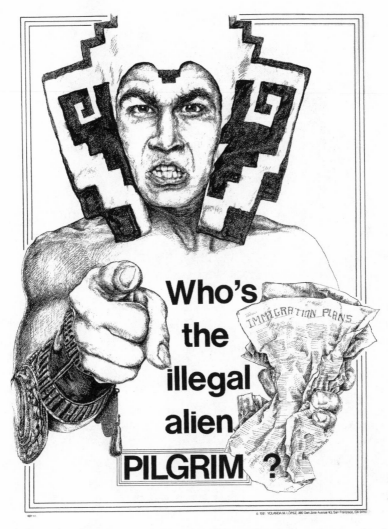

Yolanda M. López, *Who's the Illegal Alien, Pilgrim?* (1978). Pen, ink, paper. Reproduced by permission of the artist.

a Chicana artist based in Oakland, California, created a poster for the May 1 protests supporting immigrant rights. The poster was printed in a run of five thousand and distributed free around the community (Rodriguez n.d.b). On her Web site, Rodriguez describes herself as a "community poster artist" (http://www.favianna.com/). She creates posters that "reflect both national

Image in Web article titled "Between Half-Million and One Million People Protest Against Anti-Immigrant Law," by Marcus (March 25, 2006, http://la.indymedia.org/news/2006/03/151463.php).

and international grassroots struggles, and tell a history of social justice through graphics." For Rodriguez, protest posters make politics explicit and invite discussion: "They can deepen compassion and commitment, ignite outrage, elicit laughter, and provoke action." Rodriguez, however, does not define herself only as an artist; she also considers herself an educator who sees the importance in passing on her skills to the next generation of "cultural workers," just as she learned from and was inspired by artists from the *movimiento* generation. Furthermore, the educative aspect of her work is evident in the explanation she offers for creating artwork: "to translate the messages of the frontlines into works of art that can be used to educate and mobilize" (n.d.a). Rodriguez, then, is a producer of visual education, as were her artist predecessors from the Chicana/o movement.

Xico González is another young artist from California who has contributed artwork to many marches in his area of Sacramento, at times utilizing iconic images that were used in posters during the Chicana/o movement. For instance, for one of the immigrant rights marches that took place on April 10, 2006, he created the poster *Zapata—No on HR 4437*. The poster features an image of the Mexican revolutionary with his famous quote, "Es mejor morir de pie que vivir toda una vida arrodillados" (It is better to die on your feet than to live on your knees). For the march on May 1, 2006, he designed and distributed two posters for the masses. One of them, titled *¡Viva la Mujer!* (Long live the woman!), also referred to as *CheFRIDA,* is a poster that merges the image of Che with that of Mexican artist and icon Frida Kahlo. By participating in this way, González states that "as a Chicano artist, I fulfilled my mission—to empower my community through the gift that the great spirit gave me; ARTE!" (2007a, "CheFRIDA" section). González defines himself not only as an artist but also as a "cultural *activista*" (http://www.xicogonzalez.com/), which is reflected through the extensive list of educational outreach activities he has engaged in.

Reflecting on the role that arts and artists have had in the Chicana/o movement and in more recent activism around issues still affecting people of Mexican origin, there are several questions that we should continue to pose and attempt to understand. Why study the visual arts that were supported and produced during *el movimiento* and the ones produced in today's growing movements? For one, "art provides insight into the complexities of the time as interpreted by an individual artist or an artistic group" (Goldman 1994, 102). In this way, we learn more about the times of the Chicana/o movement in the 1960s and 1970s, the goals and ideologies that people held, and how the visual arts captured the political, social, and cultural narrative of that point in time. Furthermore, it allows us to begin the process of analyzing the complexities of our present day, the ways in which art is (and

Favianna Rodriguez Giannoni, *Legalization Now!* (2006). Offset poster. Reproduced by permission of the artist.

is not) reflecting our current narrative, and the function that these visual media have.

We should also ask why the inclusion of art in any social movement, march, or rally is important. Juanishi Orosco, a member of the artist collective RCAF (Royal Chicano Air Force), offers a powerful answer: "Artists give vision to the slogans, and these are lingering images that will be there tomorrow" (Macias 2006). In this sense, and at a time when we are living in a society driven by visual culture, artists operate as translators and as bridges, and therefore are forces necessary to move forward those causes they support.

So what is there to learn of the role of the visual arts and of the "pro-

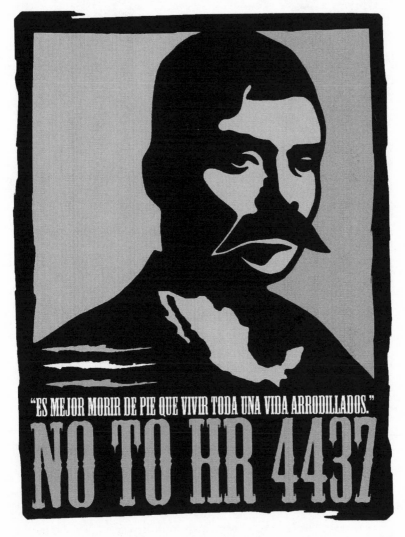

Xico González, *Zapata–No on HR 4437* (2006). Poster. Reproduced by permission of the artist.

Xico González, *¡Viva la Mujer!* or *CheFRIDA* (2006). Poster. Reproduced by permission of the artist.

ducers of visual education" in social, cultural, and political movements—whether those in the past or those taking place today? First and foremost, they play a vital part. Artists educate the masses as to the messages they want to convey through their art. However, we must be vigilant and understand that these are messages that reflect the biases, politics, and interests of the artists because, ultimately, artworks are a reflection of the perspective of their creator. As art historian Shifra Goldman reminds us, "Artists are *not* historians." She cautions us to keep in mind the advocacy position of the artist, that is, "the interpretative function of the artist with his material according to his personal politics and ideology" (1994, 102). She also reminds us that we must have a historical perspective and consider where and for whom an art piece is created.

Finally, this chapter is also an invitation for us to consider the multiple roles of artists who are interested in creating art that has a social and political impact and an educative role. Many Chicana/o artists from the *movimiento* today define themselves as "cultural workers" or fall within Ybarra-Frausto's description of "producers of visual education." As cultural workers and producers of visual education, their work has educational and political dimensions. According to scholar Henry Giroux, the pedagogical dimension of cultural work is "the process of creating symbolic representations and the practices within which they are engaged. This includes a particular concern with the analysis of textual, aural, and visual representations and how such representations are organized and regulated within particular institutional arrangements." The political dimension of cultural work speaks to projects whose intent is "to mobilize knowledge and desires that may lead to minimizing the degree of oppression in people's lives" (1992, 5). We must continue to analyze how the inclusion of visual arts and visual culture, as translated through our artists, plays a transformative pedagogical and political role in our movements today and those to come.

NOTES

1. The terms "Mexican American" and "Chicano" are used interchangeably in this chapter.

REFERENCES

Acuña, R. 2000. *Occupied America: A History of Chicanos.* 4th ed. New York: Longman.

———. 2004. *Occupied America: A History of Chicanos.* 5th ed. New York: Longman.

Chavez, C. 1966. "The Organizer's Tale." *Ramparts* (July): 43–50. http://www.hks.harvard.edu/organizing/tools/toolshome.shtml.

Cockcroft, E. S., and H. Barnet-Sánchez, eds. 1993. *Signs From the Heart: California Chicano Murals.* Albuquerque: University of New Mexico Press.

Delgado Bernal, D. 1999. "Chicana/o Education From the Civil Rights Era to the Present." In *The Elusive Quest for Equality: 150 Years of Chicano/Chicana Education,* edited by J. F. Moreno. Cambridge: Harvard Educational Review.

du Gay, P., S. Hall, L. Janes, H. Mackay, and K. Negus. 1997. *Doing Cultural Studies: The Story of the Sony Walkman.* London: Sage.

El Plan de Aztlán. n.d. http://www.sscnet.ucla.edu/00W/chicano101-1/aztlan.htm.

Galán, H. P., producer. 1996a. *Chicano! History of the Mexican American Civil Rights Movement.* Video recording. National Latino Communications Center, Galán Productions, KCET.

———. 1996b. *Taking Back the Schools.* In *Chicano! History of the Mexican American Civil Rights Movement,* produced by H. Galán. National Latino Communications Center Educational Media, Galán Productions, KCET.

Gamboa, H. J. 1998. *Urban Exile: Collected Writings of Harry Gamboa Jr.* Edited by Chon Noriega. Minneapolis: University of Minnesota Press.

Giroux, H. A. 1992. *Border Crossings: Cultural Workers and the Politics of Education.* New York: Routledge.

Goldman, S. M. 1984. "A Public Voice: Fifteen Years of Chicano Posters." *Art Journal* 44, no. 1: 50–57.

———. 1994. *Dimensions of the Americas: Art and Social Change in Latin America and the United States.* Chicago: University of Chicago Press.

Goldman, S. M., and T. Ybarra-Frausto. 1991. "The Political and Social Contexts of Chicano Art." In *Chicano Art: Resistance and Affirmation, 1965–1985,* edited by R. Griswold del Castillo, T. McKenna, and Y. Yarbro-Bejarano, 83–95. Los Angeles: Wright Art Gallery, University of California.

Gonzales, R. C. 1967. *I Am Joaquin.* Denver: El Gallo.

González, X. 2007a. *Acción.* http://www.xicogonzalez.com/toppage1.htm.

———. 2007b. *Vitae.* http://www.xicogonzalez.com/toppage1.htm.

Guzmán, K. 2005. *Self-Help Graphics and Arts: Art in the Heart of East Los Angeles.* Los Angeles: UCLA Chicano Studies Research Center.

High, F. 1997. "Chiasmus-Art in Politics/Politics in Art: Chicano/a and African American Image, Text, and Activism of the 1960s and 1970s." In *Voices of Color: Art and Society in the Americas,* edited by P. Farris-DuFrene, 118–65. Atlantic Highlands, N.J.: Humanities Press.

Hinojosa, R. 1985. "*I Am Joaquín:* Relationships Between the Text and the Film." In *Chicano Cinema: Research, Reviews, and Resources,* edited by G. D. Keller, 142–45. Tempe, Ariz.: Bilingual Review/Press.

"A History of SF State." 2009. March 20. http://www.sfsu.edu/~100years/history/long.htm.

Katzew, A. 2005. "No Chicanos on TV: Learning From Chicana/o Artists-Activists Countering Invisibility and Stereotypes in the Media Through Art." Ed.D. diss., Harvard University.

Latorre, G. 2000. "Heterogeneity in California Chicana/o Muralism." *Journal of American Studies of Turkey* 12: 25–37. http://www.bilkent.edu.tr/~jast/Number12/ Latorre.htm.

Lewels, F. J. 1974. *The Uses of the Media by the Chicano Movement: A Study in Minority Access.* New York: Praeger.

Lipsitz, G. 2001. "Not Just Another Social Movement: Poster Art and the *Movimiento* Chicano." In *Just Another Poster? Chicano Graphic Arts in California,* edited by C. A. Noriega. Santa Barbara: University of California, University Art Museum.

Macias, C. 2006. "Immigrant-Rights Protest at Capitol Is an Artful Demonstration." *Sacramento Bee,* May 2. http://www.accessmylibrary.com/coms2/summary _0286-16953249_ITM.

Maciel, D. R. 1991. "The Political and Social Contexts of Chicano Art." In *Mexico in Aztlán, Aztlán in Mexico: The Dialectics of Chicano-Mexicano Art,* edited by R. Griswold del Castillo, T. McKenna, and Y. Yarbro-Bejarano, 109–19. Los Angeles: Wright Art Gallery, University of California.

Meier, M. S., and F. Ribera. 2001. *Mexican Americans/American Mexicans: From Conquistadors to Chicanos.* 1993. Reprint, New York: Hill and Wang.

Muñoz, C. J. 1989. *Youth, Identity, Power: The Chicano Movement.* London: Verso.

Noriega, C. A. 2000. *Shot in America: Television, the State, and the Rise of Chicano Cinema.* Minneapolis: University of Minnesota Press.

Peterson, J. F. 1992. "The Virgin of Guadalupe: Symbol of Conquest or Liberation?" *Art Journal* 51, no. 4: 39–47.

Rodriguez, F. n.d.a. *Artist Statement.* http://www.favianna.com/statement/index.php.

———. n.d.b. *Legalization Now!* Offset poster no. 17. http://www.favianna.com/ port_posters/posters17.php.

Rosales, F. A. 1996. *Chicano! The History of the Mexican American Civil Rights Movement.* Houston: Arte Público Press of the University of Houston.

Smithsonian Institution. 1986. Judith Baca interviews, August 5–6. Archives of American Art, Smithsonian Institution. http://www.aaa.si.edu/collections/oral histories/transcripts/ baca86.htm.

———. 1995–96. Oral history interview with Rupert Garcia, November 10, 1995, and June 24, 1996. Archives of American Art, Smithsonian Institution. http:// www.aaa.si.edu/collections/oralhistories/transcripts/garcia95.htm.

———. 1997. Oral history interview with Gronk, January 20–23. Archives of American Art, Smithsonian Institution. http://www.aaa.si.edu/collections/oral histories/transcripts/gronk97.htm.

Sorell, V. A. 1991. "Articulate Signs of Resistance and Affirmation in Chicano Public Art." In *Chicano Art: Resistance and Affirmation, 1965–1985,* edited by R. Griswold del Castillo, T. McKenna, and Y. Yarbro-Bejarano, 141–54. Los Angeles: Wright Art Gallery, University of California.

Treviño, J. S. 2001. *Eyewitness: A Filmmaker's Memoir of the Chicano Movement.* Houston: Arte Público Press of the University of Houston.

Valdez, L., and R. Rubalcava. 1972. "*Venceremos!* Mexican-American Statement of Travel to Cuba." In *Aztlan: An Anthology of Mexican American Literature,* edited by L. Valdez and S. Steiner, 215. New York: Alfred A. Knopf.

Ybarra-Frausto, T. 1991a. "The Chicano Movement/the Movement of Chicano Art." In *Exhibiting Cultures: The Poetics and Politics of Museum Display,* edited by I. Karp and S. D. Lavine, 128–50. Washington, D.C.: Smithsonian Institution Press.

———. 1991b. "*Rasquachismo:* A Chicano Sensibility." In *Chicano Art: Resistance and Affirmation, 1965–1985,* edited by R. Griswold del Castillo, T. McKenna, and Y. Yarbro-Bejarano, 155–62. Los Angeles: Wright Art Gallery, University of California.

———. 1993. "Arte Chicano: Images of a Community." In *Signs From the Heart: California Chicano Murals,* edited by E. S. Cockcroft and H. Barnet-Sánchez, 54–67. Albuquerque: University of New Mexico Press.

CHAPTER 3

Raising a Multidimensional
Consciousness of Resistance

ALEJANDRO COVARRUBIAS

The collective *marchas* of the past decade are examples of public forms of resistance challenging a conservative backlash that has given birth to the most recent round of anti-immigrant and racist policy recommendations. They have inspired a new generation of activists to serve as catalysts to community efforts for educational justice within Chicana/o- and Latina/o-serving institutions. These collective and far-reaching efforts demonstrate the community-based nature of resistance. In this chapter, I examine a model of community-based organizations that work toward preparing young people to engage in similar acts of resistance—Agencies of Transformational Resistance (ATRs). Transformational resistance, as described by Delgado Bernal (1997), refers to oppositional behaviors to injustice that are motivated by a desire for self- and social transformation and are coupled with some level of critique of systems of domination (see also Giroux 1983). "Agencies of Transformational Resistance" is a term used to describe organizations that nurture transformational resistance (Covarrubias and Revilla 2003; Covarrubias 2005). I specifically focus on the development of a Critical multidimensional consciousness as an act of resistance and as a case study of the process of nurturing resistance among young people who ultimately engage in community-based resistance efforts.

Education and youth development fields have traditionally focused on the academic and personal development of young people without fostering a Critical and historical understanding of the context within which youth development is nurtured (Fullbright-Anderson et al. 2003). There is a tendency among these well-intentioned educators to ignore the root structural causes of inequalities. Instead, educators have focused on changing the values of young people while developing their skill set, taking a traditionally deficit perspective of development and education. Additionally, these long-established youth development approaches emphasize the development of youth from marginalized communities only, disregarding the need to enlighten youth of the dominant group in an effort to address injustice. Another weakness of youth development generally has been the misunderstanding and disconnection between youth and community development. At best, community development is expected to be connected to youth development because investment in youth is believed to eventually pay dividends for the development of the community; typically, these efforts do not directly create a space for youth in community-building efforts. This approach, not only adultist but also ultimately reactionary, does not acknowledge the historical role of young people in creating change throughout the world. The "systematic mistreatment and disrespect of young people" that adultist approaches assume are grounded in "the assumption that adults are better than young people, and entitled to act upon young people without their agreement" (J. Bell 1995). At worst, these approaches view youth as threats or nuisances that complicate community development. Agencies of Transformational Resistance work toward youth and community development that emphasize an asset-based approach where young people are actively engaged in resistance that is both personally transformational while aiming to widely transform unjust conditions and relationships everywhere.

AGENCIES OF TRANSFORMATIONAL RESISTANCE

A series of interviews, participatory observations, and a review of documents at Public Allies, Los Angeles (PALA), over the course of a year, allowed me to create the following framework of Agencies of Transformational Resistance. The ATR model describes progressive organizations as those that:

> promote a multidimensional Critical consciousness
> nurture a commitment to social justice that is broadly defined
> provide services and resources and develop skills that allow youth to
> > productively and positively engage in at least one of several forms

of empowering changes (for example, self-transformation, school
change, community empowerment, or societal transformation)

create and sustain a community of inclusiveness and love

are constantly creating and evolving a network of resistance (Covarrubias 2005)

Although this working model of ATRs offers a framework to examine and
develop progressive organizations, grassroots local movements, or institutions, it is an operational model that should be challenged and reworked.
The contributions of this study are based on the work of one nonprofit
community-based organization, PALA, and its work within a network of
other organizations and communities of progressive people in Los Angeles.

The experiences of youth who participate in PALA illustrate the characteristics of the ATR model as specifically constructed by the participants of
this study. PALA is a ten-month leadership training program that nurtures
young activists in local struggles for community justice by placing them in
apprenticeships with partner nonprofit organizations and providing contin-
uous education and training. Their mission statement asserts that they are a
"youth and community development organization that creates opportunities
for diverse young adults to practice leadership and strengthen their communities" (Public Allies 2004). The national model was developed seventeen
years ago with the intent to involve young people in community service.
Since its establishment more than nine years ago, PALA, the Los Angeles
affiliate, has been recognized as a key player in the Los Angeles progressive
scene because it has always engaged in social justice work and its staff has
developed strong relationships with local community organizers.

Critical Multidimensional Consciousness

For the purpose of this study, consciousness refers to the process of becoming aware of the ways that power is abused to create relationships of
privilege and oppression along multiple dimensions. I focus on four dimensions of consciousness in this study: class, race, sexuality, and gender. Relationships along these four dimensions are constantly reshaping people's experiences, perspectives, and opportunities as they are historically embedded in
institutions and people's psyche and are impacted by their ever-changing
realities. A Critical consciousness refers to a consciousness that has an intentional critique of relations of power. Hence, I have chosen to use a capital *C*

at the beginning of the word "Critical" to distinguish it from the more commonly used idea of critical thinking that can be apolitical and ahistorical. It includes our ability to be reflective and recognize how power relationships impact us and others, as well as how we maintain and challenge these power relations.

I investigated a Critical multidimensional consciousness that critiques the intersection of power relationships created and maintained by the constructs of race, class, gender, and sexuality. This examination is informed by recent work that utilizes Critical Race Theory and Latino/a Critical Race Theory (LatCrit) (D. Bell 1987; Crenshaw et al. 1995; Delgado 1995, 1999; Ladson-Billings 1998; Lynn 1999; Parker 1998; Solórzano 1998; Solórzano and Delgado Bernal 2001; Solórzano and Ornelas 2002, 2004; Solórzano and Villalpando 1998; Solórzano, Villalpando, and Oseguera 2005; Solórzano and Yosso 2001; Yosso 2006) in the field of education, asserting that race is a social construct and the basis of a historical and endemically racist system utilized to create and maintain inequality through its intersection with other markers used to create systems of oppression. With a transdisciplinary perspective, these theories stand in opposition to dominant views of inequality that are noncritical and sometimes one-dimensional and mostly rely on deficit thought. They also maintain the centrality of experiential knowledge to a critique of racism. Accordingly, a Critical consciousness is multidimensional (understanding the way that class, race, gender, and sexuality intersect to create oppression and privilege) and grounded in the lived experience of those who are in the process of consciousness building.

A general overview of the five elements of the model of Agencies of Transformational Resistance follows.

ATR *element 1: Raising a multidimensional and Critical consciousness.* This study captures the importance of the development of a sophisticated awareness and critique of relations of power to transformational resistance and the process by which ATRs can help in the acquisition of such a Critical consciousness. An intentional and mutually committed effort toward the development of a Critical consciousness must be put forth by both the ATR and the youth involved for this process to be successfully carried out. Formalized training sessions and opportunities to engage in dialogue and praxis are important strategies for supporting growth of consciousness and the ability to articulate it. Creating opportunities for what Freire has termed *conscientização* to happen along multiple dimensions requires a diverse community of learners, an active network of allies, and the support structure for coaching young people through an ebbing and flowing learning curve (1973, 1997). Freire's notion of *conscientização* "represents the development of the awakening of critical awareness" that occurs when *subjects* are engaged in dialogue, action, and reflection (1973, 19). Recognizing preexisting strengths of young people allows ATRs to build on the assets of youth and see them as active participants in their own growth. Finally, healthy respect and patience for the disparate development of consciousness along the dimensions of race, class, gender, and sexuality were commitments the ATR in this study made; this presents important challenges and lessons for community building and education.

ATR element 2: Nurture a commitment to social justice. The second element of an ATR is the ability and goal of an organization to nurture a commitment to social justice that is broadly defined and inclusive. Commitment to social justice in this context is defined as the commitment to engage in a process of transforming all relevant unequal and unjust relationships, whether they are personal and individual or public and systemic—both understood as political. This definition of commitment to social justice finds it important to identify the fact that unjust relationships that may happen in the home, like the exploitation or abuse of one's partner, are equally detrimental to social justice generally, as is the historical and systemic racism against People of Color that happens in large institutions. This study confirmed that an ATR could nurture a young person's commitment to social justice that widened in scope as it evolved. Evidence suggests that initially one may begin to work toward eliminating oppressive relations of power that impact one's own life, but as an Agent of Transformational Resistance recognizes the struggles of others as their own, that individual moves toward a struggle beyond the self. As this occurs, collaboration with others in a common struggle becomes necessary (Padilla 1997). Furthermore, the development of a Critical multidimensional consciousness is never independent from one's commitment to social justice, as both goals have a clearly symbiotic relationship.

ATR element 3: Develop skills and expand resources. Studying PALA highlighted another essential element of ATRs, that is, the need to provide youth with the skills and resources necessary to make change possible and probable. I found that ATRs ensure that the youth's personal needs are met by expanding the resources available to them and developing relevant and functional skills. Taking an asset-based approach to community and youth development, ATRs start from the premise that existing skills are strengths that need to be further developed and refined. The development of a Critical multidimensional consciousness can be an overwhelming revelation to a young person if not given the tools to be engaged in transforming injustice and alienating if not provided with meaningful opportunities to engage in transformational work. In addition, the burden of engaging in social justice work can be a daunting task if not connected to a supportive community and network of people doing similar work.

ATR element 4: Create and maintain an inclusive community. ATRs need to create a community of inclusiveness where injustice is grappled with as it relates to all its participants and their larger communities. The ways in which injustice impacts each individual in similar and distinct ways become an important issue for the formation of the community. A community of learners is developed where each perspective is validated and valued and everyone is responsible for and supportive of the development of all group members. More important, youth can develop in a space that is conducive to developing a Critical and multidimensional analysis because they are in a space with diverse people interested in progressive politics. A unified goal and definition of social justice may not become realized, but within this community the various struggles of empowerment are recognized and viewed as interrelated.

ATR element 5: Create and evolve a network of resistance. Recent research has explored how social networks help youth create opportunities to gain social capital and personal and political support (Stanton-Salazar 2001). Similar to this work, I found that young people in this study were given access to information that would help them navigate community-based organizations and gain the resources necessary to excel. They also emphasized their extended relationships with social justice work historically and by family affiliation in order to increase the significance of their work. Additionally, these youth found ways to utilize this network to gather information and extend their impact. This network was important for legitimizing the work of young people and offering them much needed relevant opportunities for growth, as they were typically used to being isolated in most other spaces. Furthermore, and probably most important, this network offered young people an opportunity to gain political and personal support for issues with which they were grappling. To date, research focusing on groups that nurture resistant behavior among young people and the networks these groups form has not been conducted. This study found evidence of the importance of this network of resistance in supporting the development of young people as agents of change. These networks took shape through various processes and were instrumental for the development of a Critical consciousness that was beyond the capacity of PALA to develop.

Consciousness as Historically Familial, Experiential, and Reflectively Evolving

Nurturing a multidimensional consciousness requires an intentional effort to assist youth in connecting their own understanding about personal experiences with a critique of more systemic structures of domination—the micro must connect to the macro. Furthermore, one's personal experiences with oppression and privilege must be understood in relationship to others' oppression and privilege. Coming to a Critical multidimensional consciousness involves a dynamic and endless evolutionary process of reflecting on and critiquing the intersectionality of race, class, sexuality, and gender structures of domination. Consciousness raising at PALA is also grounded in historical struggles for change against oppressive conditions. It is a process that is rooted in family history and what Dolores Delgado Bernal (2001) has termed "community memory," which refers to the string of lessons learned about injustice and passed on within communities through various culturally rooted means, like *dichos* (sayings), parables, and *cuentos* (short stories).

At PALA a Critical multidimensional consciousness starts from the premise that youth come in with the desire to create change and with the (life) experience-based foundation to develop this consciousness:

The most important thing about consciousness is that knowledge, history, and the context for the work that we do. I mean, why are people even interested in doing Public Allies if they don't have at least a beginning framework or consciousness of the need for this type of work or community service? I think that Allies come with a need identified. We mostly try to develop consciousness through our training programs, bringing up issues that we feel are really pertinent and affect the work that we want Allies to be a part of. We have to give that grounding by providing them with resources and the forum to dialogue about issues that maybe they haven't had the opportunity to dialogue about. Or if they have, they probably haven't had the opportunity to do it in such a diverse environment with so many different people. One of the main ways [we develop consciousness], is when we meet with our Allies one on one. That's another way that we develop their consciousness, by talking and reflecting on the work that they are doing with their organization, as well as just the growing and learning they are doing through the work that we make them do. (Monique, personal communication, March 22, 2001. Monique is one of the staff members who coached the young people through the program.)

Although many of the Allies come with an understanding of injustice, PALA further develops youth's consciousness through various interactive activities that force participants to be self-critical and reflective of their own experiences and build on these life stories. PALA's Asset-Based approach begins with the idea that "great leaders are catalysts for the leadership of others" (Cunningham and Mathie 2002). It embraces an ABCD perspective on leadership, believing that "(a) everyone has gifts and talents to contribute to their communities, (b) those who are often considered 'clients' of service programs should be partners and leaders in addressing public issues and (c) service and change efforts should be accountable to those who have to live with the results" (Public Allies 2004). This approach drives the development of consciousness, skills, and community building at PALA.

PALA draws on the lived experiences and family histories of the Allies to further nurture a Critical multidimensional consciousness. Juan's awareness of social injustice is rooted in his family history, as the child of two longtime Chicana/o activists, as well as his own understanding of the limited resources available to youth in his neighborhood. His interviews demonstrate his awareness of the connectedness of justice issues and how macro relations of power can influence micro experiences. He understands that consciousness is neither static nor complete. Consciousness is understood and articulated in a context-specific manner so that it is relevant for one's current situation. Similar to what I found with Juan, most of the interviewees for this study showed developing consciousnesses rooted in life experiences, previous social justice work, and lessons learned from older family members. Their emergent consciousness was often based on one or two dimensions that they perceived were most important to their lived experiences. Although the consciousness of the Allies may have already been evolving as they entered into the program, PALA further creates opportunities for youth to acquire more sophisticated critiques of relations of power by providing diverse teaching and learning opportunities that are not one-dimensional (Covarrubias 2005).

Opportunities for reflection and discussion in a safe space allow youth to examine how privilege and power impact them and how they are active participants in sustaining or dismantling injustice at different levels, including personal, institutional, and societal. PALA helps youth critically reflect on how multiple injustices are interrelated and how they impact their lives and the people they serve. This is accomplished in several ways. Weekly training sessions are broken down into skill and issue development. As explained by Ruben, the executive director of the organization, the issue development is "really more of a dialogue on issues that affect Angelinos. Our trainings fall into the context of what's going on in Los Angeles, politically, socially, and culturally . . . issues like power and privilege, like gender politics," sexual orientation, racism, ableism, and other interconnected issues of injustice (personal communication, 2001). A focus on issue development across a wide range of issues impacting Los Angeles demonstrates PALA's commitment to develop a consciousness that is Critical and multidimensional. Dialogue provides youth an opportunity to deconstruct issues being discussed and synthesize them into an evolving consciousness that is youth driven. This community dialogue becomes an active process by which members of the community of PALA, in an equal relationship among participants, together create meaning of the training sessions provided for them and the community (see Freire 1993 for a discussion of the act of and significance of dialogue). The diversity of the group further adds to a consciousness that is not only sociopolitical but also cultural and historical. The clear separation between skill and issue development demonstrates a deliberate intention to provide youth the skills necessary to impact change once they come to a self-defined understanding of transformation.

The organization provides youth a diverse setting to nurture a Critical multidimensional consciousness that is grounded in both historical liberation struggles and in personal experiences. PALA provides young people a historical perspective of issues impacting Los Angeles and complements them with personal experiences of a diverse group of youth. To that point

Monique offers: "For them to be able to share their own history, perspective, and knowledge of issues of race, class and sex will be an opportunity. We also bring in other people that have experience in the community to talk about issues of race relations, of what culturalism in Los Angeles means, and issues of homophobia. We try to address all those different topics. Our goal is to raise social consciousness by having people come talk to them [while] having the Allies share their experience" (personal communication, 2001). Training on issue development focuses on the following areas: homophobia, sexism and patriarchy, economic development, power relations, educational inequality, gentrification, immigrant experiences, the garment industry, community organizing, and people trafficking, among others. The trust built within this community makes the setting conducive to an open sharing of diverse personal experiences that the Allies had with many of these topics, as either People of Color, women, immigrants, members of the working class, queer youth, or any combination thereof. This allows youth to develop a consciousness that is both personal and multidimensional and draws on the strengths of the community.

Coaching for an Asset-Based Consciousness

An important pedagogical tool used by PALA to support the development of the Allies is the practice of coaching. Coaching involves dialogue between two individuals, the coach and the person being coached. The coach supports the Ally through the process of finding solutions for his or her own questions and is nonjudgmental and supportive. Different from a counselor or a case manager, the coach is not there to resolve issues for the young person. Through active listening, coaches guide youth through a process of self-discovery by asking thought-provoking questions. The coaching session is intended to hold youth accountable for mutually agreed-upon goals that were decided at the onset of the program. Through coaching, the young person learns to be reflective and self-critical, has the opportunity to explore ideas he or she is not ready to bring to the group, and begins to develop a self-discipline grounded in dialogue with others. This becomes an important method through which the Allies develop their own consciousness.

Although young people are constantly being challenged by the cutting-edge curriculum, they are still expected to actively participate in setting the parameters of their own development. Ultimately, they determine how far and in what directions they want to grow and rely on each other and the staff to get there. Not only is the young person respected as an active agent in creating the direction of their own development, but the process of experiential learning is given a great deal of value. Despite the many years of experience and the high level of education of each of the staff members, they have the humility to step back and be a part of the growth of the Allies and not the reason for it. This is an important characteristic of all of the staff who work at PALA because it is what allows the young people to struggle through the acquisition of their own consciousness, which in turn gives them confidence and ownership of what they have learned.

Consistent with an ABCD approach to the development of consciousness, the staff described a two-pronged approach to consciousness raising at PALA. Young people are expected to develop an individually constructed consciousness that is grounded in their own motivations and perspectives, and a consciousness of the need and complementary assets of the community. Consciousness is to be grounded in the assets of the community and the knowledge of how the community has mobilized its assets to effect change in the areas it has deemed there are needs. This process is grounded in the struggles of working-class communities of color to self-identify their needs and address them. Although I initially began this study with the intention to examine Chicana/o examples of resistance, I found that PALA would not allow for this, because an essential piece of what happens within this space is about connecting the struggles of *all* working-class communities of color throughout Los Angeles. These linkages were introduced through the training that provided a historical account of the various interconnected human rights struggles by communities of color, women, and queer folks, and especially youth participation in these struggles.

The emphasis on the lived experience of youth in the development of this consciousness is not, by any means, evidence of an anti-intellectual or anti-academic sentiment. In fact, PALA ties in scholarship and theory as often as possible to the experiential knowledge of the youth. For example, acclaimed Chicano activist scholar Rudy Acuña (1988) conducted training sessions on theoretical frameworks used to examine the experiences of People of Color. Also, youth commonly shared their own knowledge base of theory, as was the case when they shared with each other their knowledge of Paulo Freire's *Pedagogy of the Oppressed* (1997) or the utility of Augusto Boal's *Theatre of the Oppressed* (1979) for youth development. The combination of theory and practice further contributes to the development of praxis-based Critical consciousness that allows for reflection and action in a supportive community. Not only were community members responsible for their own development, but they also supported the development of each other. They looked to their communities for knowledge to build on and trusted their own sense of instinct in furthering their consciousness.

The community at PALA is a safe space, not only to explore one's identity but also to explore perspectives that Allies may not have previously had access to, limiting their ability to expand their consciousness. The organization's decidedly progressive perspective affords youth the space to feel that they can safely explore perspectives that may be taboo in other more traditional learning settings. The group's diversity also exposes youth to various valid life experiences and expands their understanding of their surroundings. This allows youth to explore dimensions of their consciousness that they have neglected or had not considered. The Allies often share each other's resources with one another as they come across them, either through e-mails, sharing of meetings, workshops, events information, or weekly Friday training sessions. This availability and dissemination of material from a Critical perspective provide people with access to a wealth of diverse and conscious perspectives that youth use to build their consciousness within a short and focused time span in the supportive space of the Allies.

Consciousness and Commitment to Social Justice

Throughout this study, evidence demonstrates that as one's Critical consciousness becomes more sophisticated and multidimensional, one's commitment to social justice becomes broader, with the individual becoming more invested in various interconnected struggles. The still evolving, budding consciousness tends to be associated to a less internalized and more narrow sense of social justice that is based on one's own identity markers (that is, class, gender, race, sexuality, and so forth), and less committed to the struggles of others because those struggles are seen as just that: the struggles of others. This seems to be associated with a limited understanding that does not recognize the intersectional nature of systems of domination and in turn the necessity for various struggles to be interrelated.

As the level of Critical consciousness rises, becoming more multidimensional and gaining a more sophisticated critique of the interrelated nature of relations of power, the commitment to social justice becomes more broadly defined to include other dimensions of justice that may not have been previously recognized as being in the interest of the person. It also becomes much more internalized, leading to a greater commitment to be involved in social justice work. Growth occurs with unpredictable spurts that are mini epiphanies alternating between plateaus in growth and times of regression to what King and Ladson-Billings (1990) have coined "dysconsciousness," which describes a state of non-Critical analysis of relationships of power that relies on deficit thinking to explain and understand social and economic outcomes or relationships; it refers to a "habit of mind" that is incomplete due to miseducation and does not allow one to challenge the status quo. The key learning in this study is that there is a growth relationship between a rising Critical multidimensional consciousness and an increasingly broader and internalized social justice commitment.

There is also evidence that whereas one dimension of consciousness may be developed to a Critical level, other dimensions of one's consciousness can remain at a tolerance level, or, much worse, at a dysconscious level. For example, there was an individual in this study whose race and class consciousness was clearly defined and Critical, but he continued to be homophobic and referred to gay men as "faggots" or "fags" in private. This expresses a still evolving consciousness that reveals that the person still remains homophobic. His consciousness is not fully Critical, as he does not see how this homophobia is destructive to others, himself, and social justice efforts generally. In one particular incident, this individual asserted that male and female identities were "too androgynous," so that it made it difficult to clearly define men's and women's roles. On another occasion he argued that problems of the home that later resulted in wider social barriers began "when women started going out into the workforce and competing against men" (Gender Politics training notes, December 8, 2000). These assertions indicate a lack of a multidimensional consciousness because they demonstrate a limited understanding of how oppressive ideas and actions toward Lesbian, Gay, Bisexual, Transgender, and Queer (LGBTQ) communities and women are connected to other oppressive relations of power that have historically targeted People of Color. A limited consciousness impedes self-reflection on the private nature of some forms of oppression that can be equally injurious. This deficit perspective would never be said or tolerated within the PALA community space. So there is an assumption by this person that if not said in this public space, it is not harmful or even homophobic.

In this study, several people successfully articulated a Critical understanding of race and class relationships, but still needed growth in understanding sexuality and gender in any Critical way. Though exceptions existed, there was a trend of people being more Critical in areas of identity and power in which they were not privileged. For example, women tended to be more Critical of gender politics, People of Color more Critical about race, and members of the LGBTQ community more Critical of sexuality. This is not surprising, as standpoint theory suggests that a marginalized perspective can lead to a more Critical analysis that is not hindered by the privilege to ignore inequities (see Delgado Bernal 1998b; and Collins 1986, 1991).

Communities Creating a Network of Resistance

Agencies of Transformational Resistance build community among diverse young people, enabling them to engage in transformational resistance as part of a supportive community of progressive youth. Through the creation of this community, one is able to create a space where the development of a Critical and multidimensional consciousness can occur. The nature of the community itself and the specific individuals who become part of a community determine the context-specific skills that are developed, the dimensions of consciousness that are tackled, and the extent to which social justice is broadly defined. On the other hand, the benefits of the community-building process itself can eventually be equally detrimental to the process of young people challenging each other's deficit thinking. This occurs when the maintenance of a cohesive community becomes more important than challenging dysconsciousness. I will provide an example of when this happened and the community members' perspectives about why it happened later in the article.

The process of community building needs to begin prior to achieving any of the previously mentioned goals for an ATR. Establishing a strong community is necessary and requires an ongoing deliberate process that is not easy to maintain. For this study, community is understood as a relationship between a group of people who are held together by similar social justice interests, progressive political commitments, social goals, or experiences. It is bound by neither time nor space. Community is not to be confused with neighborhood, which is bound by geographical, economical, or political boundaries, within which there could exist multiple competing communities or none at all. At PALA, community is not based on ethnicity, gender, class, or sexuality, although these are recognized as having been important for building and maintaining community and power. The building of community refers to the process through which a group consciously and intentionally works toward the creation of such a community.

The formation of such a cohesive internal community does not, however, isolate members from the larger communities existing externally in other spaces. In fact, it expands their access to other people, communities, and resources that can support their continued growth. This newly formed community becomes connected through various means with other existing or developing communities in other spaces, forming a wider "network of resistance." Not only do ATRs themselves create formal relationships with other communities, but young people are actively evolving this network through their participation with communities in other spaces. ATRs rely on this network to provide young people with resources to fulfill needs that they cannot meet and opportunities for growth in areas on which they do not concentrate. Young people also look to the network for models of transformational work, to participate in struggles that are connected to their existing social justice efforts but not the foci of the community in their existing space, and to expand their own knowledge and skills.

Community Building

Most Allies have not had the opportunity to be in a space of political allies. They often found themselves as a single isolated voice of progressive thought in the vast, chaotic chatter of conservative and mainstream perspectives—the one radical. In the following excerpt Wendy, an Ally, expresses the importance of this community space for her liberation in expression:

I got the support that you get being in an environment like Public Allies, where you find other people that are just as passionate as you are and are serious about it and willing to make a change. Yes, it's the support. It's the first time I heard people say, "it is ok if you're super passionate." And I started thinking, why shouldn't I be passionate. I have the right to be enraged (about injustice) if I want. I have the right to be upset, and to show that. It is ok for me to engage in dialogue and show that I am passionate about it; and not contain that and have to be professional and have to be calm, the way society says that you are supposed to act. And it's ok for me to question what my friends say. I don't have to contain myself for anybody. (personal communication, March 8, 2001)

The creation of this community of trust and support is a critical prerequisite to the practice of a mutually respectful and beneficial dialogue that leads to a Critical multidimensional consciousness. The five characteristics of ATRS become common goals that the community strives for together and individually, as they are supportive of the development of each other's consciousness, skill set, commitment to struggle, and network of resources through their community-building efforts. This community-building component appears to be the element essential for the other four to happen effectively—raising consciousness, broadening social justice, building a network, and refining skills. A cohesive community is one in which people can feel that they are on a common path toward the same goals and can expect support from each other. This community should be inclusive of diverse people, multiple perspectives, and even sometimes competing interests. The creation of such a community is a process that may be facilitated by the leadership of a community-based organization, but ultimately is shaped by the members themselves. The expressions of diverse experiences have a direct relationship to the development of a multidimensional consciousness, as young people are provided with the opportunity to learn from others' ideas. Many times young people may not have had access to these perspectives and ideas, limiting their opportunities for growth.

Community and Consciousness Raising: Struggles and Links

Although PALA recognizes the significance of building community and makes extraordinary efforts to create a sustainable community commitment and identity, there exist limitations to what could be achieved within a ten-month cycle and within the confines of the program design and funding. My conversation with Jesus, one of the Allies, was very telling of this limitation. He was very doubtful of how long he and others would maintain the relationships that they developed. Although he recognized the achievements of the organization in bringing such a diverse group of people together to work collaboratively, effectively communicate, and support each other, he believed that people would move on to other commitments after the program (personal communication, March 26, 2001). In the following excerpt Edith, another Ally, describes the types of relationships that were developed within this community:

> It was not the type of bond that you have with really close friends. We are not like the type of close friends that in a time of need you would readily make yourself available like you would to your very closest friends. But we do have a different kind of bond. I feel that I can talk about certain things more openly with them than I would to a group of people that I just met, like in a school setting. The bond was similar to what you would have with your school friends. I guess it's bigger than that because we share a lot of similar viewpoints. (personal communication, March 12, 2001)

It is obvious that the relationships that are built within this community go beyond those of your average peer in a school or professional relationship. This was one of the intentions of the PALA community-building process. The intense and sustained teamwork efforts did not, however, necessarily lead to long-term friendships, presumably because of the limited time they were together.

Hidden behind this commitment to maintain a harmonious and supportive community there appeared tensions with some of the other goals of an ATR, which ironically initially depended on the creation of a cohesive community. PALA clearly recognizes the importance of building a strong and cohesive community early. For the most part, it is successful in achieving this goal. This sets the groundwork for opening up the youth to learning from people they can trust, to some degree, and respecting everybody's perspectives. It also makes it possible for young people to provide each other feedback and hold each other accountable, to a limited extent. In the end, though, it became much more important for Allies to maintain a cohesive community than to hold each other accountable around issues of consciousness. Although admittedly this is an important decision made by the community to ensure that all perspectives are valued and that people are not silenced, some members of the community silence themselves rather than call somebody on their dysconscious perspectives in order to maintain harmony. This silencing, or lack of accountability to a common commitment to grow, limits the opportunities to emerge into higher levels of consciousness.

There were many examples when Allies found themselves disagreeing intensely with each other about various topics. Some of these differences centered on political disagreements, while others were the result of dissimilarities in perspectives grounded in life experiences. Edith described one such example when an Ally from a complex privileged background (light skinned, heterosexual, Argentinean, thirty years of age) spoke disparagingly about working-class families of color. She went as far as to suggest that the situation of low-income families was ultimately their fault for accepting it. Edith and some of the Allies asked their disapproving colleague to consider various factors related to the conditions impacting low-income communities of color. Edith pointed out that the situation of low-income communities of color is multilayered and impacted by cultural differences, deplorable housing conditions, low-income class status, issues of violence, the impact of gangs, and poor educational opportunities, as well as other issues. The more conservative thirty-year-old Ally, who happened to be the oldest Ally, held these families responsible for their own lack of social mobility, citing their unwillingness to access many government and community resources. Edith's perspective is clearly grounded in her own experiential knowledge, and that of others, about the issues faced by low-income families of color in Los Angeles. This incident ended in a willingness to agree to disagree, but also revealed a pattern that would continue to silence more progressive perspectives. There appeared to be a tolerance for a consciousness that was still developing, and sometimes blatantly dysconscious. Even though it makes sense that this tolerance for an evolving consciousness is necessary for an organization that is interested in youth development and the development of a Critical consciousness, it appeared to happen more often by the Allies not because of a need to give people space to grow but rather to ensure community cohesiveness.

The following incidents further highlight the tendency of Allies to support community at the expense of challenging a colleague. In the first incident one of the Allies, who happened to be one of the few white Allies in the group, was sharing a story with the entire PALA community about a nickname that her family had for cousins who migrated to and from Canada. The Ally's extended family had a running joke where they called this family the "snowbacks" because they were immigrants. Although the comment did not have malevolent intentions, it was inherently racist because it was derived from the word "wetback," which is used widely in the American Southwest as a racial slur toward Mexicans. When we discussed it later, I found that some of the people whom I spoke to were offended by the comment but hesitated to address it because of the importance of maintaining the community.

In another incident during an intense training on gender politics and homophobia, the same Ally who took a deficit perspective in the previous example about the condition of People of Color made a comment that was dysconscious and offensive to the trainer. The African American facilitator of the discussion stopped in the middle of the activity and respectfully challenged the Ally about her comment, pointing to the inherently homophobic perspective she was taking. Immediately, other Allies came to their peer's defense and were upset with the trainer because she had challenged the Ally. The trainer explained that questioning the Ally was intended to challenge her on her ideas and asked the group not to be afraid of conflict, suggesting that conflict is an integral part of the way we create change and how we grow. Interestingly, even in the defense of the Ally's dysconscious remarks, the other Allies acknowledged that the Ally had a tendency to make comments that were at times conservative and offensive. Nevertheless, they would not allow the community to be disrupted. When I later asked one of the Allies about the situation, he responded: "Public Allies tries to develop consciousness while maintaining the community. We try to do that among ourselves but we don't like others challenging the people in our group. We try to protect them if someone else challenges their ideas. Sometimes you can challenge a stranger's opinion but you can't if it's a friend. Public Allies is kind of mixed" (Jesus, personal communication, 2001).

The building of this cohesive community is a very long and arduous process that both the Allies and the staff work hard to maintain. Although the trainer was not a stranger in any sense to the staff, most Allies had little clue who this person was outside of the training setting. Even though they recognized that the Ally had at various points made offensive dysconscious comments, they were her own ideas and they were going to protect her right to have them and express them. The staff also rarely openly challenged young people, although in private they shared with me their desire to do so. They were concerned that the community needed to be driven by the young people and that the staff should not impose their own political views on the youth. It was also believed that the Allies needed to find their own consciousness and commitments, an acquired consciousness, not an imposed one. Anytime they felt compelled to challenge a young person, the staff chose to do it during the one-on-one coaching sessions they had with each Ally. The staff was mindful of the power relations that exist between staff and Allies and careful not to unjustly impose the power they wield over Allies. Yet Allies also confirmed in various interviews that they are "checked" within their individual meetings and challenged to critically reflect on their growth areas. ("Check" was a term that the Allies often used to describe the act of challenging other people about their inconsistencies in behavior with their politically progressive attitude, including expressing ideas that reflected dysconsciousness.)

The tension that exists between maintaining a supportive community where Allies can be themselves, with room to grow, versus a desire to want to "check" one another about areas of growth that still need to be further developed is an important one that not only Allies but also staff recognize that Allies need to struggle through. Staff understood the limitations of the relationships that are developed and chose to support the Ally in closed sessions. This is evidenced in the following quote from one of the staff members: "The reality is that they are not all the same and they are not all tight. This is something that I talk to my Allies about one-on-one because when they have an issue or when they have that debate of whether or not they should bring it up, even to another Ally or to their supervisor or to whoever they are having an issue with, its really challenging them in a personal way. Our role is to establish that strong sense of community and then to put them in dialogues and discussions that challenge their concepts about certain topics, and have them dialogue" (Monique, personal communication, March 22, 2001). Accordingly, even this apparent compromise that allows dysconscious ideas in a progressive space so as to secure a cohesive community is in itself an important learning tool. Young people are being prepared to be in a real world within diverse settings in spaces where people of opposing perspectives often come together to collaborate. It is an important element to what Public Allies refers to as "collaborative leadership."

Another key finding is that there appears to be a linkage between the level of familiarity or the strength of a relationship and the willingness to confront or challenge people about their dysconsciousness. I found evidence that there exists a meaningful connection between "level of familiarity and strength of relationship" with "willingness to challenge." The stronger the relationship one has with an individual, the more likely one is to commit energy and resources to support that person's development as it relates to consciousness and the more willing one is to take risks in challenging that person. Conversely, the less familiar one is to another person or the weaker the relationship is with that person, the more willing one is to challenge that person about their dysconsciousness, but not necessarily to commit resources. These trends may on the surface appear contradictory, but further examination suggests that they are not. It appears that the types of relationship that are developed at PALA lie somewhere on the upward swing of a parabola, such that Allies are willing to challenge each other but maybe not to the fullest, as they might with close friends or strangers. When asked about this, Edith responded: "Well at least for myself, when I have talked to my friends about these disrespectful comments or negative perspectives, I have tried convincing them. Whenever any of my friends, for example, my best friend, and I get into these conversations, we will sit there for hours and hours trying to convince each other of what's right. And usually she will say, 'I don't want to listen to you.' And I will respond, 'I have to convince you'" (personal communication, May 21, 2001). The fact that she is interested in the continued growth of the relationship and the development of her friend's consciousness makes her willing to spend hours convincing her friend about these issues, though she may not be willing to do the same thing with most of her fellow Allies. This is likely to happen because she understands that the relationship that exists with her friend is a long-standing relationship that will not be easily jeopardized because of the disagreement. On the other hand, the burgeoning relationship with fellow Allies is still fragile and susceptible to intense disagreements. Wendy, another Ally, also discussed several four-hour conversations that she had with her friends after she confronted them for using words associating women with weakness. In the same interview, she shared the opposite response to a similar situation with Allies. This is another common trend of letting things go within the PALA community or a need to be less confrontational than one would be in other settings (personal communication, March 8, 2001). After I further questioned Edith about her disagreement with the other Ally and why she would not commit the same type of energy that she had with her friends, she responded:

> Because of the kind of relationship we have at Public Allies, I felt that it was okay for her to think the way she wanted to think. I guess with my close friends I want them to think similar to the way I think. I can sometimes be stubborn with them and spend a lot of time trying to get them to think the way I think. I guess at Public Allies we've learned to respect different perspectives. We are taught that if you think a certain way that is different from me, that's okay. We also learned that it is ok for me to grow more to think like you do, or maybe you can think the way I do. I also consider where she's coming from. (personal communication, March 21, 2001)

It is evident from this statement that whereas Edith is more committed to spending the time with her friends, in the professional environment that is created by PALA, which is less personal than a friendship, she has learned to respect the experiences of others. She is also more open to the notion that these experiences create very different perspectives. The development of respect for others' perspectives then crosses over to her personal life. Edith begins to see that her openness toward others' perspectives can lead to others being open to her own ideas. Nevertheless, when asked how she would respond to a friend who would take a similar deficit framework that blames low-income people for their impoverished condition, Edith responded:

> I guess I would respond to that person really differently. I would be more upset. I think this would happen because I would begin thinking to myself, "first of all, why do you say this, if you don't even know the group of people you are talking about. You don't even know the community. You just can't come out and begin just talking like that." I would have probably felt more offended. For some reason, if I don't know you well, I don't really know where you're coming from. It might be a little more intimidating for me to challenge you because I don't

know where you're coming from. I might question, "What side are you on or what gives you the right to talk about this?" I felt like that before with one of the Allies. I have been meaning to talk to her about it, but I never have the chance to. (personal communication, 2001)

She again supports the idea that in order to be more confrontational or spend more energy confronting a person's ideas, she would need to have a very strong relationship with them. There appears to be less space for difference in opinion with those with whom she is most familiar. Even though she explains earlier the importance of respecting her fellow Allies' diverse perspectives, there seem to be doubts about a person's commitment when their comments are driven by deficit thought. Thus, there still seems to be intimidation or less interest in challenging her colleagues. It does appear to be impacted by the community space that is created and supporting this space.

Another related finding was that there was a distinction between private and public spaces when it came to challenging people's ideas. Allies confirmed that private spaces have more room for dysconsciousness than public spaces. There were times when I interviewed Allies together to capture the dynamics among people who bounced ideas off each other well within the larger group. During one interview, an Ally used the word "faggot" as an insult, and the other Ally did not challenge it. In a similar situation an Ally was characterizing Asian people as generally untrusting, and looked to another Ally for agreement. Although that person did not agree, she did not challenge the individual, either. One person even acknowledged that there are things that her family will say in private that would never be said in public spaces. When one Ally was questioned about this apparent inconsistency, he agreed that more latitude is given in private settings. He believed that we should not be checked in all spaces because that may lead people to feel censored. One of the staff members thought that this demonstrated an evolving consciousness that was not acceptable, whereas another one saw it as an expected pattern of growth. He acknowledged that growth in the area of consciousness was a long process and that the limited time that the Allies spent within the program was not enough to undo the learning that had taken place throughout the course of their entire lives.

It appears that consciousness development relies on a supportive space where youth can be *subjects* that work through their learning process. Even as there were many disagreements and even instances of dysconscious and offensive language, the Ally community recognized the need to allow for this reality. A Critical consciousness could not be forced on people, nor could one expect young people to learn everything. Allies truly needed to develop their consciousness at their own pace and work through a process of self-discovery. Nevertheless, the relationships that people have with one another impact their readiness to dedicate time and energy to confronting one another and supporting each other through this growth process. Consciousness also appears to develop first in the public spaces of a community setting where people can be held accountable (or there is a risk of accountability) and then evolves into a consciousness about and within private spaces.

CONCLUSION

In spite of the fact that young People of Color make up the majority of the student population in California and are increasing at rates that ensure they will continue to be a growing majority, they are increasingly being denied access to real opportunities for high educational attainment and resources to secure a high quality of life. Students of color are more segregated today than during the civil rights movement (Donato, Menchaca, and Valencia 1991). Push-out rates are astronomically high, and young People of Color are being diverted from schools to institutions of incarceration. Suppression rather than rehabilitation and education seems to be the direction of youth development efforts. Today, young African American and Latino men are more likely to be incarcerated than to be attending an institution of higher learning. The number of Asian youth in correctional facilities is also on the rise throughout the state. Housing in communities of color is becoming more dilapidated and less affordable. Health benefits and opportunities to maintain healthy lifestyles are increasingly scarce and difficult to attain for low-income families of color. Employment opportunities are becoming more service oriented and more labor intensive, while high-paying jobs require more advanced education and the unemployment rate is near an all-time high.

Despite these unjust conditions, People of Color continue to demonstrate resilience and engage in struggles of resistance. Transformational acts of resistance occur in various spaces that are impacted by an intersection of class-, race-, gender-, and sexuality-based forms of oppression. One place that oppositional acts of resistance are expressed is within community-based organizations. These spaces have historically served to nurture youth-driven acts of transformational resistance across various contexts. This study documents the ways these organizations support the development of a Critical and multidimensional consciousness and help young people expand their notion of social justice. Within these ATRs, young people build a community where they are able to support each other in their development.

A working model of Agencies of Transformational Resistance was presented to help move toward the development of more robust theories and models for supporting transformational acts of resistance in different spaces. These contributions to theories of resistance move us beyond the mostly passive and distant process of research to a more proactive course of action that involves expanding the capacity of these organizations by engaging in praxis. The development of a research-tested model for ATRs was thoroughly guided and supported by past research about instances of transformational resistance. These past studies guided the development of this model and drew from the notion that resistant behavior that had transformational potential needed to be guided by a conscious critique of injustice and a desire to create change that was socially just (Delgado Bernal 1997; Giroux 1983; Solórzano and Delgado Bernal 2001). However, it also adds significant contributions to the theory of transformational resistance. It has moved the theory beyond an evaluative and predictive tool to one with practical implications. Similar to other research that identifies the research process as a Critically conscious act of resistance, in this study I intentionally set out to develop a working model to better understand, but also to guide, the work of community-based organizations that were actively engaged in social justice projects. This research process then became an act of transformational resistance itself, as it was conducted through a Critical lens that was driven by a commitment to engage in work that would potentially have socially just implications.

ATRs move the theory of resistance to a tool of socially motivated and politically conscious praxis because I found ways that one could effectively use it to develop a model for progressive community-based organizations. The creation of this model was not developed during this study, but rather this study was used to capture and further develop a working model of what community-based organizations were already engaged in. This still is moving beyond the interpretive because it challenges community-based workers and scholars to grapple with this model and, in some cases, adopt the model as a practical tool for becoming actively involved in youth and community development that is asset based and has transformational intentions. The dimension of capacity building has been added to the theory of transformational resistance, which moves beyond the abstract elements of consciousness building and internalization of a vocation for social justice. This capacity-building element makes us consider the need to help youth develop the skills necessary to participate meaningfully and productively in consequential social justice projects.

This model also moves the theory of transformational resistance to a new level of understanding by evaluating the significance that community-building efforts by young People of Color can have for youth development. This study demonstrates that the most important element of the model of ATRS was the effort to build a supportive and inclusive community. The diversity of this community has direct implications for the multidimensionality of a Critical consciousness. The more diverse the community is, the more Critical perspectives about different dimensions of power young people have access to and opportunities from which to learn. This means young people could become more Critical about more dimensions of injustice. The diversity of this community also impacts the development of a more broadly defined commitment and definition for social justice. As young people were exposed to the real and diverse faces of injustice through intimate interactions in this tight community, they were able to identify and commit to a more broadly defined definition of social justice.

The community-building process is also important for the creation of a space conducive to learning. Young people are able to support each other and feel supported in a space where they understand they have a common objective to learn about how to better find their niche in social justice efforts. This commitment to a supportive community of learners also allows young people to gain support in learning skills that they lack but other young people could teach them. Although the community-building element was the most important component, it was equally important to find that it also had drawbacks. The need to constantly maintain a supportive and harmonious community where people could be open and not feel judged created the unintentional effect of allowing for dysconscious perspectives.

The benefits of using Latino/a Critical Race Theory for this research project were various. An important tenet of LatCrit is that relations of power are multifaceted, which is the foundation for the concept of intersectionality. This framework holds that injustice cannot be analyzed through one analytical lens, like class or race, but instead it must be analyzed with the premise that the intersectionality of these various relations of power (that is, race, class, gender, and sexuality) creates injustice and privilege. In this study, I found that people can exist in positions of privilege and subordination simultaneously. Therefore, in order to understand the way People of Color experience power, one must utilize an intersectional analysis of the spaces they occupy. Furthermore, in order for young People of Color to develop a Critical multidimensional consciousness, they need to embrace the notion of intersectionality to understand their roles in these multiple and intersecting relations of power. Finally, a broader and more complex definition of social justice that is inclusive of many interconnected struggles of resistance is strengthened by an intersectional framework. Hence, this study expanded the LatCrit notion of intersectionality beyond analysis of jurisprudence or formal educational institutions by utilizing intersectionality to understand the social-political spaces within which young People of Color create community, how they develop consciousness, and how they express their notions of social justice.

Nonprofit organizations, by virtue of the fact that they are corporations, tend to reflect corporate models of decision making. This model centers decision making and responsibility at the top of the organization. Studies of other models of community building may yield a different working model for Agencies of Transformational Resistance that is more conducive to serving as a catalyst for revolutionary changes. Although young people were given major roles in determining various activities and seen from an asset-based perspective, decision making was still concentrated among staff members. Because I did not see examples of youth decision making, I could not offer it as an element of the model. I would expect, however, having seen other examples of organizations that emphasize youth decision making, that this could make up the sixth element of ATRs. Having witnessed the process of self-government through community involvement implemented by the Ejercito Zapatista de Liberacion Nacional, I suspect this sixth element would include a decision-making process that was community centered. This idea requires further study.

This study has been an effort to examine how young People of Color demonstrate acts of transformational resistance within community-based organizations, despite the existence of multiple intersecting oppressive conditions. This resilience happens daily and has happened historically. In developing a working model of Agencies of Transformational Resistance, I am extending a challenge to scholars and activists to engage in dialogue, reflection, and action that will advance us to building a better-constructed model that can move us to achieve revolutionary transformations. It is my hope that this symbolic and actual discourse of resistance that is happening in many interconnected communities can move us to the evolution of a revolutionary vision that combines the need to struggle for social justice within personal and intimate relationships with the struggle to dismantle distant and oppressive relations of power.

REFERENCES

Acuna, R. 1988. *Occupied America: A History of Chicanos.* New York: Harper and Row.

Bell, D. 1987. *And We Are Not Saved: The Elusive Quest for Racial Justice.* New York: Basic Books.

Bell, J. 1995. "Understanding Adultism: A Key to Developing Positive Youth-Adult Relationships." http://freechild.org/bell.htm.

Boal, A. 1979. *Theatre of the Oppressed.* London: Pluto Press.

Collins, P. H. 1986. "Learning From the Outsider-Within: The Sociological Significance of Black Feminist Thought." In *Beyond Methodology: Feminist Scholarship as Lived Research,* edited by M. M. Fonow and J. Cook. Bloomington: Indiana University Press.

———. 1991. *Black Feminist Thought: Knowledge, Consciousness, and the Politics of Empowerment.* New York: Routledge, Chapman, and Hall.

Covarrubias, A. 1999. "LatCrit Theory and Agencies of Transformational Resistance Within the Intersection." Paper presented at the Reclaiming Voice Conference, University of California, Irvine.

———. 2005. "Agencies of Transformational Resistance: Transforming the Intersection of Race, Class, Gender, and Sexuality Oppression Through Latino Critical Race Theory (LatCrit) and Praxis." Ph.D. diss., University of California, Los Angeles.

Covarrubias, A., and A. Tijerina Revilla. 2003. "Agencies of Transformational Resistance: Dismantling Discrimination at the Intersection of Race, Class, Gender, and Sexuality Through LatCrit Praxis." *University of Florida Law Review* 55: 460–77.

Crenshaw, K., N. Gotanda, G. Peller, and K. Thomas. 1995. *Critical Race Theory: The Key Writings That Formed the Movement.* New York: New Press.

Cunningham, G., and A. Mathie. 2002. "Asset-Based Community Development: An Overview." http://www.synergos.org/knowledge/02abcdoverview.htm.

Delgado, R., ed. 1995. *Critical Race Theory: The Cutting Edge.* Philadelphia: Temple University Press.

———. 1999. *When Equality Ends: Stories About Race and Resistance.* Boulder: Westview Press.

Delgado Bernal, D. 1997. "Chicana School Resistance and Grassroots Leadership: Providing an Alternative History of the 1968 East Los Angeles Blowouts." Ph.D. diss., University of California, Los Angeles.

———. 1998a. "Grassroots Leadership Reconceptualized: Chicana Oral Histories and the 1968 East Los Angeles School Blowouts." *Frontiers: A Journal of Women Studies* 19, no. 2: 113–42.

———. 1998b. "Using a Chicana Feminist Epistemology in Educational Research." *Harvard Educational Review* 68, no. 4: 555–82.

———. 2001. "Learning and Living Pedagogies of the Home: The Mestiza Consciousness of Chicana Students." *International Journal of Qualitative Studies in Education* 14, no. 5: 623–39.

Donato, R., M. Menchaca, and R. Valencia. 1991. "Segregation, Desegregation, and Integration of Chicano Students: Problems and Prospects." In *Chicano School Failure and Success: Research and Policy Agendas for the 1990s,* edited by R. Valencia. London: Falmer Press.

Freire, P. 1973. *Education for Critical Consciousness.* New York: Continuum.

———. 1997. *Pedagogy of the Oppressed.* Rev. ed. New York: Continuum.

Fullbright-Anderson, K., K. Laurence, G. Susi, S. Sutton, and A. Kubisch. 2003. "Structural Racism and Youth Development: Issues, Challenges, and Implications." On file with the author. Aspen Institute Roundtable.

Giroux, H. 1983. "Theories of Reproduction and Resistance in the New Sociology of Education: A Critical Analysis." *Harvard Educational Review* 53, no. 3: 257–93.

King, J. 1991. "Dysconscious Racism: Ideology, Identity, and Miseducation of Teachers." *Journal of Negro Education* 60, no. 2: 133–46.

King, J., and G. Ladson-Billings. 1990. "Dysconscious Racism and Multicultural Illiteracy: The Distorting of the American Mind." Paper presented at the annual meeting of American Educational Research Association, April 16–20, Boston.

Ladson-Billings, G. 1998. "Just What Is Critical Race Theory and What Is It Doing in a *Nice* Field Like Education?" *Qualitative Studies in Education* 11, no. 1: 7–24.

Lynn, M. 1999. "Toward a Critical Race Pedagogy: A Research Note." *Urban Education* 33, no. 5: 606–26.

Padilla, L. 1997. "LatCrit Praxis to Heal Fractured Communities." *Harvard Latino Law Review/LatCrit Symposium* 2 (Fall): 341–60.

Parker, L. 1998. "'Race Is . . . Race Ain't': An Exploration of the Utility of Critical Race Theory in Qualitative Research in Education." *Qualitative Studies in Education* 11, no. 1: 43–55.

Public Allies. 2000. *Gender Politics.* Los Angeles: Public Allies, Los Angeles.

———. 2004. http://www.publicallies.org.

Solórzano, D. G. 1998. "Critical Race Theory, Race and Gender Microaggressions, and the Experience of Chicana and Chicano Scholars." *Qualitative Studies in Education* 11, no. 1: 121–36.

Solórzano, D. G., and D. Delgado Bernal. 2001. "Examining Transformational Resistance Through a Critical Race and LatCrit Theory Framework: Chicana and Chicano Students in an Urban Context." *Urban Education* 36, no. 3: 308–42.

Solórzano, D. G., and A. Ornelas. 2002. "A Critical Race Analysis of Advance Placement Classes: A Case of Educational Inequality." *Journal of Latinos in Education* 1: 215–29.

———. 2004. "A Critical Race Analysis of Latina/o and African American Advanced Placement Enrollment in Public High Schools." *High School Journal* 87, no. 3 (February–March).

Solórzano, D. G., and O. Villalpando. 1998. "Critical Race Theory, Marginality, and the Experience of Students of Color in Higher Education." In *Sociology of Education: Emerging Perspectives,* edited by C. Torres and T. R. Mitchell. Albany: State University of New York Press.

Solórzano, D. G., O. Villalpando, and L. Oseguera. 2005. "Educational Inequities and Latina/o Undergraduate Students in the United States: A Critical Race Analysis of Their Educational Progress." *Journal of Hispanic Higher Education* 4: 272–94.

Solórzano, D. G., and T. Yosso. 2001. "Critical Race and LatCrit Theory and Method: Counterstorytelling Chicana and Chicano Graduate School Experiences." *International Journal of Qualitative Studies in Education* 14: 471–95.

Stanton-Salazar, R. 2001 *Manufacturing Hope and Despair: The School and Kin Support Networks of U.S.-Mexican Youth.* New York: Teachers College Press.

Yosso, Tara J. 2006. *Critical Race Counterstories Along the Chicana/Chicano Educational Pipeline.* New York: Routledge.

CHAPTER 4

Activating Parents' Voices

EDWARD M. OLIVOS

CARMEN E. QUINTANA

The United States has a long history of ignoring the educational and social needs of bicultural communities—Latino/Chicano, African American, Native American, and others—while at the same time eradicating their strengths, such as culture, language, history, traditions, and so forth (Spring 2005).[1] Bicultural communities, however, have not always stood idly by, allowing the dominant group in society the free rein to dictate the terms of their existence. On the contrary, bicultural communities have a long record of resisting the oppressive practices of the dominant institutions of the United States and its agents. For the Latino/Chicano community, in particular, this resistance has manifested itself in many ways and through many generations; most notably, Latino/Chicano resistance has been exhibited through social movements, such as civil action, and civil disobedience, such as boycotts, walkouts, protests, hunger strikes, and so on.[2] And although generally successful in the past, the current challenge for Latino/Chicano activists rests in defining how effective these forms of resistance will continue to be and the extent to which they can serve to establish a broader support base of resistance against acts of racism and exploitation, particularly within the public school context.

The context of this book is the 1968 Chicana/o student walkouts, or "Blowouts," of East Los Angeles—one of the largest events of the early Chicana/o movement. Led by legendary Chicano teacher Sal Castro and Chicana/o student leaders, thousands of students walked out of East Los Angeles high schools to protest poor learning conditions and the lack of learning opportunities afforded to low-income Chicana/o students. Upon concessions from the Los Angeles School Board, and other political and moral victories, the 1968 walkouts demonstrated to many in "mainstream" America the political potential of an organized social movement for disenfranchised youth and communities. Moreover, the walkouts demonstrated to the nation the level of political sophistication and consciousness that existed among Chicana/o youth and communities. These victories also helped solidify the walkout as a political tool for Chicana/o activists and supporters, something that continues to this day. It is within this context of a historically successful social movement among Latinos/Chicanos that we write this chapter.

This chapter will speak to the issue of the need to improve the educational experiences of Latino/Chicano students by redefining the role of their parents and communities in the school system. As longtime education and community/parent partners, we argue that a critical element in creating schools, and ultimately societies, that respond to the particular needs and strengths of bicultural children is what parents and communities are doing as educational activists and advocates (Olivos 2003, 2004, 2006; Olivos and Quintana de Valladolid 2005; Quintana 2005). Specifically, we propose that in order to achieve Latino/Chicano solidarity for the common cause of transforming the schools to meet their own and their children's needs, all bicultural parents (and the teachers who serve them) must develop a critical consciousness that will enable them to become political catalysts that will allow them and others to "unmask" the contradictions inherent in the U.S. public education system (and in society) so that these contradictions can be identified and challenged. Therefore, we propose that efforts must be undertaken to "politicize" the involvement of Latino/Chicano parents and communities in the schools and to consider the potential and appropriateness of a new parent, student, and community social movement as a political tool for transforming the school system and society. We will use the actual voices of Latino/Chicano parents in this chapter to illustrate the problems that underlie our schools and how these problems hinder the success of Chicana/o children, as well as to highlight the consciousness and potential that exist within this community.

Although the Latino/Chicano student population in the United States comes from many diverse cultural backgrounds, Latino/Chicano students who perform poorly in school do share certain key characteristics. First, underperforming students generally have poor English abilities. According to the Pew Hispanic Center, a "lack of English-language ability is a prime characteristic of Latina/o dropouts. Almost 40 percent of Latino dropouts do not speak English well." Of the "14 percent of Hispanic 16- to 19-year-olds who have poor English language skills," their dropout rate is 59 percent (Fry 2003, iv).

A second indicator of Latinos/Chicanos who perform poorly in school is immigration status. The dropout rate for Latinas/os "born outside the United States (44 percent) is higher than the rate for first-generation Hispanic youth (15 percent)" (National Center for Education Statistics 2003, 40). This piece of data is significant given that "thirty-five percent of Latino youth are immigrants, compared to less than five percent of non-Latino youth" (Fry 2003, iii). Consequently, given these numbers, any effort to improve the academic and social achievement of Latinos/Chicanos must be tied directly to countering the anti-immigrant movement that is sweeping the United States in the early part of the twenty-first century.

Finally, a third characteristic of Latino/Chicano student underachievement, which is often ignored by policy makers, is the issue of class. Many children who perform poorly in school generally come from families who are living in poverty. A Latino/Chicano child who is "living in a family on welfare or receiving food stamps" has a greater risk of failing socially and academically than one who is living in a middle- or upper-class family (National Center for Education Statistics 2003, 68). So, while current educational reform at all three levels of the government continues to focus on issues of language and immigrant status as causal evidence of Latino/Chicano student underachievement, none makes any authentic attempt to engage the issues of class, poverty, and economic exploitation. Hence, this is the work of the social movement we envision—a movement that understands the complexity of the challenges facing Latino/Chicano students, problems that are rooted not in inherent human nature, or in cultural and linguistic deficiencies, but in the macrolevel policies of exploitation and racism (Bowles and Gintis 1976; Darder 1991; Persell 1977; Valencia 1997).

Research on the social conditions of Latinos/Chicanos in U.S. society reveals that the problems this population faces in the public school system are microrepresentations of the problems they face in broader society (Darder, Torres, and Gutiérrez 1997). That is, the school system mirrors and perpetuates the subordinate status of Latinos/Chicanos and other bicultural groups through seamless coercive and asymmetrical power relations that exist in the general U.S. sociopolitical and economic environment (Cummins 2001). Thus, the antagonistic relationships between dominant and subordinate cultures in U.S. society, which are grounded in embedded racism and the economic exploitation of racialized communities, permeate the educational context under which Latino/Chicano students are expected to achieve (Núñez 1994).

As we pass the fortieth anniversary of the 1968 East Los Angeles student walkouts and reflect back on their victories and setbacks, we cannot help but come to the realization that Latinos/Chicanos in the U.S. public school system still find themselves in the same educational quagmire as in the 1960s. Indeed, the fact remains that although the number of Latinos/Chicanos in the public school system has significantly increased during the past forty years, and pressure from politicians and the public continues to mount to improve bicultural student achievement, the educational and social attainment of Latinos/Chicanos continues to falter.

In the Los Angeles Unified School District, for example, where the 1968 student walkouts took place, Latino/Chicano students constituted more than 73 percent of the student population during the 2005–6 school year—a significant majority. Yet their educational attainment continued at levels comparable to the 1960s and before, with dropout rates hovering at 25 percent and graduation rates at 50 percent.[3] Although these numbers are not meant to specifically implicate the Los Angeles Unified School District for failing to meet the educational needs of Latino/Chicano students, or to advocate for the elimination of public education, they do nonetheless illustrate the status of Latino/Chicano students in one of the largest school districts in the country. Furthermore, they provide a large-scale picture of a trend that is virtually identical in all major school districts in the Southwest and the nation.

Within the U.S. public education system there are ever-present struggles for power, and ultimately humanity, between bicultural communities and the schools that serve them. Deeply rooted within these struggles are conflicting interests and contradictory assumptions on the part of the school system, and society in general, which preclude the success of low-income bicultural students as well as limit the authentic participation of their parents and community. In order to understand these struggles, a structural, institutional, and interpersonal analysis of the tensions, contradictions, and resistance that exist within the public school system must be used (Núñez 1994; Olivos 2006). The analysis we propose takes into account socioeconomic and historical factors as a means of studying the relationship between Latino/Chicano communities and the institution of public education. In general, our analysis suggests a broad road map for viewing the socioeconomic, political, and historical influences that affect the relationship between Latino/Chicano communities and school personnel. Simply put, we argue that the relationship between Latino/Chicano communities and the public school system is exclusively limited neither to the school campus nor to the individuals who make up the school community. To the contrary, the relationship between all bicultural communities and the school system is a microreflection of the societal contradictions and tensions in the areas of economic exploitation and institutional racism (Olivos 2006).

Because no act of domination is ever complete or unchallenged, we also acknowledge that resistance, or conflict, figures significantly in how low-income Latino/Chicano communities relate to oppressive school policies and practices and that this resistance can take separate courses. This resistance has the potential to be empowering and transformational in that it can promote authentic change within the system, making it more responsive and democratic to the needs and strengths of the community, or it can be oppressive and self-defeating in that it simply helps re-create the existing social structure, conditions, or both, which fed the resistance in the first place (Solórzano and Delgado Bernal 2001). Therefore, we propose that one of the goals of authentic Latino/Chicano community involvement in the schools is to help these parents, and the educators who serve them and their children, reflect upon and understand their roles within their schools and society, with the goal of consciously choosing the paths of resistance that will be most beneficial to them, their children, their communities, and their social order.

Our society and, as a consequence, our social institutions are rife with contradictions. These contradictions are deeply rooted and entrenched at the macro levels of economic and race relations in our society—or, in more direct terms, in capitalist exploitation and white supremacy (Barrera 1997; Kharem 2006). These two constructs form the foundation upon which our country is built. They influence our ideologies and our actions at differing levels of social interaction and are deeply embedded in our country's institutions and in the relationship between its agents and subordinate communities. Consequently, a logical starting point for analyzing the relationship between Latino/Chicano parents and the school system is through a macro-analysis of the existing social order.

Persell (1977) establishes a useful "structure of dominance" framework for analyzing inequitable educational outcomes, thus eventual social inequities, from four "levels" of our social structure: societal, institutional, interpersonal, and intrapsychic. Her framework provides a practical starting point for the very reason that it forces us to look at institutional, interpersonal, and personal inequities and contradictions through various lenses and at various levels, though always rooted in the socioeconomic environment. The paradigm for analysis we use in this chapter is greatly influenced by Persell's work in that the root of the problem for low levels of academic achievement for Latino/Chicano youth and the low levels of school participation by their parents is found in socioeconomic and historical factors that have maintained the current "structure of dominance," using the school system as one of the primary institutions for social reproduction.

In this framework, the contradictions that come to the fore at the societal level are often expressed around three broad social categories of inequality: *class, gender, and race.* These three factors become the basis of discrimination and social reproduction in our society. We constantly witness class struggles (though not as apparent in the United States as in other countries) in which poor, low-income, and working-class citizens struggle to maintain a foothold in our capitalist society in an attempt to make a living wage and to have a voice in our democracy.

Always at a disadvantage, subordinate groups are prevented from building a common movement of similar class interests, as they are constantly divided along racial and gender lines. Race and gender issues become viewed as separate struggles when in actuality they are intimately tied to class relations. These two constructs become stumbling blocks for subordinate groups who share a common class bond in that they often find themselves competing against each other in the race to the bottom to see who will become the preferred exploited group. This is best seen in the actions of racist border vigilantes, such as the Minutemen, who spread propaganda and recruit members in predominantly African American neighborhoods with the message that Mexican immigrants are taking away *their* jobs and overrunning *their* neighborhoods. Blurred by hate and generations of messages that promote white supremacy (Kharem 2006), groups like the Minutemen repeatedly exploit the class struggles of working-class Americans so that "rather than take their antagonism out on the employers and their manipulations, they often turn their wrath on the more immediate and usually more vulnerable targets," that is, Latino immigrants and their families (Barrera 1997, 23). Consequently, completely obfuscated from this struggle are the antics of corporations and their right-wing accomplices who exploit the working class by refusing to pay a living wage and health benefits simply to make a profit.

For the most part, it appears that most of American society is completely oblivious to the social contradictions that face them every day, so, not surprisingly, these contradictions often go unchallenged. There are two general reasons this phenomenon occurs. First, there are certain mechanisms at play in our social order that conceal these contradictions from the popular masses, and second, the thoughts and actions of individuals and social groups often reflect a noncritical stance that allows these inequities to go unquestioned. This same phenomenon occurs in the public school system. The overall inequities of the school system are often rationalized on the basis of deficit thinking and meritocracy, placing the blame on the individual and his or her social group and perpetuated by school personnel who accept and carry on these inequities rather than challenge them (Valencia 1997). These are the embedded tensions that underlie many of the relations and processes of socialization around which we construct meaning.

Yet not everybody in society is oblivious to the inequities or contradictions found in our county. On the contrary, there are many people who "sense" that there is a forced socialization that sets them apart unjustly. Yet rarely do these "feelings" develop into anything more concrete because we as individuals, or groups, often lack the critical consciousness and the language to name it. This did not happen in 1968, however. The East L.A. students *acted* on their feelings of dissonance. Through critical reflections with Sal Castro, college students, youth conferences, and coffee-shop discussions, these students proved that critical reflection and group consciousness raising *are* possible. The actions of these students demonstrated the possibility of looking beyond individuals as the cause of social inequity to looking at the deeper underlying structure of social and institutional inequality. It is through these actions, which are grounded in critical reflection and critical consciousness, that we see the possibility for a broad social movement for the betterment of not only the school system but society in general.

To summarize: The contradictions that surround our existence as human beings is ever present, yet only a small number of individuals are able to use it as a process for self- and social transformation. Few are the individuals who use counterhegemonic practices in their daily lives, and fewer are the teachers who use them in their teaching practices and interpersonal relationships with low-income bicultural children and their communities. The task therefore becomes creating a social movement for oppressed Latino/Chicano communities on the premise of critical consciousness and reflection. In other words, these communities must step forth with a new social movement based on the principle of social transformation and group consciousness raising. We believe that bicultural parents will be at the forefront of this struggle as they eventually tire of the abuse their children are enduring in the public school system and make explicit efforts to stop it, something we have witnessed before (Núñez 1994; Olivos 2003, 2004; Quintana 2005).

UNDERSTANDING LATINO/CHICANO DOMINATION AND RESISTANCE

The public school system in the United States is for the most part a biased and domineering institution. It imposes a worldview onto all bicultural students and their parents that perpetuates an existing social structure of inequality. This is possible via asymmetrical power relations that put Latinos/Chicanos, and other bicultural communities, in a subordinate position and deficit (racist) thinking that views People of Color as deficient and lacking, thus primarily guilty for their own subordinate status (Kharem 2006;

Valencia 1997). The U.S. myths of meritocracy and equal opportunity, which credit upward mobility solely on sheer intelligence and merit, also work to domesticate the minds of Latino/Chicano students in the school context, as they are bombarded by stories of people such as presidents and educators who tout the importance of "assimilation" into the "mainstream" while ignoring the gross inequities that these children face every day in and outside of school (Kozol 2005).

Yet there is an "incompleteness" to this domination. That is, no domination is truly complete; rather, it is always an imperfect and highly contested act. Therefore, domination must not be seen as an absolute condition or as functioning unchallenged. To the contrary, it must be viewed as a constant struggle between the dominant culture (and its agents) and subordinate cultures in multiple institutions and settings. Lareau and Horvat, for example, put forward the notion that social "reproduction is [a] jagged and uneven [process that] is continually negotiated by social actors" (1999, 38). A similar position is posed by Darder, who writes that "whether hegemony takes place in school, the mass media, or other social institutions, it must constantly be fought for [if it is] to be maintained." Darder continues by rightfully acknowledging that this is often due to the "changing nature of historical circumstances and the complex demands and critical actions of human beings" (1991, 42). And finally, posited within Marx's notion that "history unfolds dialectically," Persell also writes about the complexity of maintaining a "structure of dominance" in society. She aptly expresses: "Since complex totalities are comprised of a number of elements and tendencies, these processes may change at different speeds or in incompatible ways, leading to contradictions within the system and ultimately, perhaps, to the transformation of the system. The notion of contradiction suggests that education does not merely reproduce the social relations of production in an orderly fashion, but also contains potential for change" (1977, 8).

Thus, we argue that the contradictions that are inherent within the societal "structure of dominance" and within the institution of schooling are sources of constant tension between the dominant and subordinate Latino/Chicano cultures and ever present. Moreover, we contend that in order to clearly understand the notion of resistance, we must clearly understand that domination is a partial and dialectical process.

We find some very profound social contradictions in our country, which is touted as the most advanced in the history of the world. We find an ever-increasing number of people living in poverty and despair; we fill our prisons at significantly higher rates than many other developed nations, mostly with blacks and Latinos/Chicanos; we find the national distribution of wealth going increasingly and shamelessly from the poor and middle-income sectors of society to the upper economic segments of the nation; and we find the poor and working class fighting wars that most benefit the rich and privileged. This list can obviously go on, but for now let us just say that there is a constant overarching contradiction in the inability of the United States to match its rhetoric with its policies and practices. This in turn causes tensions at various levels of society as various groups and individuals struggle to interpret and challenge them while at the same time the dominant group works to maintain, reproduce, and legitimize them. Given this scenario, it would stand to reason that contradictions are also found in the public school system and in the educational process.

In the broader society, tensions arise from the contradictions related to economic interests, class divisions, ideological differences, and race relations—as mentioned earlier. In the school setting, quite possibly the most critical of contradictions is the public school system's inability to close the educational achievement disparity between specific social groups and middle- and upper-class white students. This is problematic to many critical educators and education advocates alike because the public education system promotes itself as a value-free, unbiased institution where every student will be allotted an equal opportunity to succeed and will be judged on his or her individual merit (McLaren 2007). Yet the consistent academic underachievement of low-income Latino/Chicano students and the treatment they and their parents receive within the schooling process bring these myths into question.

Notwithstanding this critique of the failings of the school system, we understand that free public education is a necessary institution in our country, for it does provide advancement opportunities for a small number of low-income, bicultural students who may otherwise not have them. Herein lies another contradiction: despite the general ineffectiveness of the public school system in educating Latino/Chicano children, it still needs to be available to them, more so than for the affluent, because this institution may be the only opportunity these students have to "prove" themselves and thus advance socially. It should come as no surprise, then, that it is the affluent sector of our society that often adamantly advocates doing away with public education, using, ironically and shamelessly, the low performance of low-income and bicultural students as proof of schools' failing to meet the needs of our capitalist society.

For the most part, the societal and institutional contradictions we've brought forth thus far function unnoticed, obfuscated by hegemonic socialization practices inherent in our social system. Yet these contradictions do not always go unseen. Rather, oftentimes these contradictions are exposed for what they are, and sometimes conflict is created. We believe this "awakening" for individuals from subordinate groups happens in three instances:

1. When there is *symbolic dissonance,* that is, when the contradictions between rhetoric and practice reach such "extreme levels" that they become so apparent and impossible to ignore—particularly among the greater masses.

2. When there is *personal dissonance,* as in when a person's lived experiences within the system unveil the contradictions. In other words, when what the individual or group is experiencing explicitly contradicts what they are being socialized to believe. . . .

3. Finally, when there is *critical consciousness,* as when members of the subordinate population become conscious of their subordinate roles and begin to openly resist the hegemonic workings of the dominant institutions, refusing to participate in their own oppression and domination. (Olivos 2006, 87)

The contradictions of the social system coupled with oppositional behaviors and ideologies by subordinate groups produce a less deterministic course of social reproduction than those outlined by a traditional bias theory or thought. For these reasons, the concepts of tension, resistance, and conflict figure significantly in any faithful analysis of the relationship between Latino/Chicano parents and the public school system, which can also be characterized as the relationship between subordinate groups and an institution of the dominant culture. Moreover, "models of resistance posit that domination is never as mechanistic as Social and Cultural Reproduction models would have us assume, and instead is highly contested in the dialectic between ideological and structural constraints and human agency"

(Covarrubias and Tijerina-Revilla 2003, 463). Thus, within the public education system the dialectic nature of the relationship between the schools and Latino/Chicano students and their parents is sometimes played out through submission and acceptance and other times through resistance and even conflict (Cummins 2001; Olivos 2006; Solórzano and Delgado Bernal 2001).

The issue of resistance implies that there exist contested terrains within social institutions (in our case education) in which subordinate individuals or subordinate groups are able to resist and interrupt complete domination—such as was the case in 1968 East Los Angeles. This oppositional behavior exhibited by members from subordinate groups has drawn the attention of critical educational theorists who attempt to understand how resistance functions in the relationship between the dominant and the subordinate cultures. Giroux, in particular, conveys the following: "Resistance is a valuable theoretical and ideological construct that provides an important focus for analyzing the relationship between school and the wider society. More importantly, it provides new theoretical leverage for understanding the complex ways in which subordinate groups experience educational failure" (2001, 107).

The schools' system, however, often lacks opportunities for, or demonstrates an uninterest in, understanding why and how resistance is manifested in bicultural groups and individuals. Taking the case of the Chicana/o students of the 1968 walkouts, for example, the L.A. school district initially did not care why these students were upset. To the contrary, district officials were annoyed by the fact that the student walkouts were disrupting their well-oiled socialization machine. Consequently, their response, as well as that of the Los Angeles Police Department and the state government, was to eliminate any type of resistance that disrupted the workings of this institution. This was a form of "counterresistance," which is often carried out by those in power to dismiss and silence subordinate individuals and groups and discourage them from speaking and acting out. This counterresistance is often quite effective, because the latter group often lacks the status and the power to challenge "the system" on equal footing.

RESISTANCE IN LATINO/CHICANO PARENTAL INVOLVEMENT

Essentially, the culture of the school is that of the broader society. Schools function under the same myths of meritocracy, equal opportunity, and neutrality as does our nation. These myths implant themselves into the mind-sets of the school personnel, who then use them to define the roles of Latino/Chicano parents and students in the school system. Teachers and administrators frequently assume that students and parents who are bicultural—that is, African American, Latino/Chicano, low-income, immigrant, non-English-speaking, and so forth—are somehow exclusively responsible for their academic and social achievement (and failure) (Valencia 1997). Latino/Chicano parents, on the other hand, though not necessarily disagreeing with the myths, at times challenge these views, either passively or actively (Olivos 2003, 2006).

As explained earlier, the dissonance bicultural parents experience between what the schools claim to value and what parents actually experience causes them to resist. This resistance takes on many manifestations, depending on the individual's or group's level of critical consciousness and desire to transform the system (Solórzano and Delgado Bernal 2001). For the most part, a large sector of bicultural parents chooses to simply avoid the oppressive situation, thus refusing to be present at the school. This absence of bicultural parents, however, rather than transforming oppressive school policies and practices, validates the school personnel's assumptions about them—that they are apathetic. Yet when bicultural parents *do* begin to demonstrate interest in more meaningful and active ways, school personnel keep them under close surveillance, ensuring that they do not overstep the school-defined boundaries of acceptable parental involvement. Shannon refers to this dilemma that bicultural parents face as the "paradox of minority parental involvement." The essence of this paradox is the no-win situation these parents are placed in. They are criticized by school personnel for their lack of involvement and low presence at the school yet actively dismissed or repressed when they demonstrate acts of advocacy or activism on behalf of their children or their community. In addition, whereas white parents are seen as the key to their children's success, ethnically diverse and low-income parents are viewed as barriers to their children's achievement. Shannon aptly conveys the following: "Parent involvement for minority language parents can be paradoxical. Traditionally, they are not involved and teachers complain. However, teachers also complain about the aggressive parent involvement of majority, middle-class Anglo parents. If minority language parents choose to become involved, they may be perceived . . . to be aggressive. Unfortunately, the majority parents' aggressiveness is tolerated, whereas the minority parent's [*sic*] action may be not only ignored and dismissed but also attacked as irrational" (1996, 83).

Significant to understanding the relationship between bicultural parents and the institution of public education within the analysis paradigm we propose is the notion that the contradictions inherent in society, its institutions, and in people are dialectical in nature. According to Darder, this "dialectical view begins with the fact of human existence and the contradictions and disjunctions that, in part, shape it and make problematic its meaning in the world" (1991, 80). McLaren, for his part, expresses the following: "[We must seek out] theories which recognize the problems of society as more than simply isolated events of individuals or deficiencies in the social structure. Rather, these problems are part of the *interactive context* between the individual and society. The individual, a social actor, both creates and is created by the social universe of which he/she is part. Neither the individual nor society is given priority in analysis; the two are inextricably interwoven, so that reference to one must by implication mean reference to the other" (2007, 194).

In essence what is being argued here is that the societal and institutional contradictions put forth thus far cannot be recognized as idle phenomena. Indeed, as mentioned earlier, society does not act upon the individual in a deterministic fashion. Instead, individuals and social groups are both the product and the maker of society and history. The contradictions found in society are therefore contradictions also found within individuals. Consequently, "dialectical thought seeks out these social contradictions and sets up a process of open and thoughtful questioning that requires reflection to ensue back and forth between the parts and the whole, the object and the subject, knowledge and human action, process and product, so that further contradictions may be discovered" (Darder 1991, 81).

What this means for our study of Latino/Chicano parents and the schools is that there are different modes of responsibility and accountability in the academic achievement of Latino/Chicano students and the integration of their parents in the school system. In other words, the burden of the responsibility for transforming does not exclusively lie in the parents or the school personnel; rather, it lies in both. In other words, this dialectical point of view implies that whereas the school system has a significant advantage of hegemonic status and power to contain Latino/Chicano parents, these parents must consciously assume an active and critical role in transforming the school system so that it meets the needs of not only their children but their communities as well. As a result, the plight of bicultural communities within the educational system is not one of complete despair and desperation; rather, particular school policies and practices as well as individual and collective actions on the part of the agents (that is, parents, students, administrators, and teachers) can promote more "democratic" schools (Olivos 2006).

BICULTURAL PARENTS, TENSIONS, CONTRADICTIONS, AND RESISTANCE

A fundamental flaw we find in much of the current parental involvement rhetoric is the multiple definitions given to the concept of "parental involvement" and the fact that there is no consistent agreement on what parental involvement actually means, though traditionally the inclusion of parents in the school system has been construed by educators to mean parents' supporting, not questioning or critiquing, the educators' efforts in educating their children. As a result, assumptions embedded in involving ethnically diverse parents in the educational system are complicated and have resulted in considerable tensions among stakeholders. These tensions can best be understood using two simple conceptualizations of "negative tension" and "positive tension." The former is the tension that derives from the social and institutional contradictions that serve to disempower and subjugate bicultural communities. This tension is present due to the dissonance bicultural individuals and groups encounter as they attempt to navigate what is believed to be a neutral educational institution but come face-to-face with a highly political microreflection of broader relations of domination and coercive power relations.

Positive tension refers to those instances in which historically disempowered groups—such as Latinos/Chicanos—disrupt the dominant institutions to make way for alternative ways of thinking and living, as was the case with the students in 1968. Parental involvement in our minds, therefore, is the personal and collective process of empowerment and critical understanding of broader society and the function of its institutions. It is the linking of social and civic action to that of educational advocacy. It requires individuals and groups to take critical actions in the task of unmasking these contradictions so that they become apparent to the entire school community. Indeed, ultimately the level of parental involvement cannot be determined by parental interest or measured by parental presence; rather, its success must be determined by whether the parents and the community have a voice in their collective future and in that of their children.

Transforming the school system suggests that efforts must be made to critically engage ideologies and practices that impede a collaborative and authentic relationship between the public school system and the bicultural communities it serves. This transformation process involves critiquing policies and practices currently found in the public education system through a problem-posing process—policies that reflect the inequities and coercive "power relations in the broader society" (Cummins 2001, 136). Additionally, this problem-posing process means that Latino/Chicano (and all bicultural) parents and the educators who teach their children must delve deeper into many often unexplored areas of parental involvement, particularly those related to class, race, and gender, in order to weed out the contradictions and expose them for what they are. Therefore, we put forth the idea that parental involvement must be redefined using a paradigm that will provide the space for voice, access, and the democratic participation of subordinate communities in the process of education. This paradigm further suggests that Latino/Chicano parents must involve themselves in the schools in a manner that breaks away from the school-sanctioned role of audience to that of social actor—a role that implies the possibility of a new social movement of Latino/Chicano student *and* parents working to transform the schools.

Problem posing forms the basis of our inquiry and work with parents (Olivos 2003, 2004, 2006; Quintana 2005). It is through this process of inquiry and dialogue that participants reflect upon and learn about the world and about themselves and thus engage in a transformative educational experience. Participants conceptualize the goals of their involvement and commitment to improve and create the social conditions necessary for a more democratic involvement. Through individual and collective reflection, action is taken toward resolving the issues that initiated the problem-posing process. These concepts are then internalized, which leads to further problem posing and reflection. It is through this act of questioning and inquiry that a true educational act occurs and knowledge is invented or reinvented in community with others. According to Freire, "Education as a practice of freedom—as opposed to education as the practice of domination—denies that [we are] abstract, isolated, independent and unattached to the world" (1982, 69).

We propose this process of parental involvement to challenge past research that has by and large been centered on identifying those factors within low-income bicultural families that preclude their children's academic and social success and has been focused on identifying levels and scopes of involvement that in essence do nothing to change the school or the school system but rather work only to promote the idle attendance of parents at school functions. As a result, what we propose in this chapter is that the questions of school effectiveness and social contradictions, as opposed to home improvement, must be the focus of scrutiny. These are but the first steps toward politicizing Latino/Chicano parental involvement in the public school system.

POLITICIZING PARENTAL INVOLVEMENT— LISTENING TO PARENTS' VOICES

The work of Latino/Chicano parents and parent advocates in the public school system is to recognize and engage the contradictions found within it through a problem-posing process. Specifically, Latino/Chicano parental involvement involves a deep process of critical reflection through a problem-posing dialogue that will help parents and community understand the deeply embedded contradictions of our society and our school system. Foucault similarly recognized the important task of subordinate groups in understanding and unmasking the hidden agendas and contradictions of dominant institutions, as conveyed in the following quote: "The real political task is to criticize the working of institutions that appear to be both neutral and independent; to criticize them in such a way that the political violence which has always exercised itself obscurely through them will be uncovered so that people can fight it" (quoted in Corson 1993, v).

The words of Foucault point to the importance of developing a critical consciousness among disenfranchised groups—something that was manifested in the student political movements of the 1960s—as well as a clear vision of social justice. Thus, we put forward that any Latino/Chicano parent movement must support the participation of *all* disenfranchised people in the civic life of the society in which they live. This authentic parental involvement must actively support the acquisition of knowledge that will promote the native ability of people who often have no voice in the issues that most affect their lives and the lives of their children—in this case, education. Moreover, this involvement should work to transform those practices within institutions that preclude the academic and social success of all bicultural children (Olivos and Ochoa 2006).

Over the course of our work with Latino/Chicano parents, we have come across overriding themes related to their involvement with the schools and their children's academic endeavors: racism, classism, discrimination, low standards, inequitable resources, and low expectations, to name a few (Olivos 2003, 2006; Quintana 2005). For the remainder of this section, we will present the voices of parents—voices we have collected from problem-posing involvement we have been involved in during the past decade. We will also use these voices to demonstrate how dissonance and tension are significant factors in the critical-consciousness process.[4]

A fundamental step toward "politicizing" Latino/Chicano parental involvement is identifying those issues that they feel are most pressing or urgent. Our research (Olivos 2003; Quintana 2005) demonstrates that Latino/Chicano parents are concerned about unjust and inequitable educational policies and practices that negatively impact their children as well as racist and classist educators and policy makers who denigrate their culture and their children's self-esteem. The following quote by a Latina parent in San Diego demonstrates the cognizance that these parents have about the inequitable educational opportunities afforded to the children in her community as opposed to children who come from more affluent families: "One begins to notice the difference right away, 'We don't have this. They do. This we don't have either, but they do.' One notices that the differences begin all the way from the streets. I notice and I wonder: 'Why do they have so many schools and we don't?' Our children have to get up early, at five o'clock in the morning, in order to be ready at 6 a.m. at the bus stop. Why all this? It's affecting our children." For many Latino parents, these lived experiences of seeing firsthand the contradictions between public school rhetoric of "equal opportunity for all" and the poor condition of their children's schools impact their relationship with the school (Olivos 2006).

Another concern Latino/Chicano parents have with the school system and society in general is racism. Latino/Chicano parents we have worked with have expressed feelings of discrimination based on educators' and administrators' "racist actions" against them and their children. This is noted, for example, in the quote below by a Latina parent in San Diego who recalled how Latino parents were treated different from white parents in her child's school:

> One notices the difference. If [a Latino parent] has a problem and they send a note to the principal asking for a meeting, they never get a response, the principal doesn't reply. They don't give you a response. And that's what we noticed when we were in a particular struggle. When we would send complaints, we'd never get a response. Then one day, one of the ladies that was with us, not completely but she supported us, sent the principal a letter asking for a meeting. She's American. That very same day she got a meeting. That very same day! (Olivos 2003, 175)

Since 1994's Proposition 187 in California, which targeted undocumented Latino immigrants and children, Latinos/Chicanos in the state have become more cognizant of the issue of race and how racism permeates our society. This racism became even more apparent during the early part of the 2000s as opportunistic right-wing politicians and talk-show pundits used corporate America's attack on the middle and working classes as a tool against Latinos/Chicanos. The 2004 attempt by Wisconsin congressman Sensenbrenner to criminalize to felony status undocumented immigrants and those who assist them demonstrated to many Latino/Chicano parents the extent of the racism that pervades our social fabric as a nation. Known as House Resolution (HR) 4437, this piece of legislation served as a catalyst to a "new" generation of Latino/Chicano students and parent activists that resulted in major rallies, demonstrations, and boycotts throughout the nation— culminating with the May 1, 2006, national Day of Action.

Soon after the May 1, 2006, events throughout the nation, we sat down with parents who had participated in at least one of the events and delved into their reflections on the walkouts and their perceptions about what they believed needed to be done to mobilize the Latino/Chicano community and to improve the educational and social attainment of their children and communities. These parents all had children at the elementary school in which one of the authors of this chapter worked as a teacher and faculty adviser to an English-learner advisory group. Their responses, in general, revealed to us knowledge of a racist educational system and a willingness to engage in political resistance as a form of self-defense.

Many parents we spoke to who participated in the rallies and marches believed that HR 4437 was more than an attack on immigrants; it was an attack aimed at Latino/Chicano communities and their families, and they believed that it should be stopped via education and resistance. Valeria, a parent from southern San Diego County, for example, spoke about the important role of education in the development of consciousness in a new social movement for Latino/Chicano families in the United States and in schools:

> We have been talking about education. I believe that the way to teach people is to educate them. To be a teacher, a mother, is a good way to educate a family. If there was really an interest, we could educate those people who are against this very important struggle. How much money do politicians spend when they are campaigning? A lot. Every day you see politicians on TV. Well, there ought to be organizations that educate people in the community about what the real issues are that affect the community of the foreigners as immigrants, not just Latino immigrants—in this way the people could see why we are needed, why we need each other, why we are here, and why we aren't leaving. "They" believe that we are here in the U.S. simply because we are all "dying of hunger." We came and are going to leave behind big debts—we are going to rape, steal, and terrorize, etc. For the wrongs that a few people do, the impression is left that we all do wrong. If we have been able to educate on some things by way of "the word" in much the same way we have been able to transmit our history, then why can't we educate in the same way as it relates to the struggle of the immigrant and why we are really here? This could be a solution, to transmit the message—we have to continue and not stop this protest—this message to the people.

Valeria's words transmit a powerful message of problem posing, reflection, conceptualization, and praxis. She is able to identify the problem—a problem that is greater than the immediate problems of the schools—and tie it to the contradictions found in her society. Moreover, she is able to identify those obstacles that preclude her community from moving forward as well as visualize a just and equitable society.

Many of the Latino parents we spoke to in mid-2006 expressed that the masses are here and that they are very much aware of the inequities and contradictions in our society. Many believed, however, that internalization and a long-term vision for social justice are what is missing in the Latino/Chicano struggle. They argued that planning has to be long-range and fluid to make best use of the human energy that was evident up to the May 1 national Day of Action. The boycott, protests, and marches were a good way to show that the people are not content with the status quo, and the parents agreed that their social movement was an important political response to the oppressive acts of many Americans who view Latinos/Chicanos and immigrants as enemies of the country. Diana, another parent from South San Diego, for example, said, "If people rise in protest, this country will realize that we are demonstrating our discontent. The issue of slavery is not gone. The U.S. continues its slave labor. The immigrants are its slaves! We have to unite and shout to the four winds that we have had enough!"

The symbolic and personal dissonance bicultural parents encounter in U.S. society and its institutions becomes for many parents a catalyst for questioning, resisting, and challenging the institution of public education—as well as other institutions. Complications arise, however, when "the solutions [the parents] select arise from the ascribed beliefs and values of the dominant society, [thus], they may in fact [be leading] themselves and others deeper into forms of domination and oppression" (Darder 1991, 89). Complications also arise when opportunities for reflection and internalization are not part of the problem-posing process or when a critique of social oppression is not motivated by a long-term vision for social justice, as noted in the words of Diana below:

I believe that to protest is the natural law that life gives us to express our discontent—our life-given right! Even children use the form of protest—babies will let you know when they are not content. Of course, when one gets older, one finds other ways to express discontent—dissatisfaction with status quo—and that is to protest or to boycott. I feel that what happened with our protest was good, but it would have been better if continuity was built into the protest plan. It should not only be a protest of the "illegals"; there are many "legals" that need to unite with this struggle.

A great deal of the motivation driving the resistance of Latino/Chicano parents is expressed in the need "to do something" when it comes to the issues of inequality and inequity in education and society. They regard the need to act as an important process in advocating for the rights of their children, as conveyed in the words of Teresa, a Latina parent from San Diego:

I believe that it is very important to do something. One can't say, "My friend will do it" or "'What's her name' will do it." One needs to join the struggle to see what one can do; like our newsletter is something that has helped us so that other parents, sooner or later, become involved or see that there is more information, more things to support their children, so that they can advance and take advantage of everything the school system has to offer, so that the Latino child is not always so low academically in the schools.

The voices of these parents are a powerful reminder that consciousness and praxis still exist in the Latino/Chicano community. They reflect a willingness to act, struggle, and sacrifice so that their children and their community will prevail. They also demonstrate the great potential that awaits us should this bicultural community rise once again in resistance.

SCHOOL AND COMMUNITY LEADERS, EDUCATION, AND ACCOUNTABILITY

We began by reflecting on the success of the 1968 walkouts of East Los Angeles. Now we fast-forward forty years to the current sociopolitical and economic context of Latinos/Chicanos and ask ourselves whether the walkout, or Blowout, has seen its end. That is, are popular social movements, such as walkouts, boycotts, strikes, and so forth, antiquated and out of touch within the current political climate? Moreover, is today's Latino/Chicano community, which is often seen as apathetic and uninformed, still willing to participate in a new social movement to demand social equity and equality, particularly within the educational context? Our work as educators, researchers, and community advocates has demonstrated to us that the Latino/Chicano community is still very much politically active, though their population in the United States is obviously much more diverse and larger than it was in the 1960s.

Many of our Latino/Chicano parents demonstrate an untapped critical consciousness. They are aware of the contradictions that surround their living conditions in the United States. They understand that as a people, their contributions to our society are ignored and their presence is attacked. Yet they believe that Latino/Chicano parents must take a stand to defend their children, in and outside of the public school system—as demonstrated by their participation in the schools and, more specifically, in the May 1 Day of Action. Indeed, "all measures toward the actualizing of social justice for all are *political* acts. In confronting issues of educational inequities, one does battle with issues of control, conflict and power," and this must be understood by *all* bicultural parents (Quintana 2005, 7).

We see the roles of Latino/Chicano parents in the public schools as leaders and as warriors. Quintana's study defined the warrior as "a leader [who seeks] to become knowledgeable about the responsibilities of preserving humanity. Warriors, [in her definition], act with love, compassion, and great hope and a respect for life" (2005, 4). The countless Latino/Chicano parents we have worked with throughout our careers demonstrate to us that they are seeking to be informed and included. They are willing to make the necessary sacrifices for their children to have a better life. They have also demonstrated to us that they will mobilize and take the necessary risks when it involves their children or their communities. We see that critical and social consciousness is still present in the Latino/Chicano community; it just needs to be "activated" every now and then.

In order to comprehend the nature of the tensions that exist between Latino parents and the public school system, it is also important to understand the parents' conceptions about schooling as well as their lived experiences with the public school system, for it is within these tensions that the contradictions embedded within public education come to the fore. In other words, the tensions and the contradictions rooted within the public school system (and in society in general) become more apparent when they do not align with the parents' beliefs, ideologies, or lived experiences, causing them to either resist or act against the workings of the school (Olivos 2003). When these areas of tension reach "extreme" levels of contradiction, to the point that even the most "apolitical" parent cannot ignore them, conflict arises, at times accompanied by a sophisticated political and social consciousness.

As we witness, again, the racist attitudes and actions of the dominant culture toward the Latino/Chicano population, we look back on the political tools that were effective in combating racism and exploitation in the schools and in society decades ago, and we search for the best way to organize a national movement against policies that are aimed at bicultural communities, particularly Latinos/Chicanos.[5] We believe that it will be the Latino/Chicano communities that will use the walkouts as a tool for expressing discontent and demonstrating that when it comes to advocating for and defending the rights of their children, they stand united and willing to take the necessary risks to equalize educational and social opportunities.

NOTES

This chapter is dedicated to Dr. René Núñez (1936–2006), Professor Emeritus, Chicana/o Studies, at San Diego State University: elder, mentor, colleague, activist, and friend.

1. We use the term "bicultural" rather than the term "minority" in this chapter because in the words of Darder, the latter term is often used to "linguistically, and hence politically, [reflect and perpetuate] a view of subordinate cultures as deficient and disempowered" (1991, xvi).

2. We understand that the terms "Latino" and "Chicano" are not interchangeable in the eyes of many, yet we prefer to use them both as an understanding that although the Latino/Chicano population in the United States is very diverse, they also share common cultural, sociopolitical, and economic characteristics.

3. California Department of Education, Educational Demographics Unit, four-year derived dropout rate is for the 2004–5 academic year.

4. Pseudonyms are used in this chapter.

5. Although the most recent attacks against the Latino/Chicano population are surrounded in the language of securing borders against terrorism and "illegal" immigrants, political and popular rhetoric demonstrates a clear-aimed attack against the "browning" of the United States.

REFERENCES

Barrera, M. 1997. "A Theory of Racial Inequality." In *Latinos and Education: A Critical Reader,* edited by A. Darder, R. D. Torres, and H. Gutierrez, 3–44. New York: Routledge.

Bowles, S., and H. Gintis. 1976. *Schooling in Capitalist America: Educational Reform and the Contradictions of Economic Life.* New York: Basic Books.

Corson, D. 1993. *Language, Minority Education, and Gender: Linking Social Justice and Power.* Clevedon, England: Multilingual Matters.

Covarrubias, A., and A. Tijerina-Revilla. 2003. "Agencies of Transformational Resistance." *Florida Law Review* 55, no. 1.

Cummins, J. 2001. *Negotiating Identities: Education for Empowerment in a Diverse Society.* 2nd ed. Ontario, Calif.: California Association for Bilingual Education.

Darder, A. 1991. *Culture and Power in the Classroom: A Critical Foundation for Bicultural Education.* Westport, Conn.: Bergin and Garvey.

Darder, A., R. D. Torres, and H. Gutiérrez, eds. 1997. *Latinos and Education: A Critical Reader.* New York: Routledge.

Freire, P. 1982. "Dialogue Is Not a Chaste Event." In *Comments by Paulo Freire on Issues in Participatory Research,* edited by P. Jurmo. Amherst: University of Massachusetts, Center for International Education.

Fry, R. 2003. *Hispanic Youth Dropping Out of U.S. Schools: Measuring the Challenge.* Washington, D.C.: Pew Hispanic Center.

Giroux, H. 2001. *Theory and Resistance in Education: Towards a Pedagogy for the Opposition.* Westport, Conn.: Bergin and Garvey.

Kharem, H. 2006. *A Curriculum of Repression: A Pedagogy of Racial History in the United States.* New York: Peter Lang.

Kozol, J. 2005. *The Shame of the Nation: The Restoration of Apartheid Schooling in America.* New York: Three Rivers Press.

Lareau, A., and L. Horvat. 1999. "Moments of Social Inclusion and Exclusion: Race, Class, and Cultural Capital in Family-School Relationships." *Sociology of Education* 72, no. 1: 37–53.

McLaren, P. 2007. *Life in Schools: An Introduction to Critical Pedagogy in the Foundation of Education.* 5th ed. 2003. Reprint, Boston: Pearson/Allyn and Bacon.

National Center for Education Statistics. 2003. *Status and Trends in the Education of Hispanics.* Washington, D.C.: Institute of Educational Sciences, U.S. Department of Education.

Núñez, R. 1994. "Schools, Parents, and Empowerment: An Ethnographic Study of Mexican-Origin Parents' Participation in Their Children's Schools." Ph.D. diss., San Diego State University/Claremont Graduate University.

Olivos, E. M. 2003. "Dialectical Tensions, Contradictions, and Resistance: A Study of the Relationship Between Latino Parents and the Public School System Within a Socioeconomic 'Structure of Dominance.'" Ph.D. diss., San Diego State University/Claremont Graduate University.

———. 2004. "Tensions, Contradictions, and Resistance: An Activist's Reflection of the Struggles of Latino Parents in the Public School System." *High School Journal* 87, no. 4: 25–35.

———. 2006. *The Power of Parents: A Critical Perspective of Bicultural Parent Involvement in Public Schools*. New York: Peter Lang.

Olivos, E. M., and A. M. Ochoa. 2006. "Toward a Transformational Paradigm of Parent Involvement in Urban Education." In *Urban Education: An Encyclopedia*, edited by J. Kincheloe, P. Anderson, K. Rose, D. Griffith, and K. Hayes. Westport, Conn.: Greenwood Press.

Olivos, E. M., and C. E. Quintana de Valladolid. 2005. "*Entre la espada y la pared*: Critical Educators, Bilingual Education, and Education Reform." *Journal of Latinos and Education* 4, no. 4: 283–93.

Persell, C. H. 1977. *Education and Inequality: The Roots and Results of Stratification in America's Schools*. New York: Free Press.

Quintana, C. E. 2005. "Social Justice Through the Arts: Remembering the Spirit of the Warrior." Ph.D. diss., San Diego State University/Claremont Graduate University.

Shannon, S. M. 1996. "Minority Parental Involvement: A Mexican Mother's Experience and a Teacher's Interpretation." *Education and Urban Society* 29, no. 1: 71–84.

Solórzano, D. G., and D. Delgado Bernal. 2001. "Examining Transformational Resistance Through a Critical Race and LatCrit Theory Framework: Chicana and Chicano Students in an Urban Context." *Urban Education* 36, no. 3: 308–42.

Spring, J. 2005. *The American School, 1642–2004*. 6th ed. New York: McGraw-Hill.

Valencia, R. R. 1997. *The Evolution of Deficit Thinking: Educational Thought and Practice*. London: Falmer Press.

CHAPTER 5

Black and Brown High School Student Activism

RITA KOHLI

DANIEL G. SOLÓRZANO

As Critical Race scholars, we often find ourselves in discussions about race and the debate around whether People of Color can be racist.[1] Racism, as we define later, involves structural power, something most People of Color are denied based on classifications including race, ethnicity, language, and immigration status. Based on this assertion, we feel People of Color cannot be racist; however, this idea is continually challenged in our lives by story after story of moments when blacks, Latinas/os, and Asian Americans have acted in a "racist" manner or said "racist" things to each other.[2] In many ways, we understand this sentiment because we too have witnessed numerous displays of prejudice, discrimination, and racial slurs from People of Color toward other People of Color. Like others, we have been a target of racial prejudice and discrimination by racial minorities, as well as witness to members in our own community racially discriminating against People of Color.

Thus, we are not denying that the events happened. Nor are we trying to minimize the impact that racial hatred has on its victims when the perpetrator is not white. Actually, knowing the commonalities of our oppression, it deeply concerns us when we see People of Color racially discriminating against each other. As scholars who struggle against racism, we often shy away from addressing our inter- as well as intragroup conflict. However, it is imperative that we talk about this issue, and to effectively do so we must broaden our analysis of racism beyond individuals and their actions.

We must acknowledge the structural and institutional power that fuels this conflict.

It is true that in some circumstances, one racial minority group or person can seem to have more power than another. However, when we analyze the derogatory comments of a light-skinned Person of Color about a darker-skinned Person of Color, or the racial tension among Youth of Color in overcrowded, underresourced urban public schools, we cannot overlook the fact that these events occur within institutions that are constructed, benefit, and are dominated by institutionalized white power.[3] This country was founded through the enslavement of Africans, the genocide of indigenous peoples, the war over and confiscation of Mexican land, and the exploitation of numerous Asian ethnic groups. Today, there is an overrepresentation of blacks, Latinas/os, Native Americans, and select Asian American groups below the poverty line, with substandard housing, high unemployment rates, and inadequate schools. Acknowledging these problematic social circumstances is fundamental to our understanding of racial conflict among People of Color.

Framed through Critical Race Theory (CRT), this chapter theorizes inter- and intraracial conflict between Communities of Color. As a model of solidarity building, we also highlight the Peace Week campaign of black and Latina/o high school student activists in Los Angeles, California. We must first define the conceptual framework and the concepts that guide this chapter: CRT, racism, and white supremacy.

CRITICAL RACE THEORY, RACISM, AND WHITE SUPREMACY

CRT. "CRT" is used within this chapter to centralize the role of institutional racism in the racial conflict between People of Color. The framework was developed in the 1970s among legal scholars such as Derrick Bell, Kimberley Crenshaw, and Richard Delgado to highlight race, racism, and its intersections with other forms of oppression. Over the past ten years, CRT has extended into many disciplines, including education. It is used within this field to heighten awareness about racism and educational inequity. CRT scholars have developed five tenets to guide educational research. We use each of the tenets in this project, as defined below:

1. *Centrality of race and racism.* All CRT research within education must centralize race and racism, as well as acknowledge the intersection of race

with other forms of subordination. This chapter is focused on race, racism, and its connection to power and class in the lives of Students of Color.

2. *Challenging the dominant perspective.* CRT research works to challenge dominant narratives, often referred to as majoritarian stories. This project challenges dominant narratives that pit People of Color against each other. By highlighting the role of institutional racism in the conflict between racial minorities, we challenge a divisive narrative and replace it with a counterstory of solidarity and coalition building.

3. *Commitment to social justice.* Social justice must always be a motivation behind CRT research. Committed to social justice, this project suggests a model of activism that leans on the insights of Youth of Color.

4. *Valuing experiential knowledge.* CRT scholars believe in the power of story. Building on the oral traditions of many indigenous Communities of Color around the world, CRT research values the experiences and narratives of People of Color when attempting to understand social inequality. All data in this study were collected through qualitative focus-group interviews.

5. *Being interdisciplinary.* The final tenet of CRT research is to be interdisciplinary. CRT scholars believe that the world is multidimensional, and similarly research about the world should reflect multiple perspectives. Drawing on the fields of psychology, sociology, history, and education, this project is interdisciplinary in nature. It utilizes theory and empirical research to build understanding about racism. (Solórzano and Delgado Bernal 2001)

This framework allows us to focus on the racialized experiences of People of Color, as well as redefine the concepts of racism, white supremacy, and the perceptions of our inter- and intraracial conflict.

Racism. For our purpose, Audre Lorde may have produced the most concise definition of racism: "the belief in the inherent superiority of one race over all others and thereby the right to dominance" (1992, 496). Manning Marable has also defined racism as "a system of ignorance, exploitation, and power used to oppress African-Americans, Latina/os, Asians, Pacific Americans, American Indians and other people on the basis of ethnicity, culture, mannerisms, and color" (1992, 5). Indeed, embedded in the Lorde and Marable definitions of racism are at least three important points:

(1) one group believes itself to be superior, (2) the group that believes itself to be superior has the power to carry out the racist behavior, and (3) racism affects multiple racial and ethnic groups. These definitions take the position that racism is about institutional power, something People of Color in the United States have never possessed.

White supremacy. Using and extending the work of Audre Lorde and Manning Marable, we define white supremacy as the belief in the inherent superiority of whites over People of Color in order to justify unequal and oppressive social arrangements.[4] More specifically, white supremacy is an ideology that assigns value to real or imagined differences to justify dominance over People of Color (see Memmi 1968).[5]

Our definition of white supremacy includes overt examples, such as the Ku Klux Klan and the white power movement, but it also emphasizes subtle and daily ways in which white culture is deemed superior to the culture, language, and traditions of People of Color. Bell hooks (1989) and Trina Grillo and Stephanie Wildman (1997), prominent theorists of U.S. race relations, find the term "racism" inadequate in understanding racial discrimination toward People of Color. They argue that only the term "white supremacy" appropriately identifies institutional white power as the perpetrator and source of these racial offenses. Recognizing the significance of this perspective, we thus claim that racism in the United States is synonymous with white supremacy. In this chapter, when we use the word "racism," we are also referencing "white supremacy" to acknowledge who has constructed and who benefits from racism.

The theoretical concept of racism has a marked reality in our daily world. It defines both historical and contemporary situations within the United States. Although it is an uncomfortable subject to broach, by ignoring the powerful presence and impact of racism on our society, we often prevent the progress of social justice and equity.

In 1968, fourteen years after the landmark 1954 Supreme Court case *Brown v. Board of Education* began the slow and "deliberate" dismantling of state-sponsored racial segregation in public schools, one of the chief architects of the decision, Judge Robert L. Carter, expressed his misgivings about the legal strategy of targeting the symptoms instead of the disease. He stated: "Few in the country, black or white, understood in 1954 that *racial segregation was merely a symptom,* not the *disease;* that the real sickness is that our society in all its manifestations is geared to the maintenance of *white superiority*" (247; emphasis added). In 1988, Carter continued to express lament that the NAACP lawyers had erred. He believed that "the basic barrier to full equality for blacks was not *racial segregation, a symptom*, but *white supremacy*, the *disease*" (1095; emphasis added). In 2004, decades after his first comment, in a radio interview commemorating the fiftieth anniversary of *Brown*, Carter echoed his previous sentiment: "We had the *wrong target*. This is a racist society . . . and in *Brown* we focused on *segregation*. What we should have focused on (and we couldn't see it at the time) was the elimination of *White supremacy*" (*Hear and Now* 2004; emphasis added).

It is important to note the consistency of regret in Carter's thinking as to the legal strategy around *Brown*.[6] He clearly cautions us to be ever vigilant in our legal and political strategies to dismantle racism. Carter reminds us to also acknowledge and differentiate the symptoms from the disease in our everyday struggles against racism. Indeed, in our struggle to overcome inequality (the symptom), we need to focus on attacking racism (the disease).

In this chapter we take on Carter's challenge of making sure we differentiate between symptoms and the disease when trying to understand and change the unequal conditions in which People of Color find themselves. We begin by introducing a theoretical model to explain the role of institutionalized racism and racial hierarchies in the conflict within and between Communities of Color. We will then examine this model through the case study of black and brown tension in Los Angeles schools and describe high school student activists who were able to disrupt cycles of racial oppression within their school.

A MODEL OF INSTITUTIONAL RACISM AND RACIAL HIERARCHIES

Racism is reinforced through various institutional means such as segregated housing and schools, anti–affirmative action policies, and anti-immigrant legislation. In addition, racism also takes the form of a racial hierarchy that places white culture, history, and values over the culture, history, and values of People of Color. Often, this hierarchy is sorted by phenotype and skin color, with the lightest on top and the darkest on the bottom. In this structure, People of Color frequently feel they must compete for a higher position, in part by further subordinating other nonwhite racial and ethnic groups. This "divide-and-rule" tool serves to maintain the power structure by creating a system in which People of Color blame each other for their low position in society, thus fostering inter- and intragroup conflict.

Guns and drugs are physical weapons that are constructed outside of Communities of Color, but are often pushed upon People of Color for them to hurt and keep each other in their place. We argue that, similarly, racism is a psychological weapon, constructed elsewhere, that is pushed upon People of Color for them to hurt and keep each other in their subordinate position. For example, we have witnessed racial minorities using the slurs "n*gger" and "sp*c" against each other. However, these words were not created by People of Color.[7] The power of these words comes from an intense history of institutionalized white domination, and only because of that history and power are People of Color able to use those words to hurt others.

When considering the idea of People of Color enacting racism, we feel it is necessary to challenge the notion that one Community of Color can truly be the "cause" of the lower status of another Community of Color. Instead, like Carter (1968, 1988; *Hear and Now* 2004), we feel their "racist" attitudes and actions are part of the *symptom* of the real *disease*—white supremacy— and that these actions actually work to reaffirm racist power structures.

This model of understanding racism leads us to analyze when Students of Color engage in forms of interracial conflict. What are the underlying causes (the disease) to their conflict (symptoms)? In addition, how have some Students of Color intervened in this process to work toward interracial accord and coexistence? In the next sections, we attempt to answer these questions.

Black and Brown in Los Angeles High Schools

As described earlier, racism is institutionally embedded in many facets of our society, including our public school system. It has been demonstrated that schools serving Students of Color have poorer conditions, fewer resources, and higher rates of unqualified teachers than schools that are predominantly white (Orfield and Lee 2005). Los Angeles schools reflect this trend. In 2005–6, the Los Angeles Unified School District, the second-largest district in the country, was 73 percent Latina/o and 91 percent Students of Color, but graduated only 66 percent of its student population (California Department of Education 2005–6). Many of its major high schools are overcrowded, beginning each school year with numerous vacancies and strings of long-term substitutes (Oakes, Rogers, and Silver 2004).

Within this context, racial conflict was reported at several major high schools in the area in 2005 between thousands of African American and Latina/o youth. Incidents on several campuses included racially divided acts of students hitting each other and throwing fruit and milk cartons during lunchtime (DiMassa 2005). With minimal attempts to understand the root of the tension within these Communities of Color, school officials responded with heightened security, police officers in riot gear, and locking down the schools.[8] Even neighboring schools that were not sites of any tension were locked down. Police presence was dramatically increased; forty-four officers were assigned to one of the campuses the day after an incident (DiMassa and Shields 2005). As a result, black and brown youth at these schools endured pepper spray, and many were hit with batons by police officers (Shields and Lin 2005).

As we analyze these events through the lens of our model, we begin to see how racist conditions can breed group divisions. Los Angeles, a costly and growing city, has left poor residents competing for jobs. Recent demographic shifts have changed low-income neighborhoods that have historically been black to predominantly Latina/o (Solórzano and Velez 2007), and these factors have resulted in a climate of racial tension. Schools do not exist in a vacuum, and often the racial divisions of the neighborhood can replicate themselves within the schools. However, we cannot separate racial inequity in society from the beliefs and actions of those who live there.

It is important to consider, if there were enough employment opportunities and affordable housing for the black and Latina/o residents of Los Angeles, would differences between these communities manifest in hostility? Would fights between black and Latina/o students occur in a well-resourced, well-functioning school? As explained earlier, racial and ethnic conflict is rooted in a competition for power within a racial hierarchy in which Communities of Color are forced to the bottom. The conflict, however, does not actually lead to power for racial minorities. Instead, it results in an affirmation of racism. In Los Angeles schools, conflict among black and brown students was directly connected to the conditions of those schools; in addition, the conflict led to a heightened oppression of both groups of students. This heightened oppression impedes on the learning of Students of Color, thus keeping them at the bottom of the hierarchy.

While interracial and intraracial conflict of People of Color does not always exist, it is still an obstacle in the struggle for liberation and racial equality. The Youth of Color of Los Angeles have been repeatedly degraded in the media and painted as violent and racially divided, yet many students work to challenge these notions. Downtown High School, a large new high school serving more than three thousand students, was one such site of racial tension.[9] Several fights broke out in the fall of 2005 between a small portion of the 92 percent Latina/o and 8 percent black student body (California Department of Education 2005–6). When asked about the racial climate relating to these fights, a Latina student commented that she witnessed a tension across racial lines: "Black people were showing gestures and throwing up gang signs. Kids in my class were saying that they were throwing up gang signs and looking at brown people bad, like in bad ways. And the brown people weren't going to take that, so they started fighting for no reason. Just like, if you look at me bad, I'm gonna jump you for that." This young woman believed that black and brown students felt a tension and animosity toward each. She also thought that this was the catalyst for much of the fighting.

Resembling the districtwide response to racial tension, school officials began to increase security and police presence. However, this response addressed the symptom, but did little to tackle the disease. In contrast to these measures, some of the students from a campus leadership class decided to take action on their own and began to address the larger underlying cause for these racial problems. During Peace Week, a campaign constructed to build black and brown unity, students put up posters, entered classes to give motivational speeches, and led assemblies to remind their peers of the cultural and racial similarities they share.

TREATING THE DISEASE, NOT THE SYMPTOMS

Downtown High School was recognized in the media for its student violence. A *Los Angeles Times* article explained that student fights resulted in thrown trash cans and two days of chaos. Thirty-four students were arrested, and ten were taken to hospitals, mainly to be treated for pepper spray–related injuries from police on campus (Sipchen 2006). When this occurred, the former police officer who is principal requested that social workers be assigned to campus full-time. As stated in the article, he believed that their problems had nothing to do with the school but were affecting their ability in school.

Turning to the testimonies of students, we see that although the racialized conflict of youth in this context is violent and problematic, the conflict is just a symptom of a larger disease. In a focus-group interview with four student leaders of the Peace Week campaign and their teacher, this campus is described as an oppressive place that in many ways reflects racism in broader society. Many students critiqued the heavy security presence on campus and felt locked in. Laquanza, a seventeen-year-old black female, commented: "It's like a jail at this school. . . . We have to get searched, when we get into the school. . . . When we go to lunch, we have two lunches, we don't get to really be with OUR friends—'cause they have second lunch and we have first lunch. And we have lunch at ten o'clock, and no one is really hungry at ten o'clock . . . so by the time school ends everyone is hungry." In this comment, it is clear that this young woman feels oppressed by the structure of her school. Her peers reiterated that they too felt constrained by the schedule and criminalized by the campus restrictions. They also felt offended by the daily searches of their personal belongings.

In addition to the design of the school day, the students often felt mistreated by their teachers. Like many Los Angeles schools, the school year started with several vacancies, which resulted in a culture of low expectations and disrespect of students. Maria, a fifteen-year-old Latina, describes one of her teachers: "She was really mean, she didn't really explain anything that was on the board, or any lessons that we had to do. She would just expect us to do the work and turn it in, but she never explained anything. And then it came to the point when we were just tired of her and we called [the principal] to come and get her because she was out of control. She would flick us off, she would say you guys are so stupid, you guys don't know anything." Teachers have the utmost responsibility to nurture the self-concepts and worldviews of youth. Rather than fulfilling her duties to encourage these Youth of Color, this teacher instead treated them inhumanely and set them up for failure.

Mr. L., a teacher who was part of the Peace Week campaign, added to this narrative by sharing that several teachers at the school referred to students as "stupid," as "animals," and as "rats in a cage." Unfortunately, these degrading comments are not uncommon in schools that serve black and brown youth. There is often a climate of disrespect in urban schools, and it is fundamental that we recognize this context when we analyze the actions of students in these spaces.

Brandon, a sixteen-year-old black male student, articulated this sentiment well when he commented, "This school can be very frustrating . . . so, basically [the students] are so angry that they just have to fight." Although the choice of youth to fight on campus is related to a complex host of reasons and social circumstances, Brandon emphasizes that the structure of his school plays a role in student tension and conflict. He reminds us of the connection between conflict on campus and the frustration students are made to feel in schools like Downtown High School.

CHALLENGE TO CYCLES OF RACISM

The media portrayed the students of Downtown High School in negative ways, and this was very upsetting to the youth. Many of them felt misrepresented and criminalized. In addition, all students were forced to endure increased police presence and school lockdowns. When it is examined through our model, we begin to see how conflict between black and brown youth works to maintain the racial hierarchy. Interracial fighting between black and Latina/o teenagers, induced by an oppressive context, resulted in heightened oppression within that context.

Even within a structure like this, however, several students became motivated to challenge the negative stereotypes constructed about their school and peers. Mr. L. and Ms. B., both first-year teachers and community activists, led a leadership class during the 2005–6 school year. Despite what the administration might have thought of them, they encouraged students to use their voices to take action and make a change in their school. In an interview with Mr. L., he revealed that he and Ms. B. constructed the leadership class as a space to address campus issues. Within a structured forum to problem solve the racial tension on campus, the students felt encouraged to take ownership of their school. Several student leaders emerged from the class dialogue and began a campaign to unite black and Latina/o students. Mr. L. commented:

What I really wanted to see the leadership class do was to take action— strong action around what was happening. So we brainstormed ideas and we came and put different ideas on what we could do. And at first, half, or close to half the leadership class was kind of like, "We can't do anything. What can we do?" It was people like Gaby, like

Laquanza, Maria, like Brandon, who stepped up and said, "No, we can do something! We can do something. We can make a change!" And indeed . . . I think *they* have made a change. They worked collectively, and they were able to make a change here on campus. I think each one of the students who were involved in the campus has changed, themselves.

Mr. L. pointed out the agency of students to transform the school. Although the media, administration, and many students on campus were disillusioned about the possibility for change, Gabriela, Laquanza, Maria, Brandon, and other activist youth in the leadership class believed in the good of their peers and the ability for black and brown solidarity.

As part of this unique class that challenged students to be agents of change, the youth felt both a responsibility and an empowerment to build unity on campus. In response to the negative media portrayal of their school, these students decided to put together a week of events to calm student tensions. Filled with dialogue, dance, and community speakers, they entitled this action Peace Week. A fourteen-year-old Latina student named Gabriela shared: "We've seen the news, and they portrayed us like, damn! Something real bad! And then the newspapers said we were the most dangerous campus in L.A. and the district—and that's not true because it's really peaceful

Student activists in leadership class. Reproduced by permission of Jose Lara.

around here. We just wanted to let students know that we're not that bad and we're all together right here, no matter what the news say." Along with other students in the leadership class, Gabriela believed that it was important to challenge the image of Downtown High School. She and other students were taking their school back from the negative media messages and oppressive measures of administrators and police. Gabriela felt that students should have the power. She argued, "I believe it's best that students take action rather than teachers always coming into classes and scolding, judging students, and pointing fingers at them, and in the end they start believing they got no future and what is worse is they want no future. What people don't know is that with just a little hope and motivation they will get up and start dreaming again and believing they are worth something, and can be something despite that many believe they can't and won't." In this statement, Gabriela points out that students can motivate each other, counter the negative perspectives of teachers, and reinstill a belief in each other that they are strong, capable people with much to offer this world.

In an effort to advertise messages of peace, the students of the leadership class created and mounted posters all over campus advertising phrases such as "Stop the Racism," "Stop the Violence," and "Black and Brown Unity." Much of the conflict occurred during lunchtime, so the leadership class collaborated with the school staff to play music during lunches to transform idle time into positive energy. With concern that their classmates were losing sight of shared racial and class struggles, the leadership students put together a symposium with poetry and speeches, as well as an assembly where black and Latina/o students performed dances together. They also went into classrooms and facilitated team-building activities to build community and invited Los Angeles–based community activists as guest speakers to discuss shared history. This weeklong effort was meant to break cycles of anger and conflict and was constructed as a reminder to students of black and Latina/o bonds that exist in Los Angeles, in the neighborhood, and on campus.

The students of Downtown High School responded positively to these efforts, and the campaign helped to ease much of the tension on campus. Although the week was very successful, many students felt that it should be an ongoing effort. Gabriela commented that the administration now relies on the leadership class when they start to sense conflict on campus. She

Peace Week campaign. Reproduced by permission of Jose Lara.

explained: "We need to continue to do stuff like [Peace Week], because even administrators know that that week helped bring tensions down. 'Cause even when they hear stuff, or they get little messages from people saying that something's about to start again and then they ask us to put on a rally or something, so that at lunchtime there wouldn't be tension or anything like that." As these student leaders develop positive and innovative methods to respond to fighting on their campus, they also begin to replace the oppressive tactics of the administration and gain media attention that challenges stereotypes of black and Latina/o youth. These black and brown students have redirected our attention from the symptoms to the disease. In an effort to foster unity, they have begun to challenge the system of racism that keeps People of Color divided.

LEARNING FROM YOUTH

History is filled with examples of youth leading in the struggle for racial justice. For instance, in the spring of 1951, African American students were forbidden to attend the same schools as whites in Virginia because of laws requiring or permitting segregation according to race. As a result, black students at Moton High School in Farmville, Virginia, went on strike in protest of the segregated, inferior, and overcrowded facilities at their school. In addition, they protested the fact that African American teachers were paid less than white teachers. The students and their parents, with the help of the NAACP, filed a lawsuit titled *Davis v. the School Board of Prince Edward County* in federal district court. This lawsuit was to become one of the five cases brought to the U.S. Supreme Court consolidated under the *Brown v. Board of Education* case (347 U.S. 483 [1954]). Fast-forward to the spring of 1968 in East Los Angeles, California. Students at Lincoln, Garfield, and Roosevelt high schools organized walkouts and boycotts to protest the inferior facilities and lack of a multicultural curriculum at their schools. These two events, seventeen years apart, speak to the power of youth to understand, analyze, and take action against inadequate and unequal education.

Fast-forward again to the spring of 2006, and again we see high school students engaged in civil disobedience and civic engagement to protest similar issues of educational inequality, as well as how it is manifested across black and brown racial lines. In this chapter, we examined student activism at Downtown High School as an example of resistance to structural forms of racism and attempted to answer two questions: What are the underlying causes (the disease) of the conflict (symptoms) between Students of Color? How do Students of Color intervene in this process and work toward interracial solidarity? We feel that through highlighting the experiences of these Youth of Color, the answers to these questions begin to emerge.

There is much to be learned from the students at Downtown High School and the teachers who gave them space to critically think and act on their beliefs. Gabriela shared an essay with her classmates that leaves us with a powerful message: "To make a difference will cost tons and tons of effort but if you remain standing nothing will knock you down. . . . I'm not going to make a change in a day or two; but little by little things start to change, brains start to think, and people stop being blind." Following in the footsteps of many great activists, these students crossed racial boundaries to challenge stereotypes and resist oppressive structures. Recognizing the shared history and struggle of black and brown people, the students who constructed Peace Week in the face of lockdowns and police presence were very brave. They remind us, as People of Color, that racism is not theirs. It is a part of larger institutionalized structures that are imposed on and work to divide them. We must learn the lesson(s) from these important activist youth. If we are going to successfully combat the disease of racism, we must do it collectively and in racial solidarity.

NOTES

A special thanks to the inspirational students of Downtown High School: Brandon, Gabriela, Laquanza, and Maria, as well as their teacher Mr. L. Another special thanks to John Lynch and Laura Telles for their insight and continued support of our work.

1. "People of Color" references individuals of indigenous, African, Latina/o, and Asian/Pacific Islander descent. It is intentionally capitalized to reject the standard grammatical norm. Capitalization is used as a means to empower this group and represents a grammatical move toward social and racial justice. This rule will also apply to the terms "Communities of Color" and "Students of Color," used throughout this chapter.

2. We put the term "racist" in quotes because are trying to emphasize the concept that People of Color cannot be racist.

3. Borrowing from the work of Max Weber (1922), Caroline Hodges Percell (1990), and David Jary and Julia Jary (1991), we define "power" as the reproductive or transformational capacity of institutional social structures (along with individuals or groups within those structure) to directly or indirectly control or influence the behavior of others even in the face of opposition.

4. We use the term "white" to refer to people principally of European origin who belong to the dominant group in the United States.

5. An ideology is a set of beliefs that explain or justify some actual or potential social arrangement.

6. See the Louisville (*Meredith v. Jefferson County Board of Education*) and Seattle (*Parents Involved in Community Schools v. Seattle School District No. 1*) cases in the 2006–7 term of the Supreme Court on the voluntary use of race in the selection of students in public school programs.

7. Writing is a form of speech, and because saying racial slurs can create a great deal of pain, we chose to add asterisks rather than write the words out. This is meant to honor and respect those whom the words are meant to disrespect.

8. In a student-made documentary called *Power and Pedagogy to the People*, Crenshaw High School senior Aida defines a lockdown. A lockdown on a high school campus is when police presence dominates the school. Students are forced to stay in one classroom throughout the duration of the lockdown and are not allowed to leave for any reason. If a student needs to use the restroom, the student must be personally escorted by a police officer (Institute for Democracy, Equity, and Access 2004).

9. The name of the school has been changed, teachers' names have been abbreviated, and only first names have been used for students. These changes were made for anonymity, to protect the identity of both the teachers and the students.

REFERENCES

California Department of Education. 2005–6. http://data1.cde.ca.gov/dataquest/.

Carter, R. 1968. "The Warren Court and Desegregation." *Michigan Law Review* 67: 237–48.

———. 1988. "1988 Survey of Books Relating to the Law: The NAACP's Legal Strategy Against Legal Segregation, 1925–1950." *Michigan Law Review* 86: 1083–95.

DiMassa, C. 2005. "Dozens of Police Officers Patrol Jefferson High After Race Brawl." April 20. http://www.latimes.com.

DiMassa, C., and N. Shields. 2005. "Security Tight at Jefferson High." April 19. http://www.latimes.com.

Grillo, T., and S. Wildman. 1997. "Obscuring the Importance of Race: The Implications of Making Comparisons Between Racism and Sexism (or Other Isms)." In *Critical White Studies: Looking Behind the Mirror,* edited by Richard Delgado and Jean Stefancic, 619–26. Philadelphia: Temple University Press.

Hear and Now. 2004. WBUR Boston Public Radio (90.9 FM), National Public Radio. Broadcast May 14. "Interview with Judge Robert L. Carter."

hooks, b. 1989. "Overcoming White Supremacy: A Comment." In *Talking Back: Thinking Feminist, Thinking Black,* edited by b. hooks, 112–19. Boston: South End Press.

Huber, Lindsay Perez, Corina Benavides Lopez, Maria C. Malagon, Veronica Velez, and Daniel G. Solórzano. 2008. "Getting Beyond the 'Symptom,' Acknowledging the 'Disease': Theorizing Racist Nativism." *Contemporary Justice Review* 11, no. 1: 39–51.

Institute for Democracy, Equity, and Access. 2004. "Crenshaw: Power and Pedagogy to the People." Summer Seminar.

Jary, David, and Julia Jary. 1991. *The Harper Collins Dictionary of Sociology.* New York: Harper Collins.

Lorde, A. 1992. "Age, Race, Class, and Sex: Women Redefining Difference." In *Race, Class, and Gender: An Anthology,* edited by M. Anderson and P. Hill Collins, 495–502. Belmont, Calif.: Wadsworth.

Marable, M. 1992. *Black America.* Westfield, N.J.: Open Media.

Memmi, A. 1968. "Attempt at a Definition." In *Dominated Man: Notes Toward a Portrait,* edited by A. Memmi. New York: Orion Press.

Meredith v. Jefferson County Board of Education. 2006. Oral Argument (05-915) before the U.S. Supreme Court on December 4, 2006.

Oakes, J., J. Rogers, and D. Silver. 2004. *Separate and Unequal 50 Years After "Brown": California's Racial "Opportunity Gap."* Report published by UCLA/IDEA Institute for Democracy, Education, and Access.

Orfield, G., and C. Lee. 2005. "Why Segregation Matters." *Poverty and Educational Inequality:* 1–47.

Parents Involved in Community Schools v. Seattle School District No. 1. 2006. Oral Argument (05-908) before the U.S. Supreme Court on December 4, 2006.

Percell, Caroline Hodges. 1990. *Understanding Society: An Introduction to Sociology.* 3rd ed. New York: Harper and Row.

Shields, N., and R. Lin II. 2005. "Another Brawl at Jefferson High School." May 27. http://www.latimes.com.

Sipchen, B. 2006. "Ex-Cop Walks a Tough Beat." November 13. http://www.latimes.com.

Solórzano, D. G., and D. Delgado Bernal. 2001. "Examining Transformational Resistance Through a Critical Race and LatCrit Theory Framework: Chicana and Chicano Students in an Urban Context." *Urban Education* 36, no. 3: 308–42.

Solórzano, D., and V. Velez. 2007. *Educating Students in a Changing Social, Economic, and Historical Landscape: A Visual Sociology Analysis.* Los Angeles: University of California, Los Angeles, Graduate School of Education and Information Studies.

Weber, Max. 1922. *Economy and Society: An Outline of Interpretive Sociology.* New York: Bedminster Press.

CHAPTER 6

Educational Justice and Access

XICO GONZÁLEZ

ERACLEO GUEVARA

ALEJO PADILLA

MARIANNA RIVERA

The initial intent of this chapter was to describe the implementation process of a Chicana/o Saturday school in the Greater Sacramento region located in northern California. The goal was to explore the reasons Chicana/o educators started the Saturday school and how they perceived their roles with Raza students in relation to their political ideologies and the pedagogy they practiced. In particular, this chapter was intended to answer the following questions: Are there benefits for Chicana/o educators and students to being integrated in an America-centered curriculum or school?[1] Can this integration foster an opportunity for Chicana/o teachers to provide an equitable and accessible education? Would an equitable and accessible education counter systemic institutionalized racism and provide Chicana/o students with the academic and social and political tools to maneuver the system? Interestingly, however, in the process of writing this piece, what ultimately surfaced was that this chapter was more about the pedagogical and philosophical evolution of the teachers involved with the Saturday school. Thus, we will describe the path taken to start La Academia del Barrio and also the process of reflection and practice (Freire 1970) the teachers undertook while teaching at the Saturday school.

GRUPO RAZA SCHOOL

In September 2001 a group of parents, students, community activists, and educators decided to form Grupo Raza School (GRS), a nonprofit organization that would address the K–12 academic achievement crisis facing the Raza community within the public education system and postsecondary level.[2] One avenue taken to address the stated purpose was the development of a Saturday school, La Academia del Barrio, started on January 27, 2006. It was believed that a Saturday school could make a substantive contribution to the Raza community by providing new knowledge, instilling pride, teaching leadership skills, promoting academic excellence, and developing community connectivity. Instruction would be delivered by local high school teachers and community members who shared similar cultural values and could relate to students. La Academia del Barrio would be all-encompassing and adhere to a collective democratic structure consisting of parents, students, teachers, and community members accountable to one another. Last, through the Saturday school Raza students could experience a thought process in which they would create "knowledge which is used to create and re-create reality" (Collins 2000, 212). This process would allow them to situate and recognize their historical place in U.S. schools and challenge the inequities and racism they encountered on a daily basis.

THEORETICAL RATIONALE

The Chicana/o educators involved with the implementation of the Saturday school viewed "education as the practice of freedom" (Freire 1970, 62). As a result, they felt a responsibility to incorporate perspectives on power, politics, history, and culture in relation to the school realities faced by Raza students. The integration of multiple "lenses" would help counter traditional methods of instruction in local K–12 schools.

How do these traditional methods of instruction manifest themselves in K–12 classrooms? The U.S. educational system consists of a process that perpetuates confusion, displacement, and ultimately the subordination of Raza students and other marginalized children. Historically, and in general, what Freire (1970) called a banking method was adopted. In this view of instruction teachers see themselves as the depositors of knowledge and students as empty receptacles. Teachers take on the role of all-knowing and do not acknowledge the experiences Raza students bring to school. Through this banking method, teachers fill the minds of Raza students with information that they consider to be acceptable and valid knowledge. Due to the imposed Eurocentric curriculum and disenfranchisement experienced in traditional U.S. schools, Raza students are co-opted to take on a false consciousness (Freire 1970) or a false view of their educational reality in the context of the larger society. As a result, Raza students may not question injustices or inequalities they experience as individuals or as a community. Thus, it is then important to consider who is teaching Raza students and how they are being taught.

Chicana/o Teachers: "Bridging Identity"

Various studies (Darder 1993; Galindo 1996; Weisman 2001; Berta-Ávila 2004) have shown that a major factor that influences the educational experiences of Raza students is the teachers with whom they come into contact. Carr and Klassen (1997), Gordon (2000), Southern Education Foundation (2001), Berta-Ávila (2004), and Montaño and Burstein (2006) all suggest that teachers of color play a key role in dismantling the misinformation and fear that hinder the progress of students of color. Studies suggest that students of color perceive teachers of their own ethnicities as role models, which demonstrates that teachers of color can hold roles of authority and influence (Carr and Klassen 1997; Gursky 2002; Jacullo-Noto 1991; Solomon 1997). Studies conducted by Ladson-Billings (1994), Delpit (1995), Solomon (1997), and Berta-Ávila (2004) reiterate that the ethnicity of a teacher is strongly associated with his or her personal expectations for the students with the same ethnic background. As a result, students of color feel a stronger sense of commitment to education and may be more likely to continue with school because of the support and affirmation received (Southern Education Foundation 2001; Wilder 2000).

Galindo (1996) and Montaño and Burstein (2006) believe that forging a link between the experiences of language, culture, and ethnicity and their role as Chicana/o teachers in the classroom can reinforce the concept of "bridging identity." Galindo, in particular, defines "bridging identity" as a type of identity that makes the connection between past biographical experiences with one's occupational role. With respect to Chicana/o teachers, this term specifically "highlights how past biographical identities contribute to the way that Chicana teachers define their professional role in light of their cultural minority background" (1996, 85).

For many teachers of color, their own educational experiences did reflect the social, historical, political, and economic struggles confronted in their communities. Castillo writes that as a Latina growing up, experiencing discrimination and racism due to the color of her skin and the language she spoke influenced how she saw her role as a teacher and the types of relationships she wanted to foster with her students. She states, "My experiences of being marginalized motivated me to search out for a more just and equitable system where those of us who spoke a different language or who looked different could be respected" (2002, 152). For Castillo, this meant counteracting the dominant educational views that oppress language and culture and take away the rights of Raza students.

THEORETICAL FRAME

To provide a direction, Academia del Barrio was grounded on the theory of "conscientization" as defined by Paulo Friere and followers with tenets of critical pedagogy as theoretical frameworks to comprehend the role, relationships, and approaches of Chicana/o educators when working with Raza students.

Conscientization

Paulo Friere (1970) describes "conscientization" as a process that encompasses the naming, reflecting, and acting upon of one's reality to create transformation. The process of action and reflection generates praxis from which to ground oneself. Wink interprets conscientization as having confidence in one's own knowledge, ability, and experiences (1997, 26). Hooks (1994) translates the term to mean critical awareness and engagement (1994, 14). In the context of teachers' realities in the classroom, Wink (1997) states that conscientization is the validation of one's reality, and it is having the voice to question one's own paradigms and the paradigms of institutions that are not just. Hence, in education the process of conscientization seeks the practice of freedom (Hooks 1994).

Transformational Resistance

Identifying as a Chicana/o falls within the tenets of conscientization, because those individuals also seek the physical, mental, spiritual, and material liberation of their communities. To be in a state of conscientization or to identify politically as a Chicana/o is to consciously resist the hegemonic system that is oppressive.[3] As a result, when Chicanas/Chicanos become educators, teaching becomes a political act. When hooks accounts for her experiences in education during the periods of segregation, she recalls African American educators addressing their needs as students from a similar political stance. As hooks states, for African American teachers, educating their students was deeply rooted in an antiracist struggle (1994, 2).

Critical Pedagogy

According to the work of Paulo Freire, critical pedagogy is a framework espousing an environment that fosters a problem-posing education. Hence, it is a type of learning that views "education as the practice of freedom" (1970, 62) that, in turn, consciously challenges traditional perspectives that affect directly the education of children of color (Darder 1991). Consequently, then, the role of the teacher is not just to teach to the text but to incorporate issues of power, politics, history, and culture into the lived experiences of the students (Darder 1991; Wink 1997). This alternative role ultimately fosters a setting in which teacher and student can dialogue and reflect with one another in order to create a voice leading toward transformation. For educators who view their practice in this manner, there is an unstated understanding that their work is political and geared toward equity and social justice.

A BRIEF HISTORY

In 1996 the Zapatista Solidarity Coalition (zsc) in Sacramento, along with other activists from the United States, met with the Mexican Zapatista leadership to discuss the educational, economic development, and health-care needs of the indigenous Zapatista communities. One long-term goal was the development of educational systems that would instruct and train educational promoters (*promotores de la educación*), who in turn would provide training in their communities to establish autonomous school structures. Key principles grounding the work were the concepts of autonomy and respect for indigenous culture and language.

Almost immediately, the zsc organized fund-raisers to specifically assist the Zapatistas with the building of classrooms for a school construction project called Schools for Chiapas. The zsc sold miniature Zapatista dolls to supporters and quickly raised two thousand dollars for the estimated cost of a classroom in a small town called Oventic. Over the years, the zsc continued to raise funds and gather supplies for the schools under construction.

The ZSC visited the project and encouraged others from the Sacramento area to volunteer on the construction of several schools.

However, approximately between 1998 and 1999, the ZSC was encouraged by the Zapatista leadership to focus on organizing their own centers of resistance (schools) and not so much on raising funds for the Chiapas project. At that time, one of the members of the ZSC was a student recruiter for a local university and had children who were impacted by the lack of access in the public school system in Sacramento. Motivated by the advice of the Mexican Zapatista leadership, she pushed for the ZSC to make the education of local Sacramento Raza youth a priority. Driven by a Zapatista vision of creating an autonomous educational system, a group of local Sacramento Raza community members and educators came together and created an organization to address the educational needs of their community; thus, Grupo Raza School was born.

Beginning Steps

With the inception of the GRS, meetings were held to determine the mission, goals, and next steps of the organization. A prominent figure involved in this process was Dr. Adaljiza Sosa-Riddell, professor emerita from the University of California at Davis. She played a leadership role in guiding the work of the GRS and pushed the organization to obtain nonprofit status in order to submit proposals for prospective funding to institutions such as the National Council of La Raza.

Initially, for about two years, the efforts of the GRS focused on writing grants and proposals that would assist in establishing a charter school and developing curricula from an America-centered perspective. With no real success in receiving extended funding, an opportunity emerged in the spring of 2005 to work in collaboration with a faculty member from a local community college. Gabriel Torres, of Consumes River College (CRC), was interested in offering an Introduction to Chicana/o Studies course that high school students could take for credit. To prepare for the course, GRS members met with Gabriel to codevelop the curriculum (curriculum development assistance was offered by Dr. Margarita Berta-Ávila, an associate professor at Sacramento State University as well).

The administration of the CRC and the GRS decided to offer the course on Saturdays in order to make it possible for high school students to attend.

Students were recruited from surrounding local high schools in Sacramento. In addition, because the course was offered at the CRC, CRC students could also register. Fourteen high school students completed the course that spring. Discussions took place to negotiate the possibility of continuing to teach a Chicana/o studies course on Saturdays at the CRC for the following fall semester. However, several policies were in place such as minimum GPA (3.0) and age requirements (students had to be sixteen or older) that inhibited many high school students from taking the course. Initially, the latter stipulations were not an issue because the CRC supported the efforts of the GRS and saw this school as an opportunity to reach out to the local community. Because the course received positive feedback from the students who participated, the GRS decided to forge its own efforts and develop a Saturday class or school in which policies found at the CRC would not discourage Raza students from taking classes with a Chicana/o focus.

INFRASTRUCTURE OF LA ACADEMIA DEL BARRIO

The Saturday Chicana/o studies course at the CRC offered GRS members concrete experiences from which to build. Specifically, members learned and agreed that credentialed secondary teachers with a background in teaching methods and who were aligned with the goals of the GRS should be recruited to assist in the development of a Saturday Chicana/o school, the location of the Saturday school should be in the students' community, and publicity and recruitment should focus on local high schools in the Sacramento region.

In the spring of 2005, the Bilingual/Multicultural Education Department at Sacramento State University graduated several Chicana/o educators (*maestras/os* as they called themselves) who expressed interest in working with the GRS to implement the Saturday school.[4] The maestras/os had graduated with California single-subject credentials in various areas of discipline such as Spanish, science, and social science. One exception was the teacher of art, who at the time was attending a masters of fine arts program at the University of California at Davis. With maestras/os willing to participate, the work began in the fall of 2005 with respect to finding a location and publicizing the school. Immediately, GRS members and teachers brainstormed about space that could be utilized for free and would be central to the schools from which students were being recruited. Through a personal connection, one of the maestras/os secured use of the "Sol Collective" (a local art community center). The space was adequate and would facilitate holding two classes simultaneously. Due to space limitation in the art center, the maestras/os capped enrollment at twenty students. GRS members and maestras/os began to recruit. They attended local youth conferences, recruited from the high schools they were teaching in, and advertised through Raza community Listserves.

Spring 2006: First Semester (January–May)

For the first semester of implementation (spring 2006), approximately fifteen to twenty students were recruited from local high schools in the Sacramento region. This small number was seen as necessary for two reasons: first, as mentioned, space limitations; second, the small number facilitated the opportunity to reflect thoroughly on specific aspects of instruction and the needs of the students. It was also decided that students would meet for fifteen to sixteen weeks every Saturday morning for three hours. Within the allotted time, four courses would be offered to the students: Spanish, Chicana/o art, Chicana/o history, and science. The courses, however, would be clustered in twos and taught every other weekend. For example, Spanish and Chicana/o art would be taught on the same Saturday, each for an hour and a half. The following Saturday Chicana/o history and science would be taught. The Saturday offerings would alternate between these two clusters.

The maestras/os would be present for each Saturday to offer support and consistency for one another and the students. Therefore, on the Saturday that two of the four maestras/os were not teaching, they would act as instructional assistants to facilitate group discussions or attend to individual student needs. To be responsive, reflective, and authentic to the interests and concerns of students, all maestras/os would stay after each Saturday session to assess and reflect on the instruction and identify curricular modifications for the following Saturday session.

Curriculum

The maestras/os articulated with one another to ensure that the syllabi aligned with respect to common instructional themes and projects to be addressed. Common themes the maestras/os identified (identity, struggle, resistance, and so on) would support and allow them to make concrete connections among courses. Although much preparation went into the development of the courses, the maestras/os were clear that the curriculum had to be dynamic and flexible. Thus, syllabi were subject to change each Saturday. Syllabi were developed for the purpose of structure, scope, and sequence. The input of students and what they wanted to learn played a major role in what was taught and how students engaged with the content and one another. Integrated within the curriculum were opportunities for students to participate in youth conferences, cultural events, and rallies and demonstrations related to issues of equity and justice such as immigration and labor rights. This was done to enhance the in-class instruction with "real-world" social-action activities.

Fall 2006: Second Semester (September–December)

Much was learned after the Academia del Barrio's first semester. Most important, all involved experienced the possibility of fostering an environment that respects and encourages the voices and opinions of students and maestras/os simultaneously. In other words, everyone is a maestra/o as much as they are students. In addition, maestras/os learned that it is possible to have a rigorous academic environment that is meaningful and relevant to students.

However, with gains also come lessons learned. Toward the end of the first semester, changes were made that the maestras/os and students wanted to implement for the second semester. For example:

1. Returning students had leadership roles among their peers and served as peer mentors during Saturday school sessions.

2. Interested students participated directly in the development of the curriculum similar to the previous semester.

3. Courses were offered every Saturday and not every other Saturday. Students as well as maestras/os believed it would build consistency with the curricular content.

4. The curriculum continued to be based on the lived experiences and relevant issues of student participants.

During the second semester student numbers remained consistent, yet they never grew beyond eight to ten each Saturday. Thus, if there were days that one or two students missed, it made dialogue and planned lessons difficult to implement. All students attended La Academia del Barrio on a volunteer basis. As a result, the question was posed as to whether students attending felt committed since there was no extrinsic incentive such as receiving high school credit. Another major concern during the second semester was the energy level of the teachers. The maestras/os found ways to assist each other on Saturdays, but it became difficult when all were not available to attend and offer assistance every Saturday. Therefore, a major discussion point was how a support system could be implemented so that the maestras/os would not burn out.

With these concerns in mind and as the second semester ended, the maestras/os contemplated whether there was a need to take a semester off to refresh themselves. Through the process of dialogue and reflection the maestras/os arrived at a consensus: the work could not take a break. But what could be done was to change the format of the sessions:

1. Saturday sessions would be held once a month in different Sacramento locations. Many students wanted to attend the Saturday school but did not have transportation.

2. Students would be encouraged to attend instructional sessions at different sites. The hope was that La Academia del Barrio would gain a reputation and enough student support to eventually return to weekly Saturday sessions.

3. As before, Saturday sessions would focus on specific topics related to the Chicana/o experience past, present, and future. This context would be delivered through the mediums of art, literature, history, and the Spanish language.

THE MAESTRAS/OS

As new teachers experiencing their first year in the field, the Saturday school became a space where the maestras/os could reflect on and challenge their own practices. The three hours spent together every Saturday were an opportunity to collaborate and dialogue with like-minded individuals who also viewed education as a vehicle for justice and educational equity. These maestras/os made a conscious effort not to get overwhelmed by the culture of the high schools where they taught, places they felt perpetuated low expectations and inequity toward marginalized communities. Thus, the

Saturday school became a reality check. Maestro Alejo spoke to this marginalization directly when he shared his views on how Raza and African American students at his school were denied access to their own history:

> I was sitting in a curriculum collaboration meeting with six other social science teachers, and the topic of the meeting was how we could make instructional time more efficient the following year. The discussion led with a teacher recommending that the African unit was not necessary. This teacher believed that if "not taught, it would not affect the continuity of the instructional units that are required by the state social science standards." The social science department chair, agreeing with this recommendation, asked every social science teacher if they agreed.
>
> The social studies department chair proceeded to ask the department to look at the instructional calendar to make further cuts in the units presented for the upcoming year. One teacher looked at the calendar and recommended that the ancient American civilization unit also be eliminated: "This unit can be taken out of the calendar because we teach it at the end of the year after the California state standardized exams. Therefore, the students are not accountable for this unit."
>
> I was absolutely flabbergasted at these recommendations, because with this meeting the social science department had just eliminated Africa and Latin America, two very large continents filled with billions of people and highly civilized societies, from the following year's instructional calendar. . . . It is absolutely frustrating as a new teacher to be idealistic and not teaching with like-minded teachers. Take note that these decisions were made at a school whose demographics consist of 80 to 90 percent Latin American students.

In his example, Maestro Alejo illustrated how easily Raza students can be disregarded. As a first-year teacher, he did not feel safe to share his counteropinion. Though the Saturday school's primary goal was to offer an enriching program to Raza students, it also became a training ground for new maestras/os entering the education field. They took every opportunity possible to ask each other for advice and strategies to address issues of equity at their respective school sites. Indirectly, these maestras/os developed a support system that at the same time allowed them to learn and implement the necessary tools to challenge inequities. As Maestro Alejo stated: "It is fulfilling and satisfying to teach at the Saturday school. Teaching with like-minded professionals, I do not feel like an outsider. I can freely express my opinions knowing that other teachers will not label me as radical or out of the norm."

In participating as a maestra/o, naming one's reality became prominent. For Maestro Eracleo it became clear that he felt torn between two worlds: a world that socialized him to believe that politics is not part of a student's education and the other that states that teaching is political and Raza students have a right to know this. The conflict Maestro Eracleo found himself in was one he might not have been able to identify if not involved with the Saturday school. Thus, he worked within himself to find that space where he felt confident to do the work needed to be done in the Saturday school and at his public school site. As Maestro Eracleo shares:

> We must be very careful, as we pick what material must be talked about in our daily lesson plan. There are many things going on around our world as we speak, and at times we are afraid that if we get caught up in talking about things that our kids have a different opinion as we do, we may get into trouble. But are we going to live our lives in fear? First, it was fear that *la migra* was in the barrio, and now it's fear that we talk about what our government is planning to do with us today. Are we in the land of the free? Who are we here in this land, the land where I was taught I had the freedom to speak out? Should I not teach about sweatshops in my class as I teach the different types of clothes and where they really come from? Should I not teach my kids who is really producing the clothes they wear? I feel it is very important to talk to my kids about these things. Talking to my kids about this gets the other kids thinking.

At the same time that the maestras/os personally gained from this experience, they also saw the benefits of La Academia del Barrio for the students. La Academia became an opportunity to dialogue about concepts and topics relevant and meaningful to the students. The time spent together became an opportunity to foster an environment with the students in which they gained skills to speak out, question, reflect, and act. Maestro Eracleo states:

In our school we teach our kids who they are and who they can be in life. In doing so, our kids have grown incredibly. We had kids that started off being shy and ended up demonstrating so much potential as leaders. [For example, during our Saturday sessions] we experienced this new bill that had many of us scared. We were able to talk to our students about what HR 4437 would do to our people and how we can do something about it right now. The kids that we saw as shy and quiet in the beginning broke out and participated in the marches holding signs up. They were willing to be out there chanting, asking for what we were all out there for: justice. These experiences led to many powerful discussions in class during our meetings.

Art also played a vital function in La Academia. Students were exposed to the history and role of art during the Chicana/o movement and how it came to life in the 1960s in the United States. For example, students learned how Chicanas/os engaged in reconnecting with their indigenous roots and their cultural past, and as a result came upon the art of Mesoamerican cultures through the Mexican muralists of the 1930s—Rivera, Orozco, and Siqueiros. This discovery led Chicanas/os to portray their history in barrios throughout the United States through murals and posters. Most important, students fostered the idea that art can share the message of one's community. Chicana artist Judy Baca states: "Chicano art comes from the creation of community. In a society that does not affirm your culture or your experience Chicano art is making visible our own reality, a particular reality—by doing so we become an irritant to the mainstream vision. We have a tradition of resisting being viewed as the other; an unwillingness to disappear" (1991, 21). Maestro Xico elaborates:

Art is a powerful tool in spreading the message of Chicanismo and self-determination to Chicana/o youth. Academia del Barrio students were exposed to Chicana/o art not only in a classroom setting but also in the real world. Academia del Barrio students were active participants in the fight for immigrants' rights as they marched and demonstrated against HR 4437, a bill in the Senate that proposes to make undocumented workers in the U.S. felons, as well as those that provide services to them. Academia del Barrio students were proudly holding posters made by the Brown Syndicate, a Sacramento Chicana/o artist collective that utilizes art to fight the system. Academia del Barrio students learned firsthand the importance of activism as a way to express themselves and as a way to engage in solidarity with undocumented and documented workers.

Chicana/o art encompasses visual arts, literature, poetry, culture, and history and more often than not comes alive through activism. Academia del Barrio students in their first semester were introduced to poetry in two different classes: Spanish and Chicana/o art. The instructors of both classes introduced students to the writings of Gloria Velásquez, José Antonio Burciaga, and Francisco X. Alarcón. They had the opportunity to meet and talk to Chicana poet Gloria Velásquez, author of *The Roosevelt Series* and *Xicana on the Run*. This experience was an eye-opener for GRS students and provided an opportunity to discuss culture, history, and politics through poetry.

Academia del Barrio began with four maestras/os and a vision to offer an alternative approach to learning for Raza high school students. However, when the fall 2006 Saturday sessions came to an end, what the four maestras/os had given with respect to time, planning, and teaching had been reciprocated many times over. The Academia experience helped the maestras/os gain skills in the areas of articulation, planning, collaboration, and organizing that ultimately taught them to be stronger advocates and activists at their own school sites. Overall, they became better teachers. A critical component that allowed the maestras/os to foster the latter skills was the act of reflection (Friere 1970).

THE ACT OF REFLECTION

The maestras/os understood they were starting something new with Academia del Barrio. Therefore, it was decided that a reflection component was needed after each Saturday session. Open discussions aided in analyzing what worked and what did not. These discussions were intended not to point out the flaws of each maestra's/o's teaching skills but rather to be a forum to improve the objective of educating and fostering strong Chicana/o students. A democratic process was implemented to facilitate the ideas and goals dialogued. Every maestra/o had an equal voice, all opinions were valid, and each opinion was evaluated and discussed. All decisions regarding the

Saturday school were implemented on the basis of consensus and transparency. As a result, the maestras/os developed strong and trusting relationships. The reflections became constructive and efficient. Moreover, an effort was made to integrate the ideas generated during the process of reflection with respect to curriculum and student engagement. Thus, every week lessons and instruction were revised to foster an environment in which Chicana/o students would feel motivated and inspired. The ultimate goal was that the lessons would create a situation in which the students would build on their knowledge and experiences and connect their lives to the concepts presented. For Maestro Alejo these reflection efforts came to life during one powerful moment in the fall 2006 semester:

> The lesson for the day was to discuss identity by analyzing stanzas from the poem *I Am Joaquin* by Corky Gonzales. The lesson began by students reading an assigned stanza. The class discussed the meaning of the stanza, as *la maestra* facilitated the discussion. Maestras/os began by sharing their experiences growing up as young Raza students and having an identity crisis. Halfway through the discussion, students started to participate. The students were sharing experiences that they thought were normal but in fact were examples of oppression. These experiences consisted of fellow students calling them derogatory names. The students began to realize through a collective dialogue that their experiences were oppressive.
>
> The moment the maestras/os had been waiting for presented itself with a particular female Raza student. The lightbulb of social enlightenment switched on, and the student opened up and began to analyze her experiences. She began by stating how her white friends would call her racist names. She related this experience to how she would act in her Spanish class. She admitted that she would pretend to not know how to speak Spanish by changing her Spanish accent to an exaggerated white accent. She realized that she was denying her identity, and the result was her losing part of who she was.
>
> This outcome would not have been possible without the maestras/os being able to reflect on the weekly lessons. This was also possible because we supported and respected one another.

The maestras/os received feedback from not only their peers but also their students. For many new teachers, this process might have been intimidating, but for them the feedback was critical to better serving the needs of the students in the Saturday school. Fostering an environment in which teachers' and students' voices were affirmed and acknowledged completely changed the dynamics of the teaching and learning process. They also came to understand that in working as a community (a *colectiva*—maestras/os, *estudiantes*, parents, and so forth), all are involved in teaching and learning from one another. Maestro Xico shares: "I am approaching Grupo Raza School as a community artist that is fulfilling his mission and purpose—the responsibility to transmit the knowledge that I have acquired from relatives, friends, elders, and through my studies to future generations."

Though all the maestras/os involved believed in the importance of this work, it was not until the students shared how they felt that everyone realized the influence the Saturday school was having. Natalia, a student, shared:

> Sitting through each class with students from different high schools in the Sacramento and Elk Grove districts on each side of me, who had also taken time out of their lives to come and be a part of this school, was incredible. You could see how passionate the teachers were about what they were teaching us. I'm not saying teachers at a regular school aren't passionate about what they do, but if you saw the way these teachers taught, you'd be able to see their love for the subject in their methods of teaching. They made sure we knew and were involved with who we really are. They were able to make the students as well as myself become more confident, more adventurous, and more open to trying new things.
>
> Before Academia del Barrio, I would have never imagined myself being a part of a march such as the Day Without an Immigrant march we participated in on May 1, 2006. I'd have to say, without Grupo Raza School and its wonderful people, I probably wouldn't be the person I am today. They opened a side of me I never thought I had. The time I spent at the Saturday school, as a high school senior, was a once-in-a-lifetime experience. At the beginning, we all entered this school with one goal—to be more informed and involved with our culture—and towards the end we met this goal, but at the same time became a family.

Since the last Saturday session in the fall of 2006 for Academia del Barrio, the maestras/os joined in the spring of 2007 other Chicana/o teachers in the region to form La Colectiva (The Collective). La Colectiva decided to stay under the umbrella of the GRS in order to utilize the nonprofit status for future projects.

Initially, the maestras/os met to plan for the spring '07 semester. However, they felt "burned out." This led to discussions about sustainability and the long-term mobility of La Academia. Though the maestras/os found comfort in knowing they could rely on one another and ask for help with respect to issues at the schools where they taught, it was not enough. They needed a space, outside of La Academia, that allowed them to refresh themselves and reflect critically on how they were going to keep moving forward as educators.

Keeping in mind that other Chicana/o teachers were most likely experiencing similar concerns with their own sustainability in the field, an invitation was made, to all those interested, to attend a meeting in May 2007. The objective of the meeting was to confirm, identify, and if needed establish a support group. Thus, La Colectiva was formed with the mission to serve as a support system with respect to specific issues confronted at local high school sites, help strategize plans of action with respect to specific issues and organizing efforts at school sites, organize joint events (such as marches, conferences, and social functions), and serve as a support system to foster sustainability and longevity. The group has been able to sustain itself for almost two years (spring 2007 to the present).

Finally, on a personal note, the experience of the Saturday school was an educational opportunity to learn how to organize and maintain one's spirit. La Colectiva is a result of maestras/os reaching out to one another and supporting individual struggles at schools with the Collective in mind. The maestras/os recognized that this work cannot be done alone and that they need a support group to maintain professional and personal balance and a long-standing commitment to issues of educational justice and access.

NOTES

1. An "America-centered curriculum or school" is a curriculum or school that has a focus on historical, political, economic, cultural, and social issues of the Ameri-

can continent. More specifically, the latter would focus on the experiences of Raza within the United States, Mexico, and Central and South Americas.

2. For the purpose of this study, "Raza" will be used to represent children with familial origins from Mexico, the Caribbean, and Central and South Americas. This term is preferred since it reflects a self-determination consistent with the identification of Chicana/o. "Raza" recognizes the indigenous lineage that exists on the American continent and in the Caribbean region.

3. As outlined by Darder, Baltodano, and Torres (2009), "hegemony" refers to a process of social control that is carried out through the moral and intellectual leadership of a dominant sociocultural class over subordinate groups.

4. *Maestras/os* is the Spanish translation for "teachers." However, in the context of La Academia del Barrio, "maestras/os" was how the teachers referred to one another. It also served as an act of endearment.

REFERENCES

Baca, J. 1991. "La Cultura Chicana: Voices in Dialogue." In *Chicano Art: Resistance and Affirmation, 1965–1985,* by Richard Griswold del Castillo, Teresa McKenna, and Yvonne Yarbro-Bejarano. Tucson: University of Arizona Press.

Berta-Ávila, M. I. 2004. "Conceptualizing Our Role: Reflections of Critical Xicana/Xicano Educators in the Classroom." Ph.D. diss., University of San Francisco.

Carr, P. R., and T. R. Klassen. 1997. "Different Perceptions of Race in Education: Racial Minority and White Teachers." *Canadian Journal of Education* 22: 67–81.

Castillo, G. M. 2002. "Teaching as the Practice of Freedom." In *Reinventing Paulo Freire: A Pedagogy of Love,* edited by A. Darder. Boulder: Westview Press.

Collins, D. 2000. *Paulo Freire: Una filosofía educative para nuestro tiempo.* Mexico City: Universidad La Salle.

Darder, A. 1991. *Culture and Power in the Classroom: A Critical Foundation for Bicultural Education.* Westport, Conn.: Bergin and Garvey.

———. 1993. "How Does the Culture of the Teacher Shape the Classroom Experience of Latino Students? The Unexamined Question in Critical Pedagogy." In *Handbook of Schooling in Urban America,* edited by S. Rothstein, 195–221. Westport, Conn.: Greenwood Press.

———. 1995. "Bicultural Identity and the Development of Voice: Twin Issues in the Struggle for Cultural and Linguistic Democracy." In *Reclaiming Our Voices: Bilingual Education, Critical Pedagogy, and Praxis,* edited by J. Frederickson, 35–52. Ontario, Calif.: California Association for Bilingual Education.

Darder, A., M. P. Baltodano, and R. D. Torres. 2009. "Critical Pedagogy: An Introduction." In *The Critical Pedagogy Reader,* edited by A. Darder, M. P. Baltodano, and R. D. Torres, 1–21. New York: Routledge.

Delpit, L. 1995. *Other People's Children: Cultural Conflict in the Classroom.* New York: New Press.

Espinoza-Herold, M. 2003. *Issues in Latino Education: Race, School Culture, and the Politics of Academic Success*. Boston: Pearson Education Group.

Freire, P. 1970. *Pedagogy of the Oppressed*. New York: Seabury Press.

Galindo, R. 1996. "Reframing the Past in the Present: Chicana Teacher Role Identity as a Bridging Identity." *Education and Urban Society* 29, no. 1: 85–102.

Gordon, J. A. 2000. *The Color of Teaching*. New York: Routledge/Falmer.

Gursky, D. 2002. "Recruiting Minority Teachers." *Education Digest* 67, no. 8: 28–34.

hooks, b. 1994. *Teaching to Transgress: Education as the Practice of Freedom*. New York: Routledge.

Jacullo-Noto, J. 1991. "Minority Recruitment in Teacher Education, Problems, and Possibilities." *Urban Education* 26: 214–30.

Ladson-Billings, G. 1994. *The Dreamkeepers: Successful Teachers of African American Children*. San Francisco: Jossey-Bass.

Montaño, T., and J. Burstein. 2006. "*Maestras, mujeres y mas:* Creating Teacher Networks for Resistance and Voice." *Journal of Latinos and Education* 5, no. 3: 169–88.

Solomon, R. P. 1997. "Race, Role Modeling, and Representation in Teacher Education and Teaching." *Canadian Journal of Education* 22: 395–410.

Southern Education Foundation. 2001. *Who Will Teach? The Color of Teaching*. Atlanta: Southern Education Foundation.

Weisman, F. M. 2001. "Bicultural Identity and Language Attitude Perspectives of Four Latina Teachers." *Urban Education* 36, no. 2: 204–25.

Wilder, M. 2000. "Increasing African American Teachers' Presence in American Schools: Voices of Students Who Care." *Urban Education* 35: 205–20.

Wink, J. 1997. *Critical Pedagogy: Notes From the Real World*. New York: Longman.

CHAPTER 7

The Las Vegas Activist Crew

ANITA TIJERINA REVILLA

EVELYN M. RANGEL-MEDINA

This research is a *multidimensional consciousness* analysis of the experiences lived by the immigrant rights activists of Las Vegas (see Covarrubias and Revilla 2003, 466). The focus of this study is im/migration status, but it also provides a critique of race, ethnicity, class, gender, phenotype, sexual orientation, age, and religious and spiritual orientation discrimination. This study is a *counterstory* that examines the collective experience of the Las Vegas Activist Crew, the desire of activists to create social change, and their ability to transform their communities.[1]

Undocumented im/migration is perhaps one of the most pressing dynamics of inequality in the United States and the world today; this issue is compounded by socioeconomic and political inequality. In the United States, the scope of this problem is federal, although it intersects at all levels of government. State and local entities grossly benefit from the exploitation of noncitizen populations, and they provide them with limited social services (primarily public education that is financed through property taxes paid by both undocumented and documented citizens). The "im/migration debate" is interwoven with racist and *citizenist* ideologies (defined below). At the core of the mainstream debate lies the impact that noncitizens have on this nation's economy, national identity, national security, and the changing racial and ethnic demographics of the U.S. population. What is overwhelmingly left out of this discourse, however, is the recognition of human, labor, educational, sociopolitical, and civil rights violations of a vulnerable population that ensure the economic sustenance of the world's hegemony. Sadly, this is a global reality.

CITIZENISM

Contemporary nation-states, immigration policies, and the socioeconomic and political marginalization of immigrants have created a global system founded on the subordination of noncitizens; we refer to this phenomenon as "citizenism." This term was coined during the course of this research, and it was developed through a communal production of knowledge by the authors. Broadly defined, citizenism is the ideological practice of inherent citizen superiority, the right to dominance of citizens over noncitizens, and a system of unearned advantages and privileges based on citizenship granted at birth. These systems discriminate, disenfranchise, exploit, dehumanize, and subordinate noncitizens living within mostly "developed" nation-states. Therefore, activist struggle begins with questioning the very legal foundations that relegate a marginalized existence to immigrant communities. Furthermore, we argue that the terms currently used to identify anti-immigrant discrimination, such as "nativism" and "xenophobia," do not adequately relay the ideologies used to attack and subordinate undocumented immigrants. For example, according to *Merriam-Webster's Dictionary*, nativism is "a policy of favoring native inhabitants as opposed to immigrants," and xenophobia is "a fear and hatred of strangers or foreigners." Clearly, nativism is a misnomer because "native born" can be confused with being native or indigenous to the land. Nativism is an ideology primarily espoused by U.S.-born people of European descent (that is, socially constructed "white" people) and is often used against Latina/o (and other nonwhite) immigrants, many of whom have indigenous ancestry to the Americas and the Southwest United States, such as Mexican-origin immigrants. Clearly, there is an irony that does not go uncontested when people who do not have indigenous ancestry are arguing their "native" right to the United States and are actively attempting to discriminate against people whose roots are native/indigenous to the Americas (north and south). The term "citizenism" is a rejection of white people's claim as "natives" of the United States, especially when used for the purpose of anti-immigrant or racist discrimination. In addition, xenophobia does not address the structural and institutional forms of discrimination experienced by immigrants. "Fear and hatred" of strangers or foreigners do not account for the systematic legal restrictions enforced upon immigrants by governmental, state, and local authorities, which lead to outright abusive and dehumanizing behaviors at both individual and institutional levels.

The U.S.-Mexico historical and contemporary immigration systems are an unfortunate example of citizenist systems. The United States has historically ensured the subordination of poor and "nonwhite" immigrants:

> U.S. history is full of attempts to exclude people who did not seem at the time to conform to the image of a "real American." And the treatment of immigrants has always been racialized. Over the years racial hierarchies have shifted and racial definitions changed as European immigrants gained status while Mexican and other Third World immigrants did not. Through a combination of straightforward exclusion, bureaucratic exceptions, and the creation of different mechanisms for entering the country, federal law expanded or reduced immigration based on labor needs, economic anxiety, war, and xenophobia. (Sen and Mamdouh 2008, 51–52)

Contemporarily, this is constructed under a racialized and dehumanized language of "illegality," which constructs an undocumented person as a "criminal Mexican." The majority of undocumented im/migrants in the United States emigrate from Mexico. The most recent study on undocumented im/migration estimates that "the majority of undocumented immigrants (59 percent) are from Mexico, numbering 7 million. Significant regional sources of [undocumented] immigrants include Asia (11 percent), Central America (11 percent), South America (7 percent), the Caribbean (4 percent) and the Middle East (less than 2 percent)" (Pew Hispanic Center 2010, 2). The United States has historically relied on exploited (immigrant and slave) labor to sustain its standard of living; therefore, it has enacted labor and immigration policies that ensure the continued exploitation necessary to maintain its economic foundations.

Once immigrants arrive in this country, they face a myriad of structures of domination that are part of its historical foundations (for example, racism, classism, sexism, heterosexism, environmental racism, and so forth), but their subordinate position is upheld through the social and legal construction of noncitizenship, or "illegality." Mexican elites also benefit from their migration in the form of remittances and the removal of a vast portion of its poor population that is forced to flee because of economic repression (also referred to as economic refugees). Remittances sent from immigrants from the United States are the second-largest component of Mexico's economy. Ultimately, the government benefits more from having people emigrate because the country's economy is stimulated and the government does not have to provide critical social services to this displaced population. The unequal treatment of noncitizens in the United States is justified through a criminalization of the undocumented person's labor migration, while citizens enjoy de jure civil rights and legal protections. This system is ineffective and shortsighted, much like the immigration policies created around the world. The argument of illegality is contested because immigration laws globally are unjust and irrational. We cannot continue this construction of illegality under the mantra of what is "right" and "wrong" when the premises of these laws are fundamentally inhumane and unrealistic. The idea behind citizenism is that those who are born with the right to inhabit a nation-state are entitled to more rights and protections than others. In effect, those who are not citizens (that is, undocumented people or asylum seekers) are paying taxes without representation or protection. Noncitizens are human beings with the same capabilities as citizens, and they come in all shapes, sizes, ages, genders, and sexual orientations and with a host of abilities and gifts.

THE IM/MIGRANT RIGHTS MOVEMENT

The global grassroots mobilization for im/migrant rights has brought about unprecedented events in the history of the United States. This movement is fomented by the citizenist repression of undocumented im/migrants. This movement continues to mobilize millions of people who are committed to eradicating injustice, through nonviolent strategies, and who ultimately aim to simultaneously transform this, and other intersecting, systems of discrimination. To some extent, this movement is attributed to a legislative backlash produced after the passage of HR 4437, the Border Protection, Antiterrorism, and Illegal Immigration Control Act of 2005—in the House of Representatives (with a vote of 239 to 182) on December 16, 2005. However, this peaceful uprising has deeply rooted historical and socioeconomic oppressive conditions that have led millions of people—primarily Latinas/s—to embark on a crusade for justice in the fight for human rights.[2]

Nevada is a southwestern state that has been described as "the Mississippi of the West" because of the historical segregation and racial segregation encountered throughout the state (Orleck 2005, 37–68). In Las Vegas, African American entertainers were banned from staying in hotels or patronizing casinos on the Las Vegas Strip formally into the 1950s and informally through the 1970s. Today, the legacy of this segregation remains evident on the historically African American west side of Las Vegas and has been transferred to the Latina/o and immigrant population residing primarily in North Las Vegas, but growing throughout the city. An early grassroots movement for welfare reform took place in 1971, when demonstrations organized by poor and predominantly black women were held on the Strip, especially inside the Caesar's Palace Hotel and Casino (Orleck 2005). Nevertheless, Las Vegas had never seen the extent of political mobilization that took place in 2006 as a result of the immigrant rights movement.

This local movement has been gradually growing over the last years, but its catalyst occurred on March 28, 2006, when the first citywide student walkout occurred. The height of this political mobilization is yet to be seen, yet the monumental march of May 1, 2006, will be marked in the history of this city as long as it stands, as it is estimated that eighty-five thousand people marched down the Las Vegas Strip on behalf of im/migrant rights (Pratt 2006).

Undoubtedly, Las Vegas has been changed and its political foundations have been steered in a new direction that was unforeseen by most. May 1 and most of the events leading up to it were organized and coordinated by the Las Vegas Activist Crew (hereinafter Activist Crew)—a loosely formed grassroots organization of student activists (of all educational levels) and community activists. Nationally, this grassroots initiative is present in all the major cities in this country. Locally, the power dynamics within the Latina/o community have been altered, with the Activist Crew providing a new political voice to this expanding community.

LITERATURE REVIEW

Utilizing the theoretical frameworks of Critical Race Theory (CRT), Latina/o Critical Theory (LatCrit), Chicana/Latina Feminist Theory/Epistemology, and Transformational Resistance Theory, this study provides a critical analysis of the lived experiences of the im/migrant rights activists and also critically examines the institutions (geopolitical, legal, governmental, and societal) that im/migrants confront and resist every day. All of these theoretical frameworks embrace social justice as an integral element of the research process.

The Activist Crew is a grassroots organization actively fighting for social justice in the predominantly conservative environment of Las Vegas. They are actively engaged in Activist Crew transformative leadership pedagogy where traditional notions of leadership and hierarchical frameworks are replaced with flat hierarchies. Embedded in this paradigm is the process of empowerment, transformative learning, action, and leadership development. Additionally, these activists engage in a mutual education of *conscientización* (consciousness raising) (Freire 1970). They produce grounded theories about social justice while simultaneously developing a critical consciousness. Activist Crew grounded theory is founded upon the lived experiences of youth and community activists in Las Vegas and is committed to the advancement of social justice.

Critical Race Theory

The fundamental vantage point of CRT is the centrality and intersection of race in the experience of human life, along with other intersecting positions based on class, gender, citizenship, sexual orientation, and others. Furthermore, Mari Matsuda defines CRT as "the work of progressive legal scholars of color who are attempting to develop a jurisprudence that accounts for the role of racism in American law and that work toward the elimination of racism as part of a larger goal of eliminating all forms of subordination" (Solórzano and Delgado Bernal 2001, 311). CRT, as a legal movement, challenges the dominant ideological notions of equality, color blindness, race neutrality, meritocracy, objectivity, and equality, as these are structural foundations of the institution of the law. The centrality of experiential knowledge—counterstorytelling by People of Color—is also a foundation of CRT. CRT sees the experiences of People of Color as legitimate, appropriate, and critical to understanding, analyzing, and fighting racial subordination.

Hence, controversial by the nature of its content, CRT aims to end the structural component of racism, at the same time acknowledging that racism "has never been a matter of negative attitudes but an institutionalized set of power relations" (Martínez 1998). It is this set of power relations in the law that must be examined and acknowledged in order to "fix" the injustice and oppressive lifestyles under which millions of people have lived. Another important goal of CRT is to "challenge ideologies of white supremacy and help break the oppressive bond between law and racial power" (Crenshaw et al. 1995, 20). Ultimately, the core values of CRT are justice, empowerment, and self-determination for People of Color who have been historically and systematically oppressed.

Also called into question are the mentalities People of Color have been operating under, which oftentimes are oppressive to themselves and other members of their racial and ethnic groups. CRT recognizes that People of Color can be oppressive to each other and embark on "Olympics of the oppressed," also called "oppression sweepstakes" (Martínez 1998; Moraga 2000). This behavior is the consequence of a mentality that traces its roots to colonization and slavery and continues to divide the necessary alliances of People of Color and all people who live under subordinating structures.

Latina/o Critical Race Theory

Latina/o Critical Race Theory was born in 1995 as an extension of CRT. It further examines the intersection of race with ethnicity, culture, language, nationality, color, religion, and citizenship to engage in analyses of Latina/o experiences. Henceforth, LatCrit contends that a black and white dichotomy is utilized to explain race relations and ethnicity. LatCrit focuses on the racism embedded in the historical mistreatment of Latinas/os and their communities. This type of racism against Latinas/os is implanted in immigration laws and internment camps; it is stolen land grants and silenced languages; it is invisibility and lost identity.

LatCrit is considered "outsider jurisprudence," which includes critical legal studies, feminist legal theory, critical race theory, critical race feminism, Asian American legal scholarship, and queer theory. There are two main objectives of LatCrit: "(1) to develop a critical, activist and inter-disciplinary discourse on law and policy towards Latinas/os, and (2) to foster both the development of coalitional theory and practice as well as the accessibility of this knowledge to agents of social and legal transformation" (Santiago Venator, Torres, and Valdes 2005, n.p.).

Oppositional behavior is classified under this theory as reactionary behavior, self-defeating behavior, conformist behavior, and transformational resistance. These categories are determined by the critical level of awareness of the systems of domination and the motivation to fight for social justice. This work focuses on the latter type of oppositional behavior and how activists of the immigrant rights movement fit within it. Daniel Solórzano and Dolores Delgado Bernal (2001) describe in detail the four types of resistance or oppositional behaviors. According to them, those who engage in reactionary behavior have little or no level of critical consciousness; they are not motivated for social justice and have no potential for emancipation. Self-defeating resistance possesses some level of awareness but is not motivated to fight for social justice. Conformist resistance, on the other hand, possesses the motivation to fight for self- or social transformation, yet there is a lack of a sophisticated critique of the systems of domination. Transformative resistance, unlike the aforementioned concepts, is characterized by external and internal behaviors, and it is both overt and subtle. There is a motivation to fight for social justice and a sophisticated critique of the systems of domination. Activist Crew grounded theory expands on this model by delving into the different forms of internal resistance and the levels of consciousness in which this resistance exists: consciously, spiritually, psychologically, emotionally, and physically. As indicated by one of the crew members, Neza, who was raised in Las Vegas and born in Durango, Mexico, "It is one thing to rebel psychologically and spiritually and a complete other thing to rebel physically."

The ideal of liberation, then, is essential for the Activist Crew. Particularly with the public demonstrations and the effects they have on the consciousness of the activists, the idea of liberation began expanding to reach new levels of consciousness and liberation through rebellion—a physical, spiritual, and psychological rebellion toward the institutions that have maintained the system of oppression.

Multidimensional Struggle and Consciousness

Covarrubias and Revilla write about the concept of a multidimensional consciousness, which "consists of a sophisticated critique of how multiple, intersecting structures of domination . . . interact with each other and impact one's social and political situation as part of a historical condition. Consciousness is understood as a fluid process within which those who are developing it will be at different levels at different times" (2003, 466). Hence, the intersections of race, class, gender, immigration status, sexual orientation, religious and spiritual orientation, age, and other discernible characteristics underlie the foundation of a multidimensional consciousness. Therefore, in order to defeat the structures of domination, there arises a multidimensional struggle to combat colorism, xenophobia, queerphobia, nativism, classism, sexism, ageism, citizenism, environmental racism, heterosexism, and racism. This is the internal and external struggle of the Activist Crew and its members.

RESEARCH METHODOLOGY

This research examines the activism that took place and shaped the im/migrant rights movement in Las Vegas. The study uses grounded theory, one-on-one interviews, participant action research, document examination, and analyses of daily interactions of the activists; moreover, this is grounded in our own activism and lived experiences as activist researchers. Hence, the study provides an in-depth look into activist and social justice circles that are typically unknown to academia.

We completed more than thirty semistructured interviews of Activist Crew members, which included students from all levels of formal education and community members. In the interviews, the activists discussed their experiences with im/migration, their political philosophies, and their motivations for being involved in this movement. Further, they delved into their definition of social justice and how this movement has changed their lives.

Participant observation was the primary research method utilized for this project. In conjunction with other activist researchers who have engaged in this form of research, we push to employ the concept advanced by Sandra Harding of "strong objectivity" (1992). Moreover, this project utilizes a Chicana feminist epistemology as outlined by Delgado Bernal (1998). It advances a further developed notion of objectivity, which is centered on fairness, honesty, and detachment and can be maximized when these elements are present. Consequently, this notion of "strong objectivity" examines the power dynamics of our society and how they are "exercised less visibly, less consciously, and *not on but through* the dominant institutional structures, priorities, practices, and languages of the sciences" (Harding 1992, 567). Thus, as members of several interlocking marginal groups in this society, we subscribe to the notion of relativism and to the challenge of objectivity.

By its very nature, CRT validates the experiences of People of Color, not as biased but as analytical tools to understand the dynamics and social injustice in U.S. society. Counterstory is a powerful and credible source of information of historically disempowered people(s); it is referred to as *counterstory* because it stands in opposition to the *majoritarian* story. The methods of *counterstorytelling* can take various forms, such as parables, family herstory or history, biographies, scenarios, chronicles, and narratives (Solórzano and Delgado Bernal 2001; Yosso 2006). We utilize the Critical Race Theory methodology of *counterstorytelling* to tell the story of Las Vegas activism.

WALKOUTS: *¡LA LUCHA SIGUE!* [THE STRUGGLE CONTINUES!] (1968–2006)

In March of [1968] . . . over 10,000 students walked out of the pre-dominately Chicana and Chicano high schools in East Los Angeles to protest the inferior quality of their education. For many years prior to the Walkouts, East Los Angeles community members made unsuc-cessful attempts to create change and improve the educational system through mainstream accepted channels. These formal requests went unanswered. The students received national attention and earned sup-port from numerous people and organizations both inside and outside of the East Los Angeles communities. (Solórzano and Delgado Bernal 2001, 308–9)

The 1960s are remembered in the American consciousness as tumultuous years of social upheaval, including the civil rights, LGBT, women's, American Indian, Black Power, Chicana/o, and Asian American movements. The Chicana/o movement transformed the image of the submissive "*Mexicana/o*" to one of an entire community united to fight against institutionalized discrimination. As articulated in the passage above, students led this movement as they provided a nontraditional grassroots model that gave them sufficient results. Moctesuma Esperanza, a student at the time, described the era in the following manner: "This was a time in which enough Chicano students had gained mastery of the tools that were necessary to shake up the system and had taken the ideals of the country to heart . . . and so we protested for our rights."[3]

Inspiration from the Past

Las Vegas youth were, in part, inspired by the 1968 high school walk-outs, as a recount of them was released in the HBO film *Reading. Writing. Revolution. Walkout: Based on the East L.A. Student Protests of 1968,* directed by Edward James Olmos. This film was released on March 25, 2006, and inspired not only Las Vegas youth but quite possibly youth throughout the United States. As students learned about various alternatives to change the circumstances they faced, they already held a deep understanding of the systems of discrimination that shaped their lives. A fifteen-year-old Rancho High School student articulated this point: "Although I'm not undocumented and was not brought to this country when I was young, I'm still very affected by the proposed immigration laws. Many people close to me are undocumented and limited to what they can achieve as it is so far. With these laws it would make it impossible for them to live out the American Dream. I participated in this march to show the obvious flaws that the proposed laws portray. . . . I've learned a lot by becoming involved" (Flores 2006).

Thus, largely motivated by the injustices the students faced, the Activist Crew concluded that peaceful civil disobedience would be an effective tool to advance their cause. On March 28 and March 31, there were two citywide student walkouts, the first of their kind in the history of the city, in which students from elementary, middle, and high schools walked out of school in unprecedented numbers and sparked the local immigrant rights movement. The students who participated in these events have seen firsthand the separation of their families, the future of their loved ones and themselves limited because they do not have a piece of paper—a legal permanent resident card or a birth certificate—that will allow them or their loved ones to live a life outside of the shadows and obtain a college education.

More important, the youth of Las Vegas are responsible for the awakening of this city toward grassroots political activism and the fight for social justice. Even though there had been a number of previous demonstrations that had taken place, the student walkouts were monumental to the immigrant rights movement. They began the transformation of Las Vegas, even without the initial support of the community; the students organized massive walkouts that are unprecedented in the city and local consciousness.

The Catalyst: Del Sol High School

It is important to point out that as the anti-immigrant sentiment fomented and entered the classrooms of Las Vegas, even before the nationwide actions, student mobilization and *conscientización* began. On March 16, 2006, the *Las Vegas Review-Journal* reported that approximately twenty students walked out of class after a teacher remarked to a group of Latina/o students, "Well, you guys are immigrants. You guys shouldn't even be here. I could get arrested if I teach immigrants [in reference to HR 4437], and you guys should be thankful that you're in school right now because you're immigrants" (Planas 2006).

Robert Gomez, a senior in the class who walked out, recalled this event when we met him during a march on April 1. We were deeply impressed by his *coraje* (anger) and willingness to speak out. He is representative of the rising consciousness and desire to see change from youth in Las Vegas and nationally.

These students were racially and ethnically profiled and automatically assumed to be im/migrants because they were Latina/o and were further ostracized for their perceived "illegal" status. Francisco Brieno, another student who walked out, "paraphrased his teacher's remarks: 'The illegal people come over here and get a free education. . . . You should be thankful you're in school.'" The students who walked out participated in acts of external and transformative resistance to voice their frustration. After the teacher "apologized," stating, "All I was trying to get across is that there are so many immigration laws that are not enforced," the principal, John Barlow, decided that she would not be reprimanded for the incident (Planas 2006).

However, this was not the first time that students at this school encountered racist conflict. As then cochair of El Movimiento Estudiantil Chicana/o de Aztlán (Movement of Chicana/o Students of Aztlán), known as MECHA de UNLV, Evelyn met with the principal of the school the week following the walkouts. At the meeting, the principal stated that there had been two incidents in which two black male students had been pepper-sprayed, and these incidents prompted the discrimination claims to arise. Consequently, the principal received a petition signed by fifty-nine students a month prior to the Del Sol High School walkout. This petition stated that the student either had been discriminated against or had witnessed some form of discrimination. Latina/o, black/African American, Asian/Pacific Islander, and white/Caucasian students signed the petition.

The principal further stated that most of the students who signed the petition, whom he talked to after the walkout, did not know what they were signing and that they felt as though they were happy at that school and were not experiencing discrimination. He believed that the majority of the students who signed the petition were those who "need attention," have bad grades, and have bad attendance records. After the walkout, the principal agreed to meet with the students and the community to discuss the issue. Very little came as result of these meetings. In fact, in 2007 the students tried to form a local high school chapter of MECHA, a Chicana/o student organization, and the students were denied and instead encouraged to create a multicultural organization for all students. The administration clearly missed the point on several occasions.

The students attempted different methods to call attention to their concerns, as did the students in 1968 in East Los Angeles. This particular situation exemplifies the paternalistic and dismissive attitude of the concerns presented by students of color. Del Sol High School is a microcosm of the institutionalized xenophobic undertone that is currently sweeping the United States. Hence, the student walkouts demonstrate the transformative resistance of these students as they hold a sophisticated critique of the oppressive conditions they live and the commitment to collectively fight for social justice. They took their struggle to the public and stormed the Las Vegas Strip. One student's poster message that particularly resonated with us read, "What Happened to No Child Left Behind?" The students were fundamentally critiquing the lack of access to education. Undocumented children compose approximately 16 percent (1.8 million) of the undocumented population in the United States. However, nationwide we have refused to aid these students in their quest for a higher education. Nevada, not being the exception to the rule, has considered extreme citizenist legislation for all im/migrant students. In 2006, Senate Bill 415 was introduced but not passed into law; it stated that "certain alien students are not eligible to receive certain types of financial assistance through the Nevada System of Higher Education" (Nevada Legislature 2009). Thus, when high school, middle school, college, and elementary school students decided to engage in a spiritual, psychological, and physical rebellion, they were not merely "troublemakers"; rather, they were conscious actors attempting to disassemble the segregation-based system of higher education for undocumented and low-income youth.

United We Stand, Divididos Caeremos! (United We Stand, Divided We Will Fall!)

After the walkouts, the Activist Crew created the *Students Stand Up! Newsletter* (edited by University of Nevada–Las Vegas [UNLV] undergraduate student Evelyn Flores). In response to their misrepresentation in the media, the students wrote:

Below is a list of points that led to the decision to walk out:
- We want to be heard, taken seriously, and recognized.
- We want to voice our opinion on the matter of immigration laws.
- We chose to Stand Up for our rights and those of our people who are ignored and silenced.
- We demand just laws, equal opportunity, and human dignity.
- We want it to be known that discrimination stems from fear of the unknown.
- We unite as one voice.
- We are setting stepping stones for our future children's education.
- We want to educate the youth and encourage peaceful demonstrations and student activism in our community. (Flores 2006)

This newsletter's purpose was to provide an avenue for students and community members to tell their stories, given that they never received an accurate representation of their struggle in the media. The youth faced a multidimensional struggle, including ageism, that is, discrimination based on their age. There was an overwhelming patronizing reaction throughout the community, Latina/o and otherwise, that treated the students as "ignorant," immature, and truants and further criminalized them.

Within the community, the students engaged in several meetings to discuss the issue. "Zapata," a community activist, who did not share the majoritarian and ageist sentiment, expressed the following, which summarizes the attitude toward the youth from the community: "[Hay] . . . personas que dicen que ustedes son unos niñitos que no saben lo que están haciendo . . . pero eso no es cierto, ustedes son el espiritu de este movimiento" (There are people who say that you guys are a bunch of little kids who do not know what they are doing, but this is not true. You all are the spirit of this movement).[4] The purported leaders of the Latina/o community failed to see the potential in uniting with the youth as equals in order to create a binding grassroots coalition. However, this does not include all the members of the community. There were some remarkable people whose support proved monumental.

MECHA de UNLV also proved instrumental in providing support to students during the second student walkout. After the first student walkout, student leaders from the university had lunch together. While eating *pupusas,* they tried to come to a consensus on how to proceed to support the youth and the im/migrant rights movement. Present at that meeting were students from the College of Southern Nevada (CSN), UNLV, MECHA de UNLV, Student Organization of Latinos (SOL), and League of United Latin American Citizens. At the meeting, the university students decided to support the second walkout the high school students were organizing for Friday, March 31, 2006. Contrary to media accusations, the students decided to wait three days until the end of their proficiency exams to walk out. They purposely made the decision so as to not jeopardize students' test scores on the proficiency exams, which are a requirement for graduation.

At the meeting, everyone agreed that no particular organization would take credit for helping the students and they would work together in coalition. Later that evening, in a phone conversation, the president and former president of SOL and the cochair of MECHA had a two-hour conversation in which the SOL members informed her that they would retreat from participating in the walkouts because they could be held "legally liable." They believed that supporting the walkouts would have a negative impact on their "future political careers." Two days later, SOL sent out a press release, stating the following:

> The Student Organization of Latinos (SOL) at the University of Nevada, Las Vegas, is asking its members and chapters to stay in the classrooms during the proposed student Walkouts.
>
> The mission of SOL is to promote higher education and the organization is encouraging its members to focus on the issues in an academic environment. SOL is asking its members to host debates and town hall forums at their respective schools.
>
> The Student Organization of Latinos is the oldest, student-based

Latino organization in the State of Nevada, established on the UNLV Campus in 1968. Currently, SOL has over 1,500 members and has chapters at the University, College and High School level with a combined total of 14 chapters. (Flores 2007, 1)

SOL was mistakenly given credit for organizing walkouts with the students (Lazos 2007). Unfortunately, the stance taken by SOL perpetuates a *majoritarian* narrative that wrongfully accuses students of not caring about their education if they walk out. This kind of narrative attempts to place students who choose not to exercise their right to protest as more committed to education than those who do. We argue, however, that is not the case. Furthermore, under the transformative resistance framework, not supporting the students' decision to walk out could be considered conformist resistance or self-defeating resistance (or both), because even though they had a critique of oppression (racism and citizenism) affecting students and were motivated for social justice, there may be a lack of a critical *multidimensional consciousness* that values all forms of transformative resistance. Furthermore, it is likely that ageism may be at play, as it is likely that the middle and high school students were not viewed as mature enough to make the decision of whether to walk out. Indeed, the fear about their careers being affected points to a conformist perspective rather than a transformative one that is critical of institutions and careers that maintain social injustice.

The elementary, middle school, and high school students proved to be the visionary leaders of the community when they decided to walk out again on Cesar Chavez Day (March 31, 2006), and they successfully and peacefully carried out the largest student walkout in the history/herstory of Las Vegas. In reference to the walkouts, Zapata stated, "Los estudiantes fueron la causa principal para que después las demás personas que se dieron cuenta que realmente esto iba enserio y que los estudiantes tenían razón entonces ya fue que las demás personas asistieron" (The students were the principal cause for the rest of the people to realize that this was going to happen for real and that the students were right all along was apparent. Then the rest of the people participated).

Feminist activist scholars Baumgardner and Richards write, "Superficially, high-school students are often seen as powerless. As minors, they can't vote and thus don't have the presumed value that comes with being a constituent.

. . . A more positive and accurate assessment of high-school students is that they are unique as social change-makers" (2005, 32). The students are not jaded, and they are connected to hundreds of other students—which is ideal for organizing as they demonstrated during the walkouts, which they organized primarily using MySpace, e-mail, text, and notes made during class. In Las Vegas some of them walked more than twenty miles from school to downtown and back in order to embark on a pilgrimage of justice. As Revilla articulated in an online blog:

Injustice Causes Revolution:
Reflections on the Las Vegas Student Movement
On Tuesday (3/28/06) and Friday (3/31/06), Las Vegas elementary, middle, and high school students walked out of class to protest the racist laws and attacks being made against their families, friends, and communities. The numbers of student protestors were estimated at 1000 on Tuesday and 3000 on Friday. I want to acknowledge the students' passion and motivation for this protest and recognize that throughout history the youth have been largely responsible for social change in our society. I want to further recognize the support that MECHA de UNLV and other students from CCSN [the Community College of Southern Nevada, now CSN] and UNLV offered to the students. It was indeed an inspiration to witness such amazing defenders of justice!

Saturday, there was another protest organized by high school students. It began at Rancho High School and ended at City Hall. The numbers were estimated between 250–300. Again, I want to applaud the students and community members that organized this demonstration against the xenophobia/nativism sweeping the country. It was inspiring! However, I was discouraged to see that the media portrayed the main message of this protest as a negative judgment of students' actions on Tuesday and Friday. (Flores 2006)

Students have described this movement as a "revolution"—a peaceful uprising whose ultimate aim is to liberate those who live within the shadows. Many of them indicate that it is also an intellectual revolution, in which the daily lives of those who have been impacted by the movement will never be the same. Ultimately, the words of the youth will better articulate the meaning of the movement to them. According to "Nate Guanaco Pipil," a high school senior from a predominantly Latina/o school:

> Walking out on Tuesday was probably one of the best things that I have ever done. Being surrounded by a large group of Latinos who were ready to fight for La Causa truly overwhelmed me.
>
> But now it seems as if the media is giving us nothing but negative feedback. Well let me tell them this . . . How can you call these students ignorant and uneducated?! Just because they do not know the name of the bills or what the Senate Judiciary Committee is, does not mean they are ignorant! Just by witnessing the labor their parents or families must endure on a daily basis due to their status or color of their skin makes them aware of the social injustice! So who's really ignorant?! Personally, I believe that the individual who speaks about ignorance without being aware of the oppression we face on a daily basis in this country is the ignorant one! (Flores 2006, 2)

The Activist Crew was the core organizing entity of the April 10 and May 1 actions in 2006, as well as the subsequent marches in 2007 and 2009. They also orchestrated several other important forms of activism (both external and internal) such as press conferences, newsletter publications, and other educational forums for the community. They came together during the walkouts and continue to organize into the present. Many of the students have joined with Hermandad Mexicana in Las Vegas, several Mexican federation organizations, and other community groups to form the United Coalition for Im/migrant Rights.

The year 2006 was a catalyst of unprecedented social upheaval in Las Vegas. This movement continues to be fomented by the repression that undocumented im/migrants live under citizenism. This movement continues to mobilize millions of people who are committed to eradicating injustice—through peaceful measures—and who ultimately aim to fight for justice using a *multidimensional* vision. This peaceful uprising has deeply rooted historical and socioeconomic oppressive conditions that have led millions of people to embark on a crusade for justice for human rights.

Las Vegas has never seen the extent of political mobilization that is currently taking place, particularly coming from an overwhelmingly overshadowed community such as the Latina/o community. The youth of Las

Vegas were the leaders who sparked this mobilization, given the institution-alized *multidimensional struggle* they face every day through the intersect-ing and simultaneous oppressions they endure in their lives. Even though the power of their actions is not yet acknowledged, history/herstory will prove their actions courageous and necessary. There will be an entire gen-eration of Latina/o youth who will remember the power of their collective action and the effects these actions had in transforming their lives and their environments.

May 1 and most of the events leading to it were organized and coordi-nated by the Las Vegas Activist Crew. The Activist Crew was born out of this collective action. The lessons learned by the activists were meaningful, life changing, and painful. The interviews conducted have a common link: all indicate that their lives are forever changed. On a daily basis, the Activist Crew members developed their grounded theory in their struggle for social justice. The activists engaged in a collective *conscientización* that produced and developed the theoretical concepts to explain their experiences. Hence, the local immigrant rights movement contributes to the cannon of CRT because it is a CRT movement that actively critiques the multidimensional matrix of rights.

Activist Crew grounded theory delves into the different forms of internal and external resistance and the levels of consciousness in which this resis-tance exists—consciously, spiritually, and physically. This transformational resistance becomes a process of liberation. The challenge is to continue growing and developing a critical consciousness and maintaining a critical lens in order to engage in transformative resistance. As Dr. Martin Luther King Jr. told us, "I am cognizant of the interrelatedness of all communities and states. . . . Injustice anywhere is a threat to justice everywhere. We are caught in an inescapable network of mutuality, tied in a single garment of destiny. Whatever affects one directly, affects all indirectly. Never again can we afford to live with the narrow, provincial 'outside agitator' idea. Anyone who lives inside the United States can never be considered an outsider any-where within its bounds."[5]

NOTES

The backslash in "im/migration" is used to denote two words that are used as one throughout the article: migrant and immigrant. The former denotes the movement of people within a territory (that is, the continent of the Americas), and the latter denotes the movement of people in and out of territories. This is of sociopolitical significance for the migration of Latinas/os to the United States given their indigenous/native ancestry.

1. A *counterstory* critically recounts the experiences of discrimination and resistance from the perspectives of those on society's margins; a *majoritarian* story is told by those who have historically been in power. See Yosso 2006.

2. We utilize "Latina/o" as an umbrella term to encompass the differing national identities of im/migrants, including Latin American, Hispanic, Latina/o, and Chicana/o.

3. As seen in the PBS film *Chicano! History of the Mexican-American Civil Rights Movement*.

4. "Zapata" is a self-chosen pseudonym for a community member in his fifties, born in Mexico and longtime resident of Las Vegas, who participated in the 2006 immigrant rights movement.

5. Letter from Birmingham Jail (http://abacus.bates.edu/admin/offices/dos/mlk/letter.html).

REFERENCES

Anzaldúa, G. 1987. *Borderlands/La Frontera: The New Mestiza*. San Francisco: Aunt Lute Books.

Baumgardner, J., and A. Richards. 2005. *Grassroots: A Field Guide for Feminist Activism*. New York: Farrar, Straus, and Giroux.

Covarrubias, A., and A. Tijerina Revilla. 2003. "Agencies of Transformational Resistance." *Florida Law Review* 55, no. 1: 459–77.

Crenshaw, K. 2003. "Demarginalizing the Intersection of Race and Sex: A Black Feminist Critique of Antidiscrimination Doctrine, Feminist Theory, and the Antiracist Politics." In *Critical Race Feminism: A Reader*, edited by A. Wing. New York: New York University Press.

Crenshaw, K., N. Gotunda, G. Peller, and T. Kendall. 1996. *Critical Race Theory: The Writings That Formed the Movement*. New York: New Press.

Delgado Bernal, D. 1998. "Using Chicana Feminist Epistemology." *Harvard Education Review* 68, no. 4: 1–24.

Flores, E., ed. 2006. *Students Stand Up! Newsletter*. April 5.

———. 2007. "Las Vegas Activist Crew and the Im/migrant Rights Movement: How We Transformed 'Sin City' and Our World." Honors thesis, University of Nevada, Las Vegas.

Freire, P. 1970. *Pedagogy of the Oppressed*. New York: Continuum.

Harding, S. 1992. "After the Neutrality Ideal: Science, Politics, and 'Strong Objectivity.'" *Social Research* 59, no. 3: 567–87.

Lazos, S. 2007. "The Immigrant Rights Marches (Las Marchas): Did the "Gigante" (Giant) Wake Up or Does It Still Sleep Tonight?" *Nevada Law Journal* 10: 700.

Martínez, E. 1998. *De Colores Means All of Us: Latina Views for a Multi-Colored Country.* Cambridge, Mass.: South End.

Moraga, C. 2000. *Loving in the War Years: Lo Que Nunca Paso por sus Labios.* Cambridge, Mass.: South End Press.

Nevada Legislature. 2009. https://www.leg.state.nv.us/.

Orleck, A. 2005. *Storming Caesar's Palace: How Black Mothers Fought Their Own War on Poverty.* Boston: Beacon Press.

Pew Hispanic Center. 2010. http://pewhispanic.org/.

Planas, A. 2006. "Kids Leave Class: Hispanic Students Object to Comment; Teacher Apologizes." *Las Vegas Review Journal,* March 17. http://www.reviewjournal.com/lvrj_home/2006/Mar-17-Fri-2006/news/6415969.html.

Pratt, T. 2006. "Immigrants Celebrate 'This Historic Moment.'" *Las Vegas Sun,* May 3. http://www.lasvegassun.com/sunbin/stories/sun/2006/may/03/566614677.html?im/migration.

Revilla, A. 2005. "Raza Womyn Mujerstoria." *Villanova Law Review* 50, no. 4: 799–822.

Santiago Venator, Ch., Torres, B., and Valdés, F. 2005. "LatCrit Latino and Latina Critical Race Theory." On *LatCrit Informational CD.* New York: LatCrit and Ithaca College.

Sen, R., and F. Mamdouh. 2008. *The Accidental American.* San Francisco: Berrett-Koehler Publishers.

Solórzano, D. G., and D. Delgado Bernal. 2001. "Examining Transformational Resistance Through a Critical Race and LatCrit Theory Framework: Chicana and Chicano Students in an Urban Context." *Urban Education* 36, no. 3: 308–42.

Yosso, T. 2006. *Critical Race Counterstories Along the Chicana/o Educational Pipeline.* New York: Routledge.

Learning from the Chicana/o Blowouts

MARGARITA BERTA-ÁVILA

JULIE LÓPEZ FIGUEROA

Social movements are public forums used by communities, which are often pushed to the margins of society, to voice their realities. During the 1960s, students who identified themselves as Chicana/o brought attention to the educational injustices they confronted in the schools (Chávez, 2002). The Chicana/o Blowouts raised public awareness of the lack of quality education received by students of Mexican descent, and it raised questions about what it takes to provide an inclusive and responsive education to nonwhite students. In the process of achieving clarity on the social, educational, and economic conditions that accounted for the historical and contemporary second-class status of people of Mexican descent in the U.S., students gained just cause to embrace an identity rooted in political action and social justice. Depending on where they lived in the Southwest, their sense of leadership, what constituted a challenge, and what would take priority in an action plan varied, and collectively these factors unified the students who made the personal decision to identify themselves as Chicana/o (Muñoz Jr. 1989).

Since the 1960s, the term "Chicana/o" has come to be associated with identity politics and activism of various sorts. The strategy of the time meant consciously interrupting the public landscape. It took on a more militant form to demonstrate the gravity of the unequal educational treatment students were experiencing. The Chicana/o movement exposed the role and power of majoritarian ideological frameworks that put into unquestioned practice the mistreatment of under-resourced communities (Yosso, 2005). While the original militant stance of the Chicana/o movement is historically justified, mounting efforts with allies across various communities brokered new ways to address the social structures that present challenges. Such academic disciplines as cultural studies, women's studies, queer studies along with theories like critical pedagogy, Latino critical race theory, and community cultural wealth outline the intellectual terrain framing current research methodologies from which counterperspectives emerge to interpret the existing conditions of the Chicana/o community.

Chicana/o activism in education has focused on the rights of Latina/o students, especially non-English-speaking students, and the right to bilingual educational programs. Increased efforts for the integration of Latina/o students, equal distribution of educational funding sources, and the constant struggle against alienating schooling practices such as tracking, standardized testing, the mainstream curriculum, and access to higher education have also been important issues (Gándara 1995). This symposium invites readers to gain a historical and present-day understanding of the Chicana/o movement within the institution of education, thereby revealing the varied dimensions of Chicana/o activism across time and space. The transformative educational experiences discussed in this book occur because students, teachers, scholars, and other community members consciously practiced political action through accountability, collaboration, and leadership.

WHAT IS THE SIGNIFICANCE OF THIS BOOK IN EDUCATION?

The chapters presented define a context and experience of resistance between home and school partnerships for the sake of understanding policy and practice. For example, the central theme in Olivos and Quintana situate the experiences of Chicana/o-Latina/o students within the educational system in both historical and contemporary contexts. Their work sets up a foundation to recognize that current debates about Chicanas/os-Latinas/os in the educational system are not just a response to social and political issues but are grounded in systemic educational realities that have not been addressed. This chapter represents how scholars and educators from within Chicana/o-Latina/o communities can enrich the interpretation of those realities by naming and contextualizing an educational truth that is uniquely socially constructed to be Chicana/o-Latina/o. Their work indelibly prompts a dialogue that builds on a Chicana/o epistemology within the context of education. Given their focus on critical theories, they initiate an opportunity to analyze set voiced experiences that have been marginalized. In the attempt to generate knowledge on this topic, these authors pinpoint a tension that cannot go unrecognized. That is, a Chicana/o-Latina/o epistemology cannot be fully inspired by the academic canon but also motivated by the voice of those whom the institution is supposed to serve.

Naming our educational contexts helps to understand the current effect, from the perspective of educators, community members, practitioners, and researchers in terms of roles and responsibilities or contributions to the movement. Katzew and De Katzew as well as Kohli and Solórzano reflect on the transformative nature of the movement in and through education. Katzew and De Katzew discuss the contributions of a visual art community embedded within the Chicana/o movement that sought to interrupt the public beliefs that define the Chicana/o-Latina/o experience. Because schools have permeable walls, Chicana/o-Latina/o students resonated with the campaign for a higher-quality education that was also being demanded by visual artists, or cultural workers, in protest of the larger social, political, and economic pressures of society. The Kohli and Solórzano chapter discusses racism and white supremacy as a formulated disease that up to now society has addressed only through curing its symptoms. The authors use a case-study approach to examine how black and brown students at one high school in the Los Angeles Unified School District purposefully disrupted and diffused racial tensions by inviting students to take ownership to reconstruct their lived experience and redefine how the space called school can be a vehicle for peace. Although students did not specifically use art to push an agenda for peace, the students did rely on their own modes of dissemination of the message, through art and speaking, which at a grassroots level represents what the cultural workers were doing in the Katzew and De Katzew chapter. Substantiating teaching and learning can create a space where curriculum truly becomes education for liberation.

Covarrubias and Tejeda each illustrate how creating and accessing equitable living conditions require contesting and negotiating broader social cultural landscapes beyond school. Covarrubias examines how students apprenticed within a community-based organization, Public Allies, Los Angeles. This organization cultivates activism among students through developing their consciousness as a tool to enact transformational resistance to counter the marginalization of populations whose lives are lived at the intersection of gender, class, race, and sexual orientation in order to replace deficit lenses. Tejeda frames a similar agency in the Chicana/o movement not just as manifesting in 1968. He analyzes this historical event as not only contesting what was happening in that particular moment in time. Students embodied and enacted the Blowouts to continue addressing their miseducation, a miseducation that extended beyond 1968. Movements not only are responding to the immediacy of issues but also flag the continued pattern of systemic inequalities that are far-reaching for this community. For this community in particular, Tejeda's emphasis lies in having readers grasp the deeply rooted manner in which each movement—historical and contemporary—confronts each dimension of deficit thinking that has to date afflicted the Chicana/o-Latina/o community within and beyond schools. Attaining basic human rights such as access to education, for this community, has resulted from continued activism and resistance being disenfranchised as opposed to the popular myth that all students are equally positioned to experience a quality education.

In the process of negotiating and reconfiguring "space," theories and pedagogies of (trans)formation emerge that ultimately manifest ACTION. The "action" entities students, parents, community members, and teachers take on are not static but rather ever changing due to the progress and setbacks that can occur when building a movement. For example, Revilla and Rangel-Medina speak to the concept of action through the reconfiguration of space when they describe K–12 Chicana/o and Latina/o students organizing and taking to the streets in May 2006 against HR 4437, a bill that sparked anti-immigrant sentiment. Reconfiguration and action did not occur solely due to HR 4437, but rather because students saw their worlds, their families, and what was most important to them stripped away. This forced them to shift their lens, renegotiate their space (due to circumstances), and make decisions (Action). The (trans)formation of space led to speaking out and claiming their voice. However, action does not exist without turbulence. The students learned, as well, that turbulence (setbacks) can offer insight regarding future needs. Similarly, in Xico González, Eracleo Guevara, Alejo Padilla, and Marianna Rivera's chapter we see teachers united to form a *colectiva* to counter the oppressive "space" known as schools. In doing so, they decided to go outside the "space" deemed appropriate and form a community in which students and teachers would feel safe to exhale without repercussions, a space in which they could come together to rename and reanalyze what they (teachers and students) had been taught in school in order to push back, challenge, and strategically manifest a different pedagogy or perspective when in oppressive space. However, the "action" manifested by the teachers and students came into question in the context of sustainability. How is action sustained when teachers and students are maneuvering between a reality they want and a reality they are attempting to renegotiate? As illuminated in their epilogue, sustainability can transpire if a support system exists that can assist in reflection and strategic organizing not in isolation but as a *colectiva*.

WHAT ARE SOME EMERGING LESSONS REGARDING BLOWOUTS?

Based on the experiences, struggles, and gains articulated in the chapters of this book, is there potential to formulate a Chicana/o pedagogy framework that reflects the ever-changing needs of our community in the realm of education? As the editors, we propose that yes, it can be originated. For example, each chapter highlights essential themes necessary to counter an educational system that seeks to maintain structures of inequity. At the same time, the authors ask us, the readers, to consider areas of practice necessary to self-determine our own existence. In that context, we suggest that a Chicana/o pedagogy cannot be structured within a traditional educational context that considers only teaching methodology (practice). Rather, "practice" must coexist and overlap with (1) the ability to name our circumstance, (2) the ability to create and make our space, (3) the ability to negotiate/renegotiate our space for it will not remain static, and (4) the ability to take action—keeping in mind sustainability. We do forewarn that this proposed pedagogical framework should not be viewed as a linear structure to follow. Rather, it is a framework that consists of core values always in flux and continuously interdependent of one another. This interdependent Chicana/o pedagogy can be utilized as a framework that serves as a foundation and lens from which we develop our curriculum and frame our positionality when advocating for our students' rights to an equitable education. Thus, it forms the direction and purpose of the educational practices and methodologies that we choose to enact. Keeping in mind the proposed pedagogical framework, it bears repeating that the Blowouts and current movements remind us that a collective presence through activism (Action) is often required, though not always anticipated. Perhaps there is some hesitation to participate in movements because they are often characterized as "radical."

Each of these chapters openly invites igniting local activism, within the context of the classroom and out, given the needs of students, families, teachers, and communities. However, we hope that these chapters served as a strong reminder and inspiration that having a high expectation for Chicana/o-Latina/o students is a radical idea in and of itself given historical and contemporary educational issues. These chapters promote the idea that access to education elevates the chances that students can approach their lives with all the dignity that is assumed to be parceled out to all human beings. Thus, disallowing all of us to examine new forms of identity self-formation as well as (trans)formative pedagogies and theories that people with a Chicana/o consciousness employ in their daily lives as educators, to initiate a dialogue to discuss the contemporary ways in which Chicana/o activism and identity engage the field of education, and to reflect on how Chicana/o identity and activism relate to education has stereotyped and impeded dialogue and the exchange of potentially beneficial ideas. The book dovetails those efforts to move away from deficit thinking (Valencia 1997) and instead refocus on the strengths and contributions the Chicana/o and Latina/o can make given Yosso's work that focuses on a "community cultural wealth" framework (2005). In the end, this book is a reminder that living in a democratic society requires living life with a critical eye, using your voice to name injustices, and moving your body to reflect contestation, hope, and collaboration to ensure a better future for all children.

REFERENCES

Chávez, E. (2002). *"¡Mi Raza Primero!" (My People First!): Nationalism, Identity, and Insurgency in the Chicano Movement in Los Angeles, 1966–1978*. Berkeley: University of California Press.

Gándara, P. 1995. *Over the Ivy Walls: The Educational Mobility of Low-Income Chicanos*. Albany: State University of New York Press.

Garcia, E. 1999. *Understanding and Meeting the Challenge of Student Cultural Diversity*. Boston: Houghton Mifflin.

Muñoz, C., Jr. 1989. *Youth, Identity, and Power: The Chicano Movement*. London: Verso.

Valencia, R., ed. 1997. *Evolution of Deficit Thinking*. Washington, D.C.: Falmer Press.

Yosso, T. 2005. *Critical Race Counterstories Along the Chicana/Chicano Educational Pipeline*. New York: Routledge.

CONTRIBUTORS

MARGARITA BERTA-ÁVILA is an Associate Professor in the Bilingual/Multicultural Education Department in the College of Education, California State University, Sacramento.

ALEJANDRO COVARRUBIAS is a lecturer at California State University, Los Angeles's Department of Chicana and Chicano Studies and a Visiting Faculty member at UCLA's Cesar Chavez Department of Chicana and Chicano Studies.

JULIE LÓPEZ FIGUEROA is an Associate Professor in the Department of Ethnic Studies in the College of Social Science and Interdisciplinary Studies, California State University, Sacramento.

XICO GONZÁLEZ is an artist, poet, and political and cultural *activista* based in Sacramento, California. In 2003 González was presented with the Freedom Bound Center's Dolores Huerta Activist Award by the famous Chicana activist and cofounder (along with Cesar Chavez) of the United Farm Workers Union. In 2004 González founded the Brown Syndicate, a Raza arts organization devoted to promoting Raza arts.

ERACLEO GUEVARA is a Spanish high school teacher in the Sacramento City Unified School District.

ADRIANA KATZEW is Assistant Professor of Art Education at the Massachusetts College of Art and Design (Boston).

LILIA R. DE KATZEW is chair of Chicana and Chicano Studies in the Ethnic and Gender Studies Department at California State University, Stanislaus.

RITA KOHLI serves as Clinical Faculty in UCLA's "Urban Education for Social Justice" Teacher Education Program, supporting the development of new teachers in Los Angeles schools.

CARLOS MUÑOZ JR. is Professor Emeritus at the University of California, Berkeley, in the Department of Ethnic Studies, and is Affiliated Faculty in the university's Center for Latin American Studies. He is the award-winning author of *Youth, Identity, Power: The Chicano Movement* (2007), a classic study of the Mexican American civil rights movement.

EDWARD M. OLIVOS is an Assistant Professor of Teacher Education at the University of Oregon, specializing in bilingual education and bicultural parental involvement.

ALEJO PADILLA teaches in the Social Science Department at Galt High School.

CARMEN E. QUINTANA is a bilingual fourth grade teacher in the South Bay Union School District, an ESL teacher at Chula Vista Adult School in the Sweetwater Union High School District, and an Adjunct Professor at San Diego State University and Inter American College.

EVELYN M. RANGEL-MEDINA is the Policy Director for the Green-Collar Jobs Campaign at the Ella Baker Center for Human Rights where she crafts climate, racial and economic justice policy solutions that will build a green economy strong enough to lift people out of poverty.

MARIANNA RIVERA is a Minority Engineering Program Recruitment Counselor in the School of Engineering and Computer Science, California State University, Sacramento.

DANIEL G. SOLÓRZANO is a Professor of Social Science and Comparative Education in the Graduate School of Education and Information Studies at the University of California, Los Angeles. He also has a joint appointment as Professor in the Chicana and Chicano Studies Department and is an affiliated Professor in the Women's Studies Department. He is the Director of the University of California All Campus Consortium on Research for Diversity. In 2007 Professor Solórzano was awarded the UCLA Distinguished Teacher Award.

CARLOS TEJEDA is an Assistant Professor in the School of Education in the Division of Educational Foundations and Interdivisional Studies, California State University, Los Angeles.

ANITA TIJERINA REVILLA is an Assistant Professor in Women's Studies at the University of Nevada, Las Vegas.

INDEX

Italic page numbers refer to illustrations.

consciousness: coaching youth for an asset-based consciousness, 84–86; defined, 77; dimensions of, 77; multidimensional, 5, 174–75. *See also* critical consciousness

conscientization (*conscientización*), 4, 5, 151, 172, 185. *See also* critical consciousness

consciousness raising: Las Vegas Activist Crew and, 172; relationship to community, 90–98; by women during the Blowouts, 36–37; in youth, 81–86

Consumes River College, 153–54

counterresistance, 116

counterstory, 176, 186n1

counterstorytelling, 172, 176

Covarrubias, Alejandro, 5

Crenshaw, Kimberly, 132

Crisostomo, Paula, 37

critical consciousness: "awakening" to social contradictions, 115; *conscientización,* 4, 5, 151, 172, 185; Latino/Chicano parents and, 121–22, 127. *See also* Critical multidimensional consciousness

critical education research theories, 3–5

Critical multidimensional consciousness: community building and, 90, 100; defined, 75, 77–78; developing skills in youth and, 79–80; importance of developing, 78–79, 81–86; inclusive community and, 80; networks of resistance and, 80–81; progressive organizations and, 76; relationship to community, 90–98; resistance networks and, 88–89; social justice and, 79, 86–88

critical pedagogy, 152

Critical Race Theory (CRT): counterstorytelling, 172, 176; Critical multidimensional consciousness and, 78; definitions of racism, 133–34; definitions of white supremacy, 134; development of, 132; goals of, 172–73; on interracial conflict, 173; principal tenets of, 132–33

Crusade for Justice, 32, 46, 52, 55–56

Crystal City (Tex.), 32

Cuaron, Mita, 35–36, 37

Cuba, 54

Cuban political posters, 56

cultural depravation model, 29

cultural deprivation thesis, 29–30

cultural disadvantagement model, 29–30

cultural genocide, 17–18

cultural values: *Plan Espiritual de Aztlán* and, 52–53

cultural workers, 71

culture of poverty theory, 28–39

curriculum: at Academia del Barrio, 155–56; "American-centered," 164–65n1

Davis v. the School Board of Prince Edward County, 144

Day of Action (2006), 123–24, 125

"A Day Without Immigrants" boycott, 63

"A Day Without Latinos" boycott, 63

decision making, 101

deculturalization: education and, 17–18; policies directed to Native Americans, 21–23

deficit thinking: cultural depravation model, 29; cultural disadvantagement model, 29–30; culture of poverty theory, 28–39; in education, 18–19; racial ideologies and, 18–19 (*see also* racial ideologies)

dehumanization, 3

Delgado, Richard, 132

Delgado Bernal, Dolores, 4, 75, 81, 174, 175

Del Sol High School (Las Vegas, Nev.), 178–79

Denver (Colo.): Chicano youth march in, 52; school walkouts in, 32

development rooms, 25

discourse of denial and deceit, 30

dissonance: symbolic and personal, 115

documentary films, 60–62

domination: in society and schooling, 113

Downtown High School (Los Angeles, Calif.), 138–43

dysconsciousness, 87

East Los Angeles High School Walkouts: antecedents, 1; Chicana/o educational circumstances and, 44–45; chronology of, 14–15; commemorating the ideals and practices behind, 34–40; educational circumstances of Chicana/o students preceding, 15–16; historical examina-

sion and goals, 153–54; formation of,
148–49, 152–53; Saturday school (*see* Academia del Barrio)
Guevara, Ernesto "Che," 47–48, 54, 57,
64, 67
Guitiérrez, José Angel, 32, 33, 61

"habit of mind," 87
Hall, Stanley, 24
Harding, Sandra, 175
Head Start program, 30
hegemony, 165n3
hereditarian ideas, 23
Hermandad Mexicana, 184
Herrón, Willie, 55, 59
Hidalgo y Costilla, José Miguel, 53, 61
High, Freida, 58
higher education: *El Plan de Santa Barbara,*
48; film programs, 60
high school lockdowns, 145n8
hooks, bell, 134, 151–52
House Resolution 4437, 2, 123, 124, 170
Huerta, Dolores, 49, 61

I Am Joaquin (film), 60–61
I Am Joaquin (Gonzales), 47, 60, 162
ignorance laws, 20
images and visual symbols: in the immigrant marches of 2006, 64–67, *68, 69,
70*; Mexican muralists and, 49; used
by Cesar Chavez, 50, 51–52; used by
"Corky" Gonzales, 52–53. *See also* visual
culture and art
immigrant marches of 2006: legacy of,
2–3; in response to HR 4437, 2; role of
Chicana/o artists in, 64–67; role of the
visual arts in, 62–67
im/migrant rights movement, 170–71
im/migration, 185–86. *See also* undocumented im/migration
inadequate socialization thesis, 30
inclusive community, 80
Indian Removal Act of 1830, 21
inequality: social categories of, 110–11
injustice: analyzing with Latina/o Critical
Race Theory, 101
Inside Eastside, 36–37, 39

institutional racism, 135, 136
intelligence quotient (IQ), 24
intelligence testing, 24–30
interracial conflict: in Communities of
Color, 131–32, 135, 136; Critical Race
Theory on, 173; student leadership in
challenges to racism, 140–43, 144–45;
Students of Color and, 136–43; treating
the disease, 138–40

Jackson, Andrew, 21
Jefferson, Thomas, 21
Jefferson High School (Los Angeles, Calif.),
27
journals: in the Chicana/o student
movement, 54–55

Kahlo, Frida, 67
Katz, Michael, 29
KCET station, 61
King, Martin Luther, Jr., 58, 185

La Causa, 50–51
La Mala Efe (MALAF), 55
land-grant restoration movement, 49
La Raza, 37, 39
La Raza Unida Party, 32, 49
Las Vegas Activist Crew: Las Vegas school
walkouts, 177–85; multidimensional
consciousness and struggle, 174–75; overview, 171, 172; resistance and the ideal
of liberation, 174; *Students Stand Up!
Newsletter,* 180
Las Vegas Activist Crew study: literature
review, 171–75; research methodology,
175–76
Las Vegas (Nev.): racial segregation in, 171;
school walkouts, 171, 177–85
Las Vegas Review-Journal, 178
Las Vegas Strip, 171, 179
Latina/o Critical Race Theory (LatCrit),
78, 101, 173
Latino/Chicano communities: creating a
social movement for, 112; current challenges of, 105; goals of school involvement, 109 (*see also* community school
involvement); interracial conflict and,

outs on, 32–34; underrepresentation in Congress, 47; veterans, 38

Mexican Americans in Schools (Carter), 16

Mexican American students: impact of the Blowouts on, 32–34; treatment in Los Angeles public schools, 25–28. *See also* Latino/Chicano students; Students of Color

Mexican American Youth Leadership Conferences, 38

Mexican flag, 52, 63

Mexican muralists, 49, 54

Mexican women: documentary films of, 61–62

Mexico: Olympics of 1968, 56; remittances and, 170

Minutemen vigilantes, 111

miscegenation, 24

missionaries, 20

Montoya, Malaquías, 57

Morales, Sylvia, 60, 61–62

Moton High School (Farmville, Va.), 143–44

movimiento. See Chicana/o movement

multidimensional consciousness, 5, 174–75

multidimensional struggle, 175, 185

Muñoz, Carlos, 48

muralists, 49, 54

murals: in the barrio movement, 58; by Chicana/o artists, 56; community and education in the making of, 58–59; performance art by the Asco collective, 59–60

narratives, 133

National Farm Workers, 50

Native Americans, 20–23

nativism, 168

Nava, Julian, 36

negative tension, 119

networking: by women in the Blowouts, 37

networks. *See* resistance networks

Nevada: citizenist legislation, 179; racial segregation in, 171

New Communications program, 60

New Mexico: land-grant restoration movement, 49

newspapers: activist, 36–37, 39; Chicana/o artists and, 55–56

No Movie movies, 62

Office of Indian Affairs, 21

Olmos, Edward James, 177

Olympics of 1968, 56

opportunity rooms, 25

oppositional behavior. *See* resistance

"oppressed people": subordination of, 3–4

oral traditions, 133

Orosco, Juanishi, 68–69

Orozco, José Clemente, 49

"outsider jurisprudence," 173

Oventic (Mex.), 152–53

PALA. *See* Public Allies, Los Angeles

parental school involvement: conceptualized, 119–20; dialectical nature of, 118–19; "paradox of minority parental involvement," 117; politicizing, 106, 121–26; problem posing and, 120–21; resistance in, 115–18, 125–26; tensions among stakeholders and, 119; transforming the school system and, 120

Peace Week campaign, 138, 139, 142–43, 144

pedagogy: critical, 152; Chicana/o, 192–93

Pedagogy of the Oppressed (Freire), 85

People of Color: counterstorytelling, 172; Critical Race Theory and, 172–73; interracial conflict and, 131–32, 135, 173; racial hierarchy and, 135–36; transformational acts of resistance and, 98–99; unjust conditions in California, 98

performance art, 59–60

periodicals: in the Chicana/o student movement, 54–55

personal dissonance, 115

Pew Hispanic Center, 107

Piranya Coffee House, 38–39

placards, 53

Plan Espiritual de Aztlán, 52–53

Ponitowska, Elena, 9–10

Posada, José Guadalupe, 54, 56

positive tension, 119

poster making, 57–58

poster movement, 56

posters: carried by Blowout students, 53; by Chicana/o artists, 55, 56–58; in the Chicano student movement, 53; in the immigrant marches of 2006, 64–67, *68, 69, 70*

"poverty discourse," 29

power: asymmetric relations in public school systems, 112–13; defined, 145n3

progressive organizations, 76–77

Proposition 21 (Calif.), 2

Proposition 187 (Calif.), 2, 123

Proposition 227 (Calif.), 2

Public Allies, Los Angeles (PALA), 76; Asset-Based approach, 82; "checking," 94; coaching youth for an asset-based consciousness, 84–86; collaborative leadership, 95; commitment to social justice, 86–88; community building, 89–90; consciousness raising in, 81–86; creating networks of resistance, 88–89; overview, 77; relationship between community and consciousness raising, 90–98

Public Broadcasting Stations, 61

public school systems: asymmetrical power relations in, 112–13; contradictions in and the educational fate of Latino/Chicano students, 114–15; high school lockdowns, 145n8; intelligence testing and, 25–28; Latino/Chicano parents as leaders and warriors in, 127; parental resistance to oppressive school policies, 115–18, 125–26; rationalization of inequalities in, 111; relationship of Latino/Chicano communities to, 109; relationship of Latino/Chicano parents to, 110–12, 127–28; "structure of dominance" in, 113. *See also* community school involvement; parental school involvement

push-out rates, 15

Quakers, 20

"queer," 7n1

race: centrality of, 132–33; social inequities and, 110, 111

racial hierarchies, 135–36

racial ideologies: American constructs, 19;

discourse of denial and deceit in, 30; genetic pathology model and hereditarian ideas, 23; intelligence testing, 24–30; manifestations in history, 19–20; schooling for subservience, 20–23; white racial superiority and eugenics, 23–24. *See also* racism

racialization: of social relations, 10–11

racial segregation: in California schools, 28; Robert Carter on, 134–35; in Nevada, 171; in Virginia schools, 143–44

racism: centrality of, 132–33; concerns of Latino/Chicano parents about, 122–24; Critical Race Theory on, 172–73; definitions of, 133–34; institutional, 135, 136; interracial conflict (*see* interracial conflict); Latina/o Critical Race Theory on, 173; as a psychological weapon, 136; racial hierarchy and, 135–36; student leadership in challenges to, 140–43, 144–45. *See also* racial ideologies

Raices de Sangre (film), 61

Rancho High School (Las Vegas, Nev.), 183

RCAF. *See* Royal Chicano Air Force

Reading. Writing. Revolution. Walkout. (film), 177

reflection: at Academia del Barrio, 161–63

Regeneración (journal), 55

religious symbols. *See* Virgen de Guadalupe

remittances, 170

resistance: the 1968 Blowouts and, 116; Latino/Chicano communities and, 105, 109; Latino/Chicano parents and, 115–18, 125–26; in the relationship between dominant and subordinate cultures, 116; transformational, 4–5, 98–99, 151–52, 174; types of, 174

resistance networks: building community and, 88–89; creating and evolving, 80–81

revolutionaries: inspiration to the Blowouts, 47–48; visual images of, 53, 54, 56

Right On (poster), 57

Rivera, Diego, 49

Roosevelt High School (Los Angeles, Calif.), 15, 27

Rosales, Arturo, 48